IP Issues in Corporate Transactions

A Practical Guide to the Treatment of Intellectual Property in Acquisitions and Investments

Consulting Editor **Neil Coulson**

Consulting editor
Neil Coulson

Managing director
Sian O'Neill

IP Issues in Corporate Transactions: A Practical Guide to the Treatment of Intellectual Property in Acquisitions and Investments
is published by
Globe Law and Business Ltd
3 Mylor Close
Horsell
Woking
Surrey GU21 4DD
Tel: +44 20 3745 4770
www.globelawandbusiness.com

Printed and bound by CPI Group (UK) Ltd, Croydon, CR0 4YY

IP Issues in Corporate Transactions: A Practical Guide to the Treatment of Intellectual Property in Acquisitions and Investments
ISBN 9781909416611

Table of contents

Introduction

Neil Coulson
Baker Botts LLP

Intellectual property rights are valuable. They protect products, services, goodwill and competitive commercial advantage. They are bought, sold, licensed and charged. Some are registered, some arise automatically. But all have one thing in common. They underpin many companies' commercial operations and, as a result, feature heavily in just about all corporate transactions, be they investments, acquisitions, mergers, joint ventures or commercial contractual agreements.

This recognition of commercial value is not a recent phenomenon. Two examples from the United States in the 19th century suffice to show that the economic importance of intellectual property has long been recognised. The first is from Abraham Lincoln. In his Lecture on Discoveries and Inventions, given at Bloomington, Illinois on April 6 1858 he concluded with a comment on the commercial value of patents and the patent laws, a conclusion that applies equally to all other intellectual property laws and rights:

> *[N]ext came the patent laws. These began in England in 1624; and, in this country, with the adoption of our constitution. Before then, any man might instantly use what another had invented; so that the inventor had no special advantage from his own invention. The patent system changed this; secured to the inventor, for a limited time, the exclusive use of his invention; and thereby added the fuel of interest to the fire of genius, in the discovery and production of new and useful things.*

Second is a literary example from Mark Twain in his novel *A Connecticut Yankee in King Arthur's Court*. Having been granted plenipotentiary powers, Hank Morgan sets about establishing a sound economic basis for his administration. Tellingly, he relates:

> *That reminds me to remark, in passing, that the very first official thing I did, in my administration – and it was on the first day of it too – was to start a patent office; for I knew that a country without a patent office and good patent laws was just a crab, and couldn't travel any way but sideways or backwards*

Today's commercial environment is no different. Each country has its own patent office, its own intellectual property laws. We have international conventions, starting with the Paris Convention for the Protection of Industrial Technology in 1883 and still valid today, which cover aspects of intellectual property ranging from the mutual recognition of copyright (the Berne Convention), to the establishment of the international trademark system (Madrid Agreement and Protocol). We have supra-national IP offices such as the European Patent Office, the Organisation Africaine de la Propriété Industrielle and the Office for Harmonisation of the Internal Market. We have trade agreements that address intellectual property, such as the

Agreement on Trade-related Aspects of Intellectual Property Rights, and we have the continual tension between monopoly IP rights and anti-monopolist anti-trust laws.

Any corporate transaction will involve intellectual property regardless of the business or businesses involved, even if the intellectual property extends only to goodwill and perhaps a registered trademark protecting the services offered. This means that an understanding of IP rights, how they are protected, how you can deal with them, and what you need in an agreement to assign title, license the rights and make sure that as a buyer or seller, or joint venture partner, you have adequate protections, is fundamental.

A full analysis of IP rights worldwide is outside the scope of this book. Its aim is to present to the reader an overview of the key IP issues that arise. For the IP specialist, it provides an aide memoire; to the corporate, commercial or generalist lawyer, it provides an overview of intellectual property and an understanding of how intellectual property fits into transactions, and how the issues that arise can affect those transactions. Its main focus is on intellectual property under English law, but the issues raised have international relevance and the content of the chapters applies internationally as well as domestically.

From identifying the key IP rights and the differing considerations depending on the types of transaction, the early chapters then take the reader through the due diligence process and the contractual negotiation of protective warranties and indemnities. As I have intimated above, while all transactions will involve intellectual property, in some industries intellectual property is the keystone of commercial activity and any transaction in these sectors will involve a particular and detailed consideration of the IP rights involved with issues specific to the sector concerned. These are addressed in the specific chapters on transactions in technology and telecoms, life sciences, fast-moving consumer goods and media. Finally, we have two chapters that put intellectual property in a wider context. Firstly, and always importantly, how is it valued? The value of the intellectual property has implications for deal price and the extent to which contractual protections and comfort are needed. Secondly, we look at the anti-trust position with an analysis of how intellectual property and anti-trust are forever linked in any corporate transaction.

Every issue that arises will have its own dynamic depending on the transaction. With thanks to each of the authors, the chapters in this book put those issues into context, helping IP requirements to be recognised and enabling those requirements to be addressed.

Neil Coulson is an intellectual property partner at Baker Botts LLP and chairs the IP departments in the firm's London and Moscow offices. He has worked across all the key industry sectors, including oil and gas, engineering, chemicals, electronics, pharmaceuticals and biotechnology, and fast-moving consumer goods. Neil advises, in particular, on cross-border technology licensing issues, standalone IP agreements and on intellectual property in the context of corporate and commercial transactions. According to the Legal 500, *he "combines the rare mix of detailed legal knowledge, a practical, commercially-minded approach and significant experience" and has the "perfect combination of legal expertise and commercial acumen".*

Intellectual property rights

Clive Thorne
Wedlake Bell LLP

Intellectual property (IP) law concerns legal rights associated with inventive efforts or the establishment of commercial reputation and trade secrets.

The rights fall into different types depending upon whether they represent creative effort such as copyright, patents and designs or whether they represent branding and marketing rights, such as trademarks and passing off. Some of the rights are protectable by registration, including patents, trademarks and designs. Others such as copyright are protectable once the entitlement to the right is established as a matter of evidence.

In each case, the relevant IP law is designed to ensure the existence of the right as a 'chose' in action which can then be dealt with as an item of personal property, eg, licensed or enforced against third party infringement.

The rights covered in this chapter include patents, trademarks, copyright, designs, confidential information and quasi-IP rights such as the database right.

The rights in this chapter are identified by reference to legislation and common law in the United Kingdom. However, as is stated in relation to each below, IP rights are national or supra-national rights that exist in each country of the world and there is equivalent legislation at common or civil law for these rights around the world. Sometimes this is the same, sometimes it is similar, sometimes it is different. For any corporate transactions, rights may well need to be assessed on an international basis. This chapter provides details of the types of IP rights that apply and can be used as an aide memoire when looking at the position around the world.

1. Patents

Patents are designed to provide the owner of the patent a monopoly right in the invention set out in the patent. There are two patent systems, both governed by the Patents Act 1977: the first is a United Kingdom domestic patent granted by the UK Intellectual Property Office, the second is a European Patent Convention patent granted by the European Patent Office situated in Munich. Generally the provisions of the UK Patents Act 1977 are framed so as to have the same effect as the corresponding provisions of the European Patent Convention. Each country (almost without exception) has its own national or supra-national patent system.

Patents are granted for a 20-year term from the date of filing of the patent. Under the system of Supplementary Protection Certificates for medicinal products, certain pharmaceutical patents can be renewed up to a maximum of 25 years to take into account the lengthy period from the date of filing the patent to the marketing of the patented pharmaceutical once the regulatory requirements are completed.

The filing date is the date when the patent application is received by the patent office. The application must indicate that a patent is being applied for, identify the applicant and contain a description of the invention for which the patent is sought or a reference to an earlier relevant application made by the applicant. The applicant then has a period of 12 months during which he must file one or more claims and an abstract of the invention and pay the necessary fee.

Section 5(2) of the Patents Act 1977 provides that an invention can claim the priority of an earlier invention filed within the preceding 12 months if the later application is supported by matter disclosed in the earlier application. Thus an inventor may apply for a UK patent for his invention and then within 12 months apply to the European Patent Office or other national or supra-national office, designating a number of member states, and the priority date will be that of the original UK patent.

The patent specification should contain a description of the invention and be sufficiently detailed to enable a person "skilled in the art" to work the invention.

The patent claims define the invention for which protection is required and will often consist of a number of claims, some of which may be in the alternative. Section 14(5) of the Patents Act 1977 requires that the claim shall:

- Define the matter for which the applicant seeks protection;
- Be clear and concise;
- Be supportive by the description; and
- Relate to the invention or to a group of inventions which are so linked as to form single inventive concepts.

The claims must be novel, consist of an inventive step, ie, not obvious, and be capable of industrial application. If any of these requirements are absent, the patent is at risk of being found invalid.

In *Biogen Inc v Medeva Plc* the House of Lords gave guidelines as to the meaning of inventive step: "sometimes, it is the idea of using established techniques to do something which no one had previously thought of doing. In that case, the inventive step will be doing the new thing. Sometimes it is finding a way of doing something which people had wanted to do but could not think how."[1]

The invention must be new and must not already have been available to the public. This is defined by the Patents Act 1977 section 2(1) which states that an invention is new if it "does not form part of the state of the art". Section 2(2) describes the "state of the art" as comprising all matter made available to the public before the priority date of the invention whether "by written or oral description, by use or in any other way". A claim may be anticipated by the priority date either where the priority date describes something that falls within the scope of the claim such that it enables the invention as claimed to be worked or where the inevitable result of carrying out what is described falls within the claim.

---

1 1997 RPC 1.

Industrial application is defined in Section 4(1) of the Patents Act 1977 such that an invention is capable of industrial application if it can be made or used in any kind of industry including agriculture. Exclusions from this are the methods of treatment of human or animal bodies by surgery or therapy or of diagnosis practised on human or animal bodies; however, pharmaceuticals are capable of industrial application.

Section 1(2) and (3) of the Patents Act 1977 contains exclusions from patentability:

- A discovery, scientific or theoretical or mathematical method;
- A literary, dramatic, musical or artistic work, or any other aesthetic creation whatsoever; and
- A scheme rule or method for performing any mental act, playing a game or doing business or a program for a computer for the presentation of information.

Patents may be dealt with by way of assignment or licensing whether exclusive or otherwise. They may also be charged or mortgaged as in the case of other personal property.

2. Trademarks

Worldwide trade marks may be applied for domestically under national law or under the international "Madrid Protocol". If the former applications will be made in the national trademark registry. In the latter procedural rules exist for obtaining trademark registrations internationally by a single application. In practice an application will be made designating the international registration as applying in particular countries.

There are two systems of trademark protection in the United Kingdom, both of which are governed by the Trade Marks Act 1994 which was passed to implement the EU Trademarks Directive (EC No 40/94).

Traditionally trademarks have been regarded as marks of origin to identify the goods and services as emanating from a particular manufacturer and also as a property item to protect commercial reputation and goodwill. With the development of branding strategy the latter has become increasingly important. The CJEU has held that National Court should interpret trademark law in accordance with EU law and the Trademarks Directive. This means that the CJEU is the final court of appeal for determining issues of trademark law.

Article 2 of the Trademark Directive defines a trademark as: "A trademark may consist of any sign capable of being represented graphically, particularly words, including personal names, designs, letters, numerals, the shape of goods or of their packaging, provided that such signs are capable of distinguishing the goods or services of one undertaking from those of other undertakings."

It should be noted that the mark must be capable of being represented graphically and also capable of distinguishing goods or services of one undertaking from the those of others. CJEU case law has confirmed that the requirement of being represented graphically must:

"... enable the sign to be represented visually, particularly by means of images, lines or characters so that it can be properly identified ... clear, precise, self-contained, easily accessible, intelligible, durable and objective".[2]

The Trade Marks Act 1994 introduced, for the first time, the ability to register sounds, smells and colours as trademarks provided they are capable of being represented graphically.

Shapes may also be registered as trademarks including the shape of goods or their packaging, provided that they have distinctive character.

Grounds for the refusal of registration are set out in Article 3 of the Trademark Directive and include the following:

- Trademarks which are devoid of any distinctive character;
- Trademarks which consist exclusively of signs or indications which may serve in trade to designate the kind, quality, quantity, intended purpose, value, geographical origin or the time of production of the goods or rendering the service or other characteristics of goods; and
- Trademarks which consist exclusively of signs or indications which have become customary in the current language or bona fide and established practices of the trade.

It is also not possible to register trademarks on the relative ground of an earlier registered or unregistered trademark right. An earlier trademark is defined as one having an earlier application date which gives the trademark seniority.

Article 4 makes specific provision for identical trademarks, similar trademarks and identical or similar marks to earlier trademarks where the earlier mark has a reputation and where the use of the sign would either take advantage of or be detrimental to the distinctive character or the repute of the earlier mark.

Article 5 of the Trademark Directive sets out the rights conferred by a registered trademark. These are exclusive rights so that the proprietor is given the right to prevent the use of a sign in the course of a trade by a third party without the proprietor's consent.

In order to constitute infringement the offending mark must be used in a trademark sense as an indicator of origin. Thus for example use of a mark in a cartoon or satirical paper is unlikely to constitute infringement.

3. Passing off

Numerous jurisdictions have unfair competition laws governing the use of IP rights and protecting from unfair trading practices. A good example is the Australian Trade Practices Act. In the United Kingdom there is no express unfair competition law; instead the common law tort of passing off (which also applies in most common law jurisdictions) provides effective protection from deceptive trading practices.

English law protects goodwill and reputation and recognises the common law tort of passing off designed to protect trading goodwill and reputation. In the leading case of *Erven Warnink v J Townend & Sons (Hull) Limited ("Advocaat")*[3] the House of

---

2 *Ralf Sieckmann v Deutsches Patent- und Markenamt,* Case C-273/00 paragraph 55.
3 [1979] AC 731.

Lords set out the requirements for a successful claim for passing off as follows:

- A misrepresentation;
- Made by a trader in the course of trade;
- To respective customers of his or ultimate consumers of goods or services supplied by him;
- Which is calculated to injure the business or goodwill of another trader (in the sense that it is a reasonably foreseeable consequence); and
- Which causes actual damage to a business or goodwill of the trader by whom the action is brought or will probably do so.

In *Reckitt & Colman Products Ltd v Borden Inc ("Jif Lemon")*[4] the requirements were simplified by the House of Lords as follows:

- The existence of the claimant's goodwill;
- A misrepresentation as to the goods or services offered by the defendant; and
- Damage (or likely damage) to the claimant's goodwill as a result of the defendant's misrepresentation.

Goodwill is normally shown as a result of history of offering goods or services under the particular mark or get-up, or professional reputation. It must be established in the course of trade. Passing off is shown by the misrepresentation, which is largely a matter of evidence based upon evidence of confusion arising from the misrepresentation made by the defendant.

4. Copyright

A series of international treaties, primarily the Berne Convention, provide that almost every country is obliged to give copyright protection within its jurisdiction. Thus citizens of Berne Convention countries will generally be entitled to copyright protection for their works in other Berne Convention countries.

Copyright is a property right that subsists in certain specified types of works as provided for by the Copyright Designs and Patents Act 1988. Examples of the works in which copyright subsists are original literary and artistic works, films, sound recordings, performers' rights and computer software.

The 1988 Act gives the owner of the copyright subsisting in the work the exclusive right to do certain acts in relation to the work such as making a copy, broadcasting or selling copies to the public.

If a third party carries out one of the acts restricted by copyright without the consent or licence of the copyright owner the copyright owner is entitled to sue for infringement of copyright. The Act incorporates defences to infringement such as fair dealing with the work.

Generally the term of copyright is 70 years from the end of the calendar year in which the creator died although specific copyrights are given specific terms. For example copyright in a sound recording expires 50 years from the end of the calendar year in which it was made.

4 [1990] 1 All ER 873.

Section 1(1) of the 1988 Act lists the works in which copyright can subsist as being:

- Original literary, dramatic, musical or artistic works;
- Sound recordings, films or broadcasts; and
- The typographical arrangement of published editions.

There is a requirement for originality which means that the work must be new or innovative. The work should be independently created and be the independent work of the author. The leading cases have indicated that the author must expend "skill and labour" on the creation of the work. The threshold for originality in England is relatively low.

Generally copyright will not protect ideas such as the plot of a work of fiction.

"Literary work" has been interpreted in case law as covering work which is expressed in print or writing irrespective of the question whether the quality or style of the work is high. Dramatic works include works of dance or mime. A musical work is a work consisting of music exclusive of any words or action intended to be sung, spoken or performed with the music.

An artistic work is defined by Section 4(1) of the Act as including a number of different types of work:

- A graphic work, photograph, sculpture or collage, irrespective or artistic quality;
- A work of architecture being a building or a model for a building; or
- A work of artistic craftsmanship.

Section 4(2) defines a graphic work as including:

- Any painting, drawing, diagram, map, chart or plan; and
- Any engraving, etching, lithograph, woodcut or similar work.

Problems of interpretation have arisen with the definition of works of artistic craftsmanship and the courts have required the existence of some artistic quality.

In order for copyright to subsist in a work under Section 1(3) of the Act the qualification requirements must be satisfied either by reference to the author of the work, or by reference to the country of first publication or in the case of a broadcast, the country of first transmission. A network of international copyright conventions ensures that copyright is protected worldwide so that a citizen of a Berne Copyright Convention country would be entitled to enforce copyright in the United Kingdom and vice versa.

The author of a work is the person who creates it. In the case of a literary or artistic work this is the person who writes or designs it. The author of a piece of music is its composer and the author of a photograph is the photographer. In the case of a broadcast the author is the person making the broadcast. The author of a sound recording is the producer and the joint authors of a film are the producer and principal director. In the case of a commissioned work the author remains the copyright owner so that it is necessary for there to be an assignment to the commissioner. Works created by an employee in the course of his employment will generally vest with the employer.

The acts restricted by copyright under Section 16(1) of the Act include exclusive right to:

- Copy the work;
- To issue copies of the work to the public;
- To rent or lend the work to the public;
- To perform show or play the work in public;
- To communicate the work to the public; and
- To make an adaptation of the work or do any of the above in relation to an adaptation.

In order for there to be infringement it is necessary that a substantial part of the work has been taken. In the seminal decision of *Ladbroke (Football) Ltd v William Hill (Football) Ltd* the House of Lords held that substantiality must be decided by its quality rather than its quantity.[5] The reproduction of a part which by itself has no originality will not normally be a substantial part of the copyright and therefore will not be protected.

Copying is defined by Section 17 of the Act so that for example Section 17(2) defines copying in relation to a literary, dramatic, musical or artistic work as "reproducing the work in any material form". This does not extend to reproducing the idea underlying the work.

In addition to primary infringement of copyright there are other acts of infringement known as "secondary infringements" in which case the infringement must be undertaken by a person with knowledge of or reason to believe that the copies are infringing copies. Secondary infringement involves inter alia the following activities:

- Importing into the UK other than for private or domestic use;
- Possessing or dealing with an infringing copy;
- Making import into the UK, possessing in the course of business or selling, letting for hire, offering or exposing for sale or hire.

The Act contains remedies for civil proceedings by way of damages or on account of profit as well as criminal proceedings designed to deal with intentional infringement whereby the infringer knows or has reason to believe the work is an infringing copy of a copyright work.

Defences to copyright infringement include lack of title in the work, lack of substantiality so that the work is not infringed as well as specific defences of fair dealing including, for example, non-commercial research or private study, incidental inclusion of the work in a photograph, criticism, review and reporting current events. There is also now a defence of parody.

5. Designs

Design protection varies according to the jurisdiction. Some jurisdictions accord protection under copyright law, others under patent law. In the United States there is a system of registerable Design Patents. In Germany and Austria there is a system of registerable Utility Models or *"Gebrauchmaster"* for a maximum 10-year term.

5 [1964] 1 WLR 273.

Similar systems exist in Italy and Spain. Australia has a system of "innovation patents" for a term of eight years.

Until the Copyrights Designs and Patents Act 1988 designs in the UK were protected either as registered designs under the Registered Designs Act 1949 or by copyright on the basis that there was a three-dimensional infringement of the two-dimensional copyright drawing. The Copyrights Designs and Patents Act 1988 introduced a new form of design protection known as UK unregistered design right designed primarily to protect functional designs, generally for a period of no more than 10 years. The term of protection under the Registered Designs Act 1949 was increased to 25 years from the date of first marketing.

In 2002 an unregistered and registered community design was introduced by the Registered Designs Regulations by way of the Council Regulation EC6/2002 on community designs.

The current design regime therefore is:

- Registration as a UK design under the Registered Designs Act 1949;
- UK unregistered design right;
- Unregistered community design;
- Community registered design; and
- Residuary artistic copyright protection.

5.1 Registration under the Registered Designs Act 1949

Under Section 1(2) Registered Designs Act 1949 design is defined as "... the appearance of the whole or part of a product resulting from the features of, in particular the lines, contours, colours, shape, texture or materials of the product or its ornamentation".

A design must be new and have individual character so that the overall impression it produces on the informed user differs from the overall impression on such a user by any design which has been made available to the public before the relevant date.

Features of appearance of a product which are dictated solely by the product's technical function are excluded from registration. However, this does not prevent registration of design which includes such features. For example, the solely functional terminal block which was the subject of *AMP v Utilux*[6] would still be incapable of registration under the current law.

The initial registration period is five years from the date of registration of the design but may be renewed for subsequent five year periods up to a maximum of 25 years.

5.2 UK unregistered design right

In order for design right to subsist in a design it must be an original design. There are also requirements for qualification which must be satisfied and the design must be fixed in some tangible form by recording it in a design document or by making an article to the design.

Design is defined as the "design of any aspect to the shape or configuration (whether external or internal) of the whole or part of an article".

Design right does not subsist in:

---

6 [1972] RPC 103.

- Methods or principles of construction;
- Features of shape or configuration which:-
  - Enable the article to be connected to, placed in, around or against another article so that either article may perform its function (the "must fit" exception); or
  - Are dependent upon the appearance of another article of which the article is intended by the designer (creator of the design) to form an integral part (the "must-match" exception).

Originality is not defined in the legislation save that Section 213(4) states that a design which is "commonplace in the designer field at the time of its creation" is not original.

5.3 Community registered design right

Article 3(a) of the Community Design Regulation states that the definition of design is "the appearance of the whole or a part of a product resulting from the features of, in particular, the lines, contours, colours, shape, texture and or materials of the product and/or its ornamentation". A design must be new and have an individual character. A design is new if no identical design or one whose features differ only in immaterial details has been made available to the public either before the date of filing for a registered community design or in the case of the unregistered community design before the design was made available to the public. A period of grace of 12 months is allowed without destroying novelty where the disclosure in question is by or through the designer or in breach of confidence.

There are a number of exceptions to registration, for example where the features of appearance of a product are solely dictated by the product's technical function and there is also a "must fit exception".

The term of protection of the designs which are registered at the Office for Harmonization in the Internal Market (OHIM) is 25 years.

Although registration gives an exclusive right, the rights in a community registered design are not infringed by:

- Acts done privately and for non-commercial purposes;
- Acts done for experimental purposes; and
- Acts of reproduction for the purposes of making citations or teaching if they are compatible with fair trade practice, do not unduly prejudice the normal exploitation of the design and mention the source.

5.4 Unregistered Community design

This is essentially a transitional right which has a term of three years. It has the same basis as for a Community registered design right except that to prove infringement you must additionally show that the design has been copied.

5.5 Copyright in artistic works applied industrially

There is a residuary copyright protection for artistic works which are "applied industrially", that is to say, as soon as the design is applied to more than 50 articles.

The usual rules relating to copyright and in particular infringement apply. The term was recently extended to 70 years after the author's life, from 25 years as provided for in the 1988 Act.

6. Confidential information and trade secrets

Most jurisdictions afford protection for trade secrets.

There are essentially two methods of protecting trade secrets or confidential information in English law, either by way of contract such as a non-disclosure agreement or obligations of confidentiality in a contract of employment. Alternatively the law of breach of confidence creates in certain circumstances an equitable obligation of confidence which the courts are prepared to enforce.

The leading authority remains *Coco v AN Clark (Engineers) Limited* where the requirements to enforce confidential information were set out:[7]

- The information must have the necessary quality of confidence about it;
- The information must have been imparted in circumstances importing an obligation of confidence; and
- There must be an unauthorised use of that information to the detriment of the party communicating it.

The leading case which has clarified the principles applicable to the employee relationship is *Faccenda Chicken Ltd v Fowler* which concerned the wrongful use by an ex-employee of sales information.[8] The Court of Appeal held that if there was a contract of employment the employee's obligations were to be determined from that contract but in the absence of any express terms the employee's obligations would be implied. In particular there was an implied term imposing a duty of good faith or fidelity on the employee. This was more restricted post-employment than that imposed during the course of employment. The nature of the obligation would depend upon the nature of the employment and whether confidential information was generally handled, the quality of the information and the extent to which the employer stressed the confidential nature of the information.

A more recent development has been the interpretation by the courts of Article 10 of the Human Rights Convention within the Human Rights Act 1998 and the acceptance by the highest courts of a right of privacy subject to disclosure in the public interest. The leading case is *Campbell v Mirror Group Newspapers Ltd* where the House of Lords stated that the law of breach of confidence had developed to such a stage that it represented the UK's implementation of the Human Rights Convention, rights of privacy and freedom of expression.[9]

7. Database right

Database right protects the format of the collation of the data in the database. The data itself may also be protected by literary copyright.

---

7 1969 RPC 41.
8 1986 1 All ER 617.
9 2004 2 AC 457.

Database right was introduced by EU Directive 96/9/EC to provide a *sui generis* remedy for the legal protection of databases.

A computer database is a collection of data stored on computer media usually in the form of a computer file or files and will frequently include lists of clients or products, drawings and photographs. A computer database generated by a computer is a copyright work under the 1988 Act. However since the Copyright and Rights Databases Regulations 1997 it seems unlikely that both database right and copyright will exist simultaneously.

The leading interpretation of database right is *British Horseracing Board v William Hill* (2001 RPC 612) involving a database containing details of racehorse owners which gave a fairly broad interpretation of the right, and the tort of wrongful extraction from the database.[10]

Database right protects the format of the collation of the data in the database. The data itself may also be protected by literary copyright.

8. Semiconductor topography design right

Integrated circuits known as silicon chips are generally manufactured from layers of materials with different patterns formed by the processes of etching the layers of the materials. EU Directive 87/54/EEC, which came into force on 7 November 1987, gave a *sui generis* right (generally called a "topography right") in the layout of an integrated circuit. This was replaced with an amended right under the Design Right (Semiconductor) Regulations 1989 which came into force on 1 August 1989. For the purpose of the Regulations, the semiconductor topography must be original. It is not original if it is commonplace in the design field in question at the time of its creation. The duration of the right depends on whether the topography is commercially exploited. Normally the term of the right is 10 years from the end of the year in which it was first commercially exploited anywhere in the world, subject to a maximum term of 15 years.

10 2001 RPC 612.

Types of transaction

Richard Binns
Lydia Torne
Simmons & Simmons LLP

---

1. Share purchases

One of the most common types of corporate transaction is the purchase of a business by way of a share sale. Under this model, the purchaser will acquire 100% of the shares in the target business and thereby assume all of the previous owner's assets and liabilities.

A purchaser will want to assess the status of the target business, in particular: (i) the quality of its key assets; and (ii) the extent of its liabilities, as these will affect viability for continued growth and profit and the extent of the risk the purchaser will incur, both of which will factor into the overall valuation of the target business.

1.1 Due diligence

All businesses will have some degree of intellectual property, even if it is only copyright in their administrative paperwork. However, an increasingly competitive market means that businesses are being compelled to innovate to maintain their market position and it is this innovation, protected by various IP rights, that is often a key attraction for a purchaser. In such cases, it will be particularly important for a purchaser to conduct appropriate due diligence to assess the status of the relevant IP assets. Such diligence should include verifying whether:

- the target has the right to use the intellectual property it relies on and will still be able to do so following the sale;
- the target is subject to any particularly onerous contractual terms under its licences-in or licences-out of intellectual property or if such agreements have relevant change-of-control provisions;
- the intellectual property is subject to challenge by a third party;
- the target is infringing a third party's intellectual property (eg, a consultancy that developed intellectual property for the business but did not assign its rights in that intellectual property to the target); and
- there are any encumbrances on the intellectual property.

The extent of the due diligence can vary from a full due diligence report providing details on all information obtained (both positive and negative) through to an exceptions only report that includes only key negative issues reaching a certain materiality threshold.

In some cases a purchaser may choose not to conduct formal due diligence on a target and instead rely solely on contractual protection (such as warranties and indemnities). This may be particularly helpful where the timescale for the deal is limited or the business is not considered to be particularly rich in intellectual property.

Due diligence can reveal significant issues with IP assets, particularly problems related to the ownership of the relevant intellectual property. Whereas copyright works created by employees in the course of their employment duties will automatically vest in their employer under English law, the works of consultants will not. This can lead to gaps in ownership of key IP assets. Further, the position with respect to ownership of employee works differs in other jurisdictions. For example, in certain Middle Eastern jurisdictions, employers do not automatically own employees' copyright works, nor can employees prospectively assign all works they create in the course of their employment to their employer. Consequently, a purchaser will want to ensure that copyright works have been periodically retrospectively assigned to the target.

The purchaser will also need to consider among other things: (i) the effect of the proposed transaction on the parties' tax structures and liabilities, including whether intellectual property owned by the target will need to be subsequently hived off to an IP holding company within the purchaser's group; (ii) how to protect intellectual property and confidential information known to third parties that will no longer be connected to the target (eg, former consultants and the seller's other group companies); and (iii) whether the sale or any connected licensing arrangements are permitted under competition law.

When negotiating with public entities, information provided may be subject to a freedom of information request by a third party (eg, a competitor) with which the public authority may be compelled to comply. Care should therefore be taken when considering what to provide to the public body and how best to try to ensure such information is protected as commercially sensitive information.

1.2 Impact of due diligence

If material issues are identified, a purchaser will need to assess their impact on the wider transaction and either accept the resultant risk or request specific protections from the seller. For example, a purchaser may require:

- a reduction in the sale price (this might correlate to the perceived reduction in value of the target as a result of the issue or the cost to rectify the issue);
- the issue to be rectified (eg, by requiring the seller to obtain an assignment of material intellectual property owned by a consultant as a condition precedent[1] to the sale);
- a different deal structure (eg, by converting a share sale to an asset sale in order to permit the purchaser to cherry pick assets and leave behind liabilities or hiving off certain assets into a special purpose vehicle (SPV) to be subsequently sold);

1 Sometimes a purchaser may agree to such actions being a condition subsequent to the sale. However, in such cases the parties will need to clearly establish what the effects will be if this condition is not satisfied.

- an indemnity to compensate the purchaser if a potential risk comes to fruition (eg, litigation is brought against the target for infringement of a particular third party's intellectual property);
- transitional arrangements to be put in place in order to permit the target to continue with its business after the sale while the purchaser implements an alternative solution (eg, a licence to use intellectual property owned by another member of the seller's group until the purchaser can replace that intellectual property or remove the business's reliance on it).

If none of these options is suitable or possible the purchaser may decide to abort the deal.

1.3 Warranties and indemnities

Whether or not the purchaser has conducted due diligence, it will usually seek warranty protection regarding the state of the business at the sale date and that, for example, the target has the right to use all intellectual property that it uses in the operation of its business at the sale date. Where due diligence has identified particular concerns, a purchaser may push for a warranty on this point in order to try to encourage the seller to disclose against that warranty. In this way, warranties can uncover issues and add to the due diligence process. However, once an issue is disclosed, a warranty cannot be enforced against the seller in connection with that disclosed issue (assuming it has been fairly and properly disclosed).

The extent to which warranties are given depends on the balance of negotiating power between the parties. It is common for warranties to be heavily negotiated, with sellers seeking to keep the number of warranties they give to a minimum and to qualify those indemnities by restricting them by awareness, materiality and time. Sellers may also seek to ring-fence their IP warranties, meaning that wider warranties (eg, those regarding dispute resolution) will not cover IP disputes. This will usually result in a purchaser requiring ring-fenced disclosures. In this case, disclosures in respect of broader dispute resolution will not apply in respect of IP disputes and each will need to be specifically disclosed.

Where an issue has been identified by due diligence and/or warranties, a seller may request an indemnity to reduce its risk of potential future liability. The scope of an indemnity will usually be limited to the specific issue and the seller will usually seek to restrict its liability under an indemnity as much as possible. For example, a seller may: (i) seek to impose a cap on the amount recoverable under the indemnity or a minimum threshold which must be met to trigger the indemnity; (ii) exclude certain types of loss; or (iii) restrict the indemnity to a certain period of time. The final form of an indemnity (and the extent to which it does in fact minimise a purchaser's potential liability) will depend significantly on the balance of negotiating power between the parties.

1.4 Transfer process

As mentioned above, in a share sale the purchaser will assume all the assets and liabilities of the target. It is therefore not necessary to specifically assign the relevant

IP assets – their ownership will automatically transfer. Equally, there is no need to record the transfer in ultimate ownership of the target as it will not affect the name of the owner on the intellectual property register. However, when conducting due diligence, purchasers should check for change of control provisions in the target's key contracts that may permit the other party to terminate the contract in the event of a change of ultimate ownership in the target.

2. Asset purchases

A purchaser may prefer to enter into an asset purchase rather than a share purchase on the basis that it allows it to purchase the key assets of the target, without taking on its liabilities.

2.1 Due diligence

Under this model, once the relevant assets have been identified, the purchaser will need to conduct similar due diligence to that outlined in section 1.1 above. This process can give rise to similar issues to those referred to above, such as the target not owning the rights in the relevant IP asset. Additional issues can arise in connection with the transfer of key licences: assignment may be prohibited under the terms of the licence and/or the consent to an assignment or novation can be withheld by a third party. Further, in an asset sale context there may be deeper concerns regarding an asset's reliance on the intellectual property of another member of the seller's group or on intellectual property that is still owned by the target but not the subject of the sale.

Sales involving a government entity may give rise to additional considerations that could affect deal structure and negotiation strength. For example, the government entity is likely to be subject to various disclosure obligations, including under the Freedom of Information Act 2000, which could result in documents and correspondence being made publicly available. In addition, where retained assets are reliant on assets that have been sold, the government entity may be able to rely on statutory or crown rights (which give it the right, as a matter of law, to use certain IP rights in certain circumstances, assuming they are being used for the services of the Crown) to avoid transitional licensing arrangements. However, in practice this does not often happen and there may be a requirement to formalise the arrangements, including terms relating to compensation.

2.2 Warranties and indemnities

Similar warranty and indemnity protection will be sought in respect of the purchased IP assets as under section 1.3 above.

2.3 Transfer process

In an asset sale, the seller will need to specifically assign to the purchaser each IP asset. This assignment might be dealt with in the body of the asset purchase agreement along with other assets being transferred. Alternatively, the parties sometimes prefer to include an obligation in the main asset purchase agreement to execute a separate assignment deed in respect of the IP assets, which is included as a schedule to the asset purchase agreement. This can be helpful where: (i) the parties wish to keep separate any liability for IP-related warranties and indemnities from the asset purchase agreement more generally; or (ii) conversely, the parties wish to keep all issues of liability and consideration in the main agreement so that the intellectual property assignment is a pure standalone assignment that the parties can use in the recordal process without having to disclose the wider (and sensitive) terms of the sale.

It is important that the purchaser promptly records itself as the owner of that IP asset at the relevant intellectual property registry. Broadly speaking, as a matter of English law, the assignment will only be effective against a third party once it has been recorded on the relevant register. Consequently, if a purchaser does not record that it has obtained title to that IP asset, and a bona fide third-party purchaser for value, without notice, subsequently acquires rights in the IP asset from the seller, the purchaser may not be able to enforce its rights against that third party and until it is registered as proprietor it will not be able to enforce its rights against third parties generally.

The asset purchase agreement should include a requirement for the parties to provide each other with assistance, to execute all documents and do all things necessary in connection with this process. Depending on the jurisdiction where the IP asset subsists, recordal processes range from the relatively straightforward to the convoluted, involving powers of attorney, confirmatory deeds of assignment and official forms (which may need to be notarised and/or legalised). Where large portfolios of registered intellectual property are being assigned, the purchaser may wish to consider obtaining an estimate from an IP practitioner for the costs of the recordal process (perhaps focusing on key markets of interest in the first instance) as the costs involved can be significant and a purchaser may come under pressure to agree to absorb those costs. These post-completion matters are addressed specifically in Chapter 10.

2.4 Licensing

As mentioned above, in some cases the target business or assigned IP asset will be reliant on intellectual property retained by the seller or a third party to which it will no longer have access post-sale. For example, the target may use (without a formal licence) bespoke software that has been created by another member of the seller's group and that is integral to the operation of its business. In such cases, the purchaser will need to ensure that it obtains a right to use the relevant software until it can remove the target's reliance on the asset. The reverse position may also be true, where the target has developed intellectual property that is used by the rest of the seller's group and for which the seller will require a licence post-sale.

Other types of licence may also be required, such as a run-off trademark licence. This will permit the seller/purchaser to use the sold/retained mark for a limited period while it migrates its business across to a new trademark. This may be particularly important where the business has lots of premises, products or other real assets that will need to be rebranded over a period of time.

These types of licence can be set out in the main body of the sale documents, but are often set out in separate licence agreements that are included as schedules to the transaction documents. This is because the parties may wish to include detailed ancillary provisions regarding the arrangement such as quality control provisions, warranties and indemnities and additional termination rights. These licences may vary in duration and can be provided for no further charge (particularly where they are given for a short period of time) or for a fee. They will usually be non-exclusive in scope (thereby permitting the licensor to use the intellectual property itself or exploit it via third parties) and permit the licensee to use the licensed intellectual property only to the extent and in the manner in which it was used prior to the sale, with no right to any improvements or upgrades to that intellectual property.

In any of these licences, it is quite common to see a right for the licensor to terminate if the licensee challenges the validity of the licensed right. This makes commercial sense: (a) if a party has challenged the intellectual property, the working relationship is likely to be irreparably damaged; and (b) it is likely to deter the licensee from challenging the intellectual property (thereby preserving the licensor's monopoly). However, the new Technology Transfer Block Exemption Regulation[2] (which came into force on May 1 2014) now provides that, in a non-exclusive licence, a termination right of this nature will fall outside the scope of the block exemption (and will need to be assessed on a case-by-case basis as to whether it has an anti-competitive effect on the market). This change could assist a non-exclusive licensee to take a licence of an IP asset the validity of which it can then challenge, without fear of losing its licence in the event that its legal challenge is unsuccessful. This is potentially an empowering change for licensees and licensee purchasers should bear it in mind as a means to maximise their position.

3. Initial public offerings

Companies may want to undertake an initial public offering (IPO) for many reasons. Most commonly, IPOs are used to raise finance, but also for an increased profile or to permit the business to engage in other activities such as employee share schemes or to permit existing shareholders to easily exit the business.

As part of the IPO, a company will need to provide a prospectus giving potential investors a detailed understanding of the business, its strengths, weaknesses and risk factors so that they are able to make an informed decision about their investment. In order to prepare the prospectus, the company and its advisors will usually undertake detailed due diligence. The due diligence process (business, financial and legal) for IPOs is often more thorough than that used for acquisitions of the types set out in sections 1 and 2 above, because it is not possible to rely on contractual protections (such as warranties and indemnities) in the same way and the penalties for presenting a misleading prospectus are significant. The due diligence will result in the preparation of a report to the company setting out in detail (among other things) the state of the business, its strengths and weaknesses, market position, financial position and legal risks and liabilities. The due diligence report helps to inform the prospectus, but also provides some comfort to the company and its

2 Technology Transfer Block Exemption Regulation 316/2014, OJ 2014 L93/17.

directors (and to an extent the bank sponsoring the IPO), who will be responsible for the content of the prospectus. It also assists the company in valuing the business and setting the share price (see section 5.3 for further information regarding the valuation of IP assets).

Where the company is an innovator business, such that much of its future revenue and profit may depend on its ability to protect and enforce its innovations, it will be particularly important for the company to follow the steps below:

- Step 1: identify relevant intellectual property;
- Step 2: assess the validity and enforceability of that intellectual property;
- Step 3: assess the extent to which the intellectual property is infringed by third parties;
- Step 4: verify its freedom to operate using that intellectual property; and
- Step 5: based on the foregoing, understand the real value of that intellectual property.

Accordingly, IP lawyers will usually be engaged for the first four steps and an accountant (sometimes with the assistance of a lawyer) will be engaged for Step 5. This fifth step is looked at in more detail in Michelle Korman and Stephen Robertson's chapter on IP valuation. Step 1 will require collaborative working with the company to understand what its material IP assets are. This can be facilitated by asking the company to complete a set of due diligence questions, the answers to which can reveal the starting point for the investigation. It will then be for the lawyers to investigate these rights. It will also be important to identify any material licensing-in of intellectual property on which the company may be dependant, as the termination or breach of this licence may be a considerable risk factor for the business. Where the company has registered IP rights around the world, it may need to engage local attorneys in the various jurisdictions to provide an assessment of those rights.

Once the due diligence report is finalised, lawyers will usually be engaged to prepare the section of the prospectus on legal risk factors for the business. It will be important to ensure that the information provided in the risk factors section is comprehensive, easy to understand and factually accurate. Bearing in mind that IP rights (and their commercial impact) are not necessarily widely understood, it will be important to convey the significance of these rights and any potential risks in a measured way. For example, it is very hard (if not impossible) to say categorically that an IP right is valid and enforceable unless it has been confirmed as such by a court of competent jurisdiction (and even then courts in different jurisdictions have been known to reach different conclusions as to validity when considering equivalent patents covering the same invention). However, for many investors, not being able to state that an IP right is valid may be a matter of immediate concern. It is therefore important to ensure that risk factors are couched in the correct terms so as not to raise concerns unduly, but to flag real issues. Equally, where the business operates in a regulated market, care will need to be taken in drafting the prospectus to ensure that, while it emphasises the strengths of the business and its products and services, the prospectus does not inadvertently breach applicable regulations. For example, a prospectus for a pharmaceutical company will need to ensure that, in describing the strengths of its current product portfolio, it does not inadvertently promote a prescription-only medicine to the public, which is prohibited.

4. Joint ventures

Joint ventures are common corporate structures that allow parties to pool their strengths to develop and exploit a particular product or service. These structures allow the parties to remain independent while contributing towards a common goal. There are many structures that can be considered as a joint venture transaction, including:

- incorporating a limited company with the relevant parties as shareholders;
- establishing a limited liability partnership with the relevant parties as members;
- establishing a limited partnership with the relevant parties as members; or
- a pure contractual arrangement where no separate entity is established. The specific considerations for joint ventures are looked at in more detail in Chapter 5.

With multiple parties, all with different backgrounds, each looking to achieve different goals from the joint venture, it can be challenging to reach an agreed position on key points such as intellectual property. It can be helpful in the first instance to get the parties to agree a broad set of principles regarding ownership, exploitation and enforcement of intellectual property, which can then form a framework for the parties to work with. Any agreement will need to consider:

- granting the joint venture entity access to the participants' background intellectual property. The agreement will need to provide for the parties to identify and disclose relevant intellectual property and the terms on which it can be used, for example, on a non-exclusive basis for the purpose of performing its obligations under the joint venture project only;
- the apportionment of ownership of intellectual property generated by the joint venture entity (known as the 'foreground intellectual property'). For example, will the intellectual property be owned by the joint venture entity that generated it or will it be owned by one or all of the participants? If the intellectual property will be owned by one participant, will it be the same participant in all cases or will certain participants own intellectual property in respect of certain technical fields of interest?;
- cross-licensing of intellectual property generated by the joint venture entity. If the participants own the foreground intellectual property, this will need to be licensed (at least) to the joint venture entity (if one exists) in order for it to be able to use the intellectual property as part of its day-to-day activities. It may also be necessary to license the foreground intellectual property to other participants in the joint venture;
- provisions regarding access to intellectual property (both background and foreground) upon the dissolution of the joint venture or exit of one party (in a multi-party joint venture). For example, in a tripartite joint venture, if one party chooses to exit, will its background intellectual property continue to be

licensed to the joint venture entity and will the exiting party continue to own and/or have the right to use any foreground intellectual property?; and

- provisions regarding who will be responsible for the filing, prosecution and maintenance of any intellectual property generated by the joint venture entity and who will bear the costs of that action. For example, it may be that the allocated owner of the IP right is responsible for, and shall bear the cost of, filing, prosecuting and maintaining that intellectual property. However, this could give rise to disproportionate costs for one participant if their intellectual property faces particular challenges. Further, the parties should consider what will happen if the party responsible for filing for registered protection does not wish to do so – will the other participants have a right to do so instead and if so, in whose name and at whose cost?

The parties will also need to consider the impact of the introduction of the unified patent court (UPC). Currently, a patent owner who wishes to enforce patent rights across Europe must do so on a country-by-country basis. The UPC (which is scheduled to open in 2015 or early 2016) will provide a single forum through which patents can be enforced and challenged on a pan-European basis. A unitary patent will also be introduced that will provide protection for the entire European Union (excluding Spain and Italy) in one right (rather than numerous national rights). Patent owners can opt out of the jurisdiction of the UPC, thereby avoiding a central attack on their patent rights (ie, an invalidity action in the UPC that invalidates all the owner's patent rights for that invention across Europe). However, only the proprietor of the patent can opt out; consequently, the terms of any joint venture agreement should set out whether the parties wish to opt in or opt out of the UPC's jurisdiction and, if the latter, they should contain provisions compelling the proprietor to do so. This can be quite a controversial decision as the opt-out will apply to all patents for that invention in Europe. A proprietor cannot opt out in respect of the United Kingdom only because its UK licensee would prefer not to be subject to the UPC's jurisdiction. Consequently, where a party licenses patents in the same patent family to different licensees in different territories of Europe it will need to make a decision regarding the treatment of these patents in all such jurisdictions for all licensees.

Sometimes, irrespective of the corporate structure of the joint venture, the parties may establish a separate company (an IPCo) whose sole purpose will be to hold and manage intellectual property. For example:

- the participants will license their background intellectual property to the IPCo;
- the IPCo will license this intellectual property to any end joint venture entity;
- the IPCo and joint venture entity will have an agreement in place under which the joint venture entity assigns all its rights in any intellectual property generated as part of the joint venture project to the IPCo, which will own it and license it back to the joint venture.

This creates one central owner of IP rights, which can file, prosecute and maintain protection of the intellectual property generated, as well as grant access to intellectual property upon exit (eg, the participants may each have a non-exclusive licence for all intellectual property generated by the joint venture). Another benefit of an IPCo of this nature is that it may be established in a tax-efficient jurisdiction for IP assets.

5. Corporate venturing

Corporate venturing can cover a wide range of financing options, including angel funding, seed funding, venture capital investment, unsecured and secured lending by banks and monetisations.

Where the business being invested in relies heavily on innovative products or services for its development and future revenues, potential investors will want to scrutinise the quality of its IP protection to ensure that the business is in the best possible position to maximise its growth and revenues. In particular, investors will look to verify: (i) the extent to which inventions, trademarks, designs and other materials are capable of registrable protection and are in fact registered; (ii) whether the ownership or validity of the IP rights has been challenged (or is vulnerable to challenge) by a third party; (iii) the extent to which use of the intellectual property may infringe a third party's rights and freedom to operate; and (iv) whether the intellectual property is being infringed by a third party.

This principle will apply in respect of all funding. However, each type of funding brings its own particular concerns.

5.1 Angel and seed funding

As angel and seed funding occur at such an early stage in the life of a business, an investor's key concern is likely to be whether the business's innovation is protected from being freely copied by third parties – the monopoly afforded by IP protection will often be crucial to the development of a successful start-up business. As the level of investment in angel and seed funding is often comparatively lower than funds raised through the other means listed above and comes at a stage where the business's internal operations are less well established, investors may be less thorough in their due diligence and simply seek assurance that the key intellectual property is adequately protected. Although the level of equity given in return for this funding is relatively low, allowing the investor a more limited degree of control over the business, the business will be in a difficult position as it is likely to be keen to obtain any investment at that stage and the lender will know this. As a result, the borrower's bargaining power may be considerably lower than the lender's.

5.2 Venture capital

The amount of investment provided though venture capital is significantly higher than that raised through angel and seed funding, as is the equity given in return. A venture capital company will be looking to invest with a view to making the business profitable as soon as possible in order to sell off the business and realise its investment in a short period of time. Consequently, a venture capital company will usually conduct extensive independent due diligence into the state of the business's assets before assessing whether to invest. If issues are identified, to the extent that these can be rectified the high degree of equity afforded to the venture capital investor will usually give it the ability to bring about those changes if needed.

When a venture capital investor comes to sell the funded business, it is likely to resist giving any form of contractual protection in respect of the assets being purchased on the basis that it is not sufficiently familiar with the business and its operations (notwithstanding its own extensive due diligence prior to becoming involved with the business). Any purchaser will therefore need to be able and willing to rely on its own due diligence of the business in order to verify the assets being purchased. As part of this due diligence process, it can be helpful to gain access to the original owners of the business who procured venture capital funding as they are likely to be the driving force of the business and be aware of any material issues.

5.3 Secured and unsecured lending

Historically, banks have shied away from providing secured or unsecured lending to businesses that rely heavily on IP assets. There are many reasons for this, one of which being the inherent difficulty of valuing IP assets.

(a) Valuation

One of the key difficulties with intellectual property valuation is that, in all cases, the valuer must make assumptions regarding the IP assets, such as the validity and likely useful life of the intellectual property, which, if incorrect, can have significant implications. Furthermore, each of the three common IP valuation methods (cost,[3] market[4] and income[5]) involves its own (potentially problematic) assumptions. For example, on a historical cost-based valuation, while the amounts incurred may be concrete, this method assumes that the initial outlay by the business in creating the intellectual property matches the real-world value of the asset, which is often incorrect. Examples might be (i) the enormous investment made by pharmaceutical companies into the development of a new drug compound that subsequently fails to obtain a marketing authorisation; and (ii) the relatively small expenditure incurred in creating a brand name that goes on to accrue significant goodwill (for example, Forbes recently valued the Apple brand at $124.2 billion[6]). A valuation can only ever be one person's opinion at a particular time based on a potentially artificial, constructed basis, which does not necessarily provide a sound basis against which banks can lend.

It is these types of problem, particularly for small and medium-sized enterprises, that have led to an increased interest in how to improve debt financing against intellectual property, both at the UK and EU level. In particular, the European

---

3 Where the value of the IP asset is linked to the actual cost incurred by the business in creating the asset.

4 Where the value of the IP asset is linked to the amounts generated under arm's length transactions for similar assets.

5 Where the value of the IP asset is linked to the revenue that the business will accrue as a result of owning the IP asset.

6 Forbes, *The World's Most Valuable Brands*, available at www.forbes.com/powerful-brands/list/.

Commission has appointed a specialist intellectual property valuation panel to consider issues associated with IP valuation and the impact it can have on businesses' ability to raise finance. This has culminated in the publication of a report[7] that made a number of suggestions to try to improve the current position, namely:

- establishing a database containing anonymous information on IP transactions to try to provide benchmarks for valuation purposes;
- creating a central body to oversee the practice of IP valuation rather than rely on lawyers, accountants and other non-specialised practitioners;
- establishing a risk-sharing loan guarantee scheme to facilitate intellectual property secured lending by banks; and
- requiring the mandatory management report to include a report on key IP assets of the business.

It remains to be seen to what extent these suggestions will be adopted, but, in any event, it does suggest that the recent trend in providing IP assets as security will continue.

(b) Secured lending

As industry becomes more aware of, and seeks to rely on, its intellectual property, we are seeing an increase in the number of debt finance deals that are relying on IP assets as security.

A lender's preferred position will usually be to take a mortgage or other fixed charge over key registered IP assets, with a floating charge over all other assets (including other intellectual property). This approach should afford the lender the greatest amount of comfort – the fixed charge gives it the highest degree of control over the asset and the fact that it is a registered asset, (i) makes it easier for the lender to carry out due diligence; and (ii) allows the lender to record its interest in the asset on the relevant register.

Seeking to rely on unregistered rights – such as copyright – as security can prove more problematic as it can be difficult to identify these assets (there may be a significant volume of works) and to comply with due diligence requirements (eg, proving that the borrower is the author and/or owner of such works). However, for certain businesses (such as software companies) this copyright is likely to be one of the most valuable assets the business has to leverage for debt.

In other cases, the borrower's most valuable asset may be a licence of an IP asset (which may be material to the operation of its business and/or generate an income or revenue stream), in which case the lender may be willing to lend in return for a security interest in the licence itself. This type of security is considerably more complex and will require the parties to enter into a detailed agreement, which will sit alongside the underlying licence agreement, controlling the borrower's actions under the licence (eg, termination).

---

7 European Commission, *Final Report from the Expert Group on Intellectual Property Valuation*, available at http://ec.europa.eu/research/innovation-union/pdf/Expert_Group_Report_on_Intellectual_Property_Valuation_IP_web_2.pdf#view=fit&pagemode=none.

(c) *Unsecured lending*

In addition to secured lending, we have recently seen a growing interest in unsecured lending by financial institutions in connection with intellectual property. As part of the EU's innovation strategy, it is aiming to increase the ability to exploit intellectual property across the EU and to help IP-rich businesses to access funding that they may previously have struggled to obtain due to the intangible nature of their assets. Accordingly, the European Investment Bank has established InnovFin Large Projects under which it provides unsecured loans from €25 million to €300 million, backed by funds under Horizon 2020. These loans are aimed at improving access to risk finance for research and development projects. Without security, the banks will be looking for other contractual mechanisms to provide reassurance that they will recover their investment, such as controls over how the funds are used and the extent to which the borrower can take actions that may affect the recoverability of those monies. Equally, the borrower will be looking to retain maximum freedom to operate its business as it sees fit without the lender taking control. The difficulty is trying to find a middle ground that both parties can accommodate. This requires a good understanding of the other's concerns and each of the parties' bottom line requirements.

5.4 Monetisations

It is becoming increasingly common for intellectual property owners to monetise their assets. This is essentially where an intellectual property owner sells its right to future revenues in respect of an IP asset to a third party in return for an immediate upfront fee. Monetisations can be undertaken for a number of reasons including: (i) cash flow – the need for a lump sum now, rather than incremental payments in the future; and (ii) risk hedging – where an intellectual property owner is concerned that its IP asset may be subject to a successful challenge in future, it may prefer to obtain a smaller lump sum up front rather than run the risk of not receiving any royalty income in the future. There are a number of structures that can be adopted for these transactions, the most common being the intellectual property owner assigning its right to receive revenues under a relevant agreement to the purchaser. However, this structure can prove problematic where, for example, (i) the underlying agreement requires a consent to the assignment of rights that cannot be obtained; or (ii) both the assignor and assignee wish to have certain related rights under the underlying agreement (eg, the right to confidential information such as royalty reports); or (iii) the intellectual property owner still has an obligation (at its own cost) to maintain, defend and enforce the relevant IP asset (which can be costly if an action arises and negates the benefit of receiving the slightly reduced upfront amount). Other structures include putting in place a contractual obligation on the licensor to have revenues it receives paid directly into the other party's bank account or into an escrow account (in order to permit any necessary deductions before release). However, this arrangement has its own difficulties, not least of which is the fact that the other party is likely to require a more direct right of access to the funds for which it paid in advance.

6. Insolvency

Sales and other dealings involving an insolvent or distressed intellectual property owner can differ significantly in approach to solvent sales as the actual or threatened insolvency may cast an overarching shadow on the transaction. For example, an insolvency practitioner acting on behalf of the intellectual property owner is unlikely to be willing to incur any liability in connection with the transaction and is therefore unlikely to give any warranty or indemnity protection in connection with the sale. Rather it will be looking to give a bare assignment or licence of those rights the intellectual property owner may have. The purchaser will need to conduct its own due diligence and satisfy itself as best as possible as to the status of what it is purchasing, which can be quite difficult when purchasing unregistered IP rights such as copyright. However, while a purchaser will not usually have the benefit of express warranties and indemnities from the seller, it may still have the benefit of certain statutory implied terms under the Unfair Contract Terms Act 1977 (particularly if standard terms and conditions are used) and this should be considered carefully.

When purchasing IP assets from an insolvent or distressed intellectual property owner it is worth remembering that the process for recording the transfer of that intellectual property may be more complex than usual. For example, the documents will need to be executed by the insolvency practitioner, which will usually look to include additional exclusion of liability wording in any documents it executes, which may not be acceptable to some local registries. Indeed, some local registries may struggle significantly with the idea of an insolvency practitioner acting on behalf of a proprietor at all. Where the assets concerned are foreign IP rights (eg, French trademark registrations or German patents), it should be remembered that local law requirements will apply and need to be complied with.

In the context of IP licensing, the parties will sometimes try to contractually provide for what will happen in the event that one party becomes insolvent. For example, a licensor may seek to provide an immediate right for it to terminate the licence in the event that the licensee becomes insolvent. Conversely, a licensee is likely to want to leave its licence in place in the event of a licensor's insolvency as it will want this to continue and any sale of the asset to be subject to its licence. However, if the licensee is not able to enforce, maintain or defend the licensed intellectual property, the licensor's insolvency may result in an exclusive licensee losing the monopoly afforded to it under the licence. In order to protect this monopoly a licensee may try to put in place some sort of right of first refusal to purchase the intellectual property or seek to have the intellectual property assigned to it upon the licensor's insolvency. These types of arrangement should be approached with caution as they may constitute a transaction at undervalue, which, as a matter of English law, can be set aside by an insolvency practitioner. Licensees who have concerns regarding the liquidity of a licensor may wish to consider including contractual checks on the financial health of the licensor, purchasing the intellectual property at the outset, structuring payments to avoid large upfront payments (thereby minimising the risk of losing significant sums of money) and requiring IP assets to be placed in escrow for release upon insolvency.

IP due diligence in corporate transactions

Paul Davies
EverEdgeIP

1. Introduction

Trade and transactions have always included an element of due diligence, from biting coins to check hardness and ensure they are pure gold to complex due diligence for a corporate transaction. In any exchange where the value is freely determined between the parties, substantial responsibility falls on the parties to ensure they are receiving their desired value from the trade.

Traditionally, intellectual property has formed part of corporate transactions although often not as an identifiable part of the transaction in its own right. Mergers were conducted based on perceived strategic value or identified revenue-bearing activities. While other forms of property would be suitably accounted for and valued, intellectual property was incorporated as part of a non-specified margin payable over other assets in the transaction.

In more recent decades, intellectual property has been increasingly identified as a specific asset in transactions. Regardless, in most circumstances, the assets have been transferred as part of a going concern with the value attributed to the revenue of the business being purchased.

As IP theory and value have evolved, the attribution to intellectual property has increased. Liquidity of IP assets has also improved, leading to an increased volume of transactions of intellectual property alone. Even in those transactions where the business as a whole is sold, intellectual property may constitute 80% or more of the asset base and more regularly forms the strategic reason for purchase.

However, unlike the majority of assets in which title and value is relatively well defined, intellectual property is still far less certain. Even the existence of the rights is in doubt. Copyright only exists if the work is original; a patent is only of value if valid and enforceable, a trade secret of value if confidential. Entitlement to the rights is often subject to the history of the derivation of the work, idea, process or method. Despite registration of many rights, validity and ownership may be subject to challenge. Even those rights in which ownership is not in doubt and validity beyond reproach provide only a right to litigate, not a right to produce. The rights may still be impaired by the existence of more powerful rights in the hands of third parties.

All of this makes the due diligence process complex and without a defined end. A patent, depending on the laws of the jurisdiction concerned, may require novelty and inventiveness over all published materials regardless of their obscurity. Hence validity can never be positively proven. No amount of searching will provide a conclusive answer. No enquiry can be sure to guard against poorly compiled information on the origins of a work. There must always be risk.

The purpose of due diligence is to lower that risk. Zero risk is unachievable.

Simply to make life more difficult for those charged with the process, transactions are usually timeline driven and a budget must be maintained commensurate with the value of the transaction.

It is a simple fact that there is never enough time and never a large enough budget to do all the due diligence that may be desired.

Hence the process becomes one that is not driven by a formulaic process. Instead strategy must be determined and employed to ensure that the limited resources are put to best use in the time available and the risks that remain are transferred, mitigated or accounted for in the value paid. This chapter seeks to provide some guidance on a strategic approach to this problem.

2. Aims of the due diligence process

The aims of the due diligence process have already been alluded to in the preceding section. The goal of the process is to ensure that the parties involved are obtaining fair value in the transaction. As we have seen in Richard Binns and Lydia Torne's chapter on types of transaction, the majority of transactions comprise the receipt of cash or a cash equivalent, thus providing security over the value obtained for the seller. In contrast, the purchaser is buying assets of uncertain value and effect. For both, reduction of uncertainty is advantageous. It provides greater certainty to the buyer and in consequence, increases the value paid for the seller.

So where does the risk lie? Every transaction involving intellectual property combines a legal, a business and a financial element in the valuation of the asset. Is the asset legally owned? To what business use can the asset be put? What is the value to be derived from that use? Typically due diligence has been conducted on the legal element because of the relative ease of doing this compared with an uncertain business or financial assessment. With intellectual property becoming an asset of greater strategic value, the business and financial elements begin to dominate.

The value of intellectual property is a function of the use to which it is to be put. Hence the value and the risks associated with ensuring that value is obtained cannot be divorced from the reasons behind the transaction itself. If the risks to obtain that value are to be minimised by the due diligence process, the process must also take into account the strategic reasons for the transaction.

In general, transactions where intellectual property forms a significant part of the value are conducted for one of four reasons:

- the purchase of technology. The intellectual property behind the technology provides the know-how and technical details to transfer the technology together with any patent rights that may otherwise preclude the purchaser from pursuing the technology. The purchase is generally by an organisation having access to channels for the exploitation of the technology that is greater than that of the seller. The most important strategic aim of the intellectual property after purchase is to support and protect the products;
- the purchase of channel. This is the purchase of market share or access

through the acquisition of customer lists, reputation and trademark rights. Although technology rights may be transferred as part of the overall transaction, their relevance to the value being paid is significantly less;
- the purchase of assets to support commercialisation. This relates to the specific purchase of intellectual property to support existing market efforts or provide assets for assertion. This usually involves the purchase of a portfolio of assets to increase the purchaser's own portfolio and place the purchaser in a better or dominant position in the IP landscape. In this instance the strength of registered assets or the portfolio of such registered assets as a whole is paramount;
- the purchase of assets to supply freedom to operate. Here the greatest strategic aim is to ensure the assets are not in the possession of others and used against the purchaser. While the strength of the registered assets is important in the context of price setting, the post-transaction implications of validity are not. The intention may be to shelve the assets.

Each of these scenarios provides a very different valuation methodology for the assets. Consequently, the due diligence to support the business case based on each valuation needs to be different.

Thus far the discussion has considered primarily the aims of the buyer. The seller is assumed to be receiving cash or a cash equivalent and it is the buyer that has the primary interest in performing due diligence. However, this is far from the case in many instances.

The seller has two main interests in performing good due diligence of its own. These are:
- to drive value into the transaction. A good due diligence process in advance can increase the value offered. As risk is reduced, a potential buyer can attribute greater certainty to the realisation of the strategic value;
- to minimise risk post-transaction. Many transactions will carry warranties or indemnities against the seller with claw-back provisions should the buyer suffer a loss. At a minimum, a seller is likely to be required to provide a warranty around ownership of the rights in question.

Despite the potential value lift from the presentation of good due diligence by the seller, greater effort is likely to be made in risk mitigation. At best the seller is motivated to provide the appearance of good due diligence for value but is not motivated to find issues that would impair value unless they also lead to risk management under a warranty or indemnity. On this basis, while the seller will carry a burden, the greater burden is likely to fall on the buyer in ensuring true value in the transaction.

A further point of distinction in due diligence for transactions relates to the volume of assets being transacted. This also informs the strategy to be taken to complete the due diligence.

A transaction involving a small portfolio is likely to involve a few key assets, which act as the motivation for the transaction. These key assets will contribute the majority of the value to the deal and if few enough in number, can be the subject of detailed review.

In contrast, the purchase of a portfolio of hundreds or thousands of assets is beyond individual analysis or valuation. Furthermore, the outliers that contribute significantly more or less than an average value have a diluted effect on the portfolio valuation. In such instances, the analysis changes from a detailed review of specific assets to a review of the quality of the portfolio as a whole and how this aligns with the strategic aims of the purchaser.

While the majority of the strategic aims in due diligence reside with the buyer, the seller's due diligence should take a similar view. The seller will wish to present a portfolio with the highest degree of confidence in its ability to meet the buyer's strategic aims.

3. Questions to ask and searches to run

The methods by which due diligence is conducted will again depend on the importance of various parts of the portfolio. Regardless, some standard operations are likely to be used with variations on the reliance on each operation being a function of the rights in question.

To obtain information, initial questionnaires may be used in conjunction with searches of the public records. A mix of both will be important in identifying various issues.

To determine the right mix for a particular due diligence, it is necessary to consider some of the fundamental issues that might detract most from the value proposition put forward to engage in the due diligence process.

There are a number of generic impairments to an IP portfolio that would have relevance regardless of the nature of the transaction.

The first of these is the matter of the identification of all the rights that should form part of the transaction. It is remarkably common for rights to be left behind with the seller. If that seller is subsequently wound up as a legal entity, recovery of those rights or transfer to the intended buyer can be problematic. Identification of the rights commences with both questions and public record searches of the organisations involved on the side of the seller, both past and present.

With the organisations identified, a mixture of three types of search is appropriate:

- proprietor searches – for trademarks, patents and design rights, full searches may be run on international databases to ensure the rights identified initially by the proprietor cover all the rights that should be transferred. Note the limitations of databases that either (i) may not hold the records for some individual and generally less regular countries; and/or (ii) may show only granted rights, not pending applications. If rights in any such countries are suggested by the proprietor's records, these will need to be investigated in the countries themselves. Particularly for a share purchase, care needs to be taken that the proprietor is in fact the company in which shares are being acquired, or is a company controlled by that company;
- inventor searches – specifically relating to a patent portfolio, inventors noted

in previous proprietor searches can be cross-checked for inventions standing in the individual's name. This may require supplementary information from the seller to confirm relevant dates of employment for critical inventors;
- online or market presence searches – particularly for trademark portfolios, unregistered trademarks used by the seller in association with the goods and services may carry significant brand equity and yet not be identified with the normal provision of a schedule of registered rights. Market research on the seller and its online presence may ensure these are identified early in the process and incorporated in the transaction.

A more significant difficulty arises with respect to transactions based on technology rather than specific, identifiable registered assets. In such transactions, unregistered rights in the form of trade secrets, confidential information and know-how are likely to form a greater proportion and generally an essential element of the transaction.

To perform due diligence in relation to such a transfer of technology, a questionnaire is unlikely to be able to predict the full extent of documentation and knowledge that should be included in the transfer. Interviews with key technical staff of the seller and buyer may be required.

The enquiries during technical interviews should concentrate on the form and location of the technical data necessary to implement the technology. If the technology is reduced to practice, products may be available and if in full-scale manufacture, the products will already be supported by a significant number of drawings of the product itself, tooling drawings and operating parameters. The copyright in all such documents needs to be included in the rights transferred.

Even with this range of material, a significant portion of knowledge can be lost in the transfer if additional inquiries are not made.

Know-how in the production, design or use of a technology may come in two forms. The first relates to the information needed to replicate existing products or processes post-transaction. This is the positive knowledge of what or how to manufacture, design or use products. This is supported by existing technical documentation of final products.

The second form is often neglected and relates to the negative knowledge within an organisation. This is the knowledge of what not to do. This knowledge is held in the documentation of failed prototypes, previous research or marketing entries or methodologies that have been tried and failed. Although such information may not be of significant value in the replication of the technology in its current form, it may be remarkably valuable during the subsequent evolution of the technology post-transaction, particularly where some or all technical staff of the seller may be lost to the buyer.

In general, the form and identity of this negative knowledge is only uncovered through detailed interviews with technical staff.

Once the rights associated with the seller have been identified, it is necessary to determine the level of relevance of the rights to the transaction. This will determine the extent of further investigation applied to individual or families of assets.

Search and analysis tools such as Innography exist to provide some form of comparative value to a patent portfolio and potentially identify rights of particular importance. Searches of this type are critical to the initial analysis of the value proposition and strategic value of a portfolio. If this analysis has been done in assessing a deal at the outset, portfolio items of particular value may have already been identified. If not, this type of analysis may be useful to determine which rights deserve greater inspection.

Should the transaction involve trademarks and brand equity, the relative market penetration of each brand may be equated, in most instances, to the revenue gained from the goods and services and hence the relative importance may be related directly to the revenues of each brand. One further consideration in this aspect is relatively new brands that may not have achieved full penetration as yet but for which significant cost has been incurred on advertising and preparation of the market. Both the revenue and advertising spend for related brands in the previous 12 months would be relevant.

Should the analysis of the overall transaction highlight specific assets of significant value (relative to the remainder), prior art searching may be performed to clarify the likelihood of a grant of pending rights or to confirm the validity of granted rights. Again, with due diligence budgets constrained, some reliance may be placed on prior art of record for granted rights or examined applications. This reliance should be treated with some caution and generally used for matters in which several family members in different jurisdictions have undergone a search to counter the constraints official budgets place on the amount of searching performed by examiners in each jurisdiction.

4. How to treat existing litigation

Due diligence for either party in a transaction seeks to remove as much post-transaction risk as possible. For the seller, having disposed of the rights, the greatest risk is a claim under any warranty provisions supplied as part of the transaction. These warranty provisions are likely to be hotly contested in the negotiations and any existing or threatened litigation will form a large portion of the negotiation.

Generally, existing and threatened litigation will be dealt with by a disclosure letter. The intent of the disclosure letter is to limit the liability of the seller on the basis that the purchaser is fully aware of the risks at the time of purchase. Of course, such a limitation needs strict definition and will only extend to the disclosures made. Hence the purchaser will limit any exclusion of the warranty. This makes it incumbent on the seller to ensure the disclosure is as complete as possible.

Full disclosure includes:

- the full file on the litigation itself held by the seller;
- copies of all opinions issued, both during and prior to the litigation. Opinions may have been provided and held in files relating to the asset itself, such as the registration file. It is imperative all such opinions are produced; and
- all evidence already compiled.

In addition to the disclosure above, the purchaser needs to ensure that the litigation can be maintained, if desirable to do so. Hence all documents to fulfil discovery requirements and support the evidence need to be identified and passed on on transfer.

Further, testimony either in person or by affidavit may be required as the litigation progresses. Access to staff of the seller to provide such evidence should be arranged on reasonable terms. To the fullest extent possible, the evidence should be obtained early to mitigate the risk of the seller's employees no longer being available.

Determining the merits of the case and hence the impact on the value of the transaction is also a function of the value of the asset in question. If the litigation is in respect of an asset of minor value to the transaction as a whole, little consideration needs to be given provided it is only the asset itself that is at risk. If the risk is in relation to product, damages are a critical assessment.

Existing legal opinions need to be treated with caution. Most legal opinions are produced with at least some bias in favour of the interests of the client. Indeed, even if an opinion is quite positive in relation to the merits of a case, it is likely that the other side has received similarly positive opinions on their case. Were this not so, there would be much less prospect of the dispute extending to actual litigation. Hence, any further opinions required to assess the merits should be provided by an independent party that is not already associated with the litigation and it needs to be made clear that they will not be taking over the litigation in the future. This removes all self-interest in the generation of the opinion itself. It is especially important to obtain at least one opinion from a source other than one that may have filed or prosecuted rights around the asset in question.

All opinions should be scrutinised for implications on damages in instances where infringement of a product is at issue. It should be noted that an adverse opinion may expose the defendant to damages in the United States for flagrant infringement and, conversely, favourable opinions provide some defence against an argument of flagrant infringement. With the potential for triple damages for flagrant acts, the findings of these opinions are critical. Again, this also highlights the importance of obtaining independent opinions. The opinions in the possession of the seller may reflect the commercial reality of potential damages, but are unlikely to provide an unbiased opinion on the risk of infringement.

5. Jurisdictional issues

For the purchaser, the value and weight given to rights in different jurisdictions is an area of considerable variation and, like the rest of the assessment, largely driven by the strategic purpose of the transaction.

If rights are obtained to support the sale and production of product, the comparative value of the assets may be related to the current or intended revenues in each jurisdiction. In contrast, if the rights are obtained for the inherent sale value of the assets themselves, non-US rights are likely to be of significantly less value despite the size of relative markets. This discrepancy is one constantly borne out in real world market transactions where the US rights are the driver of, perhaps, 80% of the value of the transaction of a family of assets. This rule of thumb is also industry dependent and a function of the higher levels of liquidity of US IP assets compared to those in other jurisdictions.

If the non-US rights do form a significant value in the transaction, care needs to be taken in assessing the validity, term and ability to enforce the rights. While membership of the World Trade Organisation and other trade-related agreements have increased the harmonisation of the treatment of intellectual property, there is still ample variation in relation to many of the rights.

Patent law is perhaps a more harmonious field of law and hence greater reliance on a consistent position in relation to patents in different countries may be applied. However, grace periods provided over early disclosure by the applicant in territories such as the United States, Canada and Australia are not replicated in Europe, China and elsewhere. Hence the validity of the assets in question must be considered on a jurisdictional basis. Usually this consideration would be obtained by applying a strict rule over prior disclosure and isolating those assets for further consideration in respect of which this may have been compromised.

Many patent assets are compromised by the actions of the applicant prior to filing. This is not a rare occurrence and all disclosures of the technology protected by the patent, often by cross-reference to non-disclosure agreements with third parties that are disclosed by the seller, should be checked, if budget restrictions allow.

Similarly, the status of trademarks, especially those not the subject of registration, varies considerably. Common law jurisdictions and those with mature unfair competition law are more likely to assign value to unregistered trademarks on the basis of the reputation gained to date. In contrast, other jurisdictions such as China provide little protection over unregistered marks and the importance of filing and registration takes on much greater emphasis.

A further area of significant concern in the transfer of intellectual property across jurisdictions relates to trade secrets, when knowledge of the trade secret itself is held in multiple jurisdictions.

A trade secret IP strategy relies heavily on proactive management of the trade secret and employment law for control over those that are privy to the secret itself. The major provisions of employment law used to assist in the protection of trade secrets are confidentiality provisions and restraint of trade provisions. While confidentiality provisions are generally universally understood and upheld across jurisdictions, a specific breach of confidentiality is often difficult to prove once staff move across to new employers. The restraint of trade provisions are of greater use in such instances.

The limitation on restraint of trade is that many jurisdictions either do not recognise the validity of such provisions under local employment law or the restraint is seen as being jurisdictionally limited regardless of the global nature of the business itself. A restraint under the law of the United Kingdom is unlikely to be able to be applied to staff that shift to a competitor with headquarters in Asia, regardless of the overlap in markets between the company and its competitor.

Individual country employment law may also dictate compensation to inventors. For example, in Germany there is a mature regime whereby inventors are routinely compensated for their inventions. Although this is primarily of concern to the seller, the purchaser may wish to ensure there is no subsequent claim arising from inadequate compensation that may impair the validity of the rights obtained. This is likely to form part of and be captured by the warranty provisions in a transaction. Regardless, any reliance on warranty provisions should be avoided if possible in favour of prevention and ensuring the seller has dealt with any of the issues.

A yet further aspect of note in multi-jurisdictional transactions is the issue of attorney–client privilege where discussions and instructions are passed between attorneys in various countries. This issue becomes apparent only upon litigation but even those rights not yet subject to litigation must be considered as likely to be so in the future. Ultimately it is only the power of litigation that drives value into most IP asset classes.

Different jurisdictions may have different levels of attorney–client privilege and, more importantly, many of the companies operating in the international IP arena may not be law firms. Hence while local law may provide some special privileges for practitioners in that country, this may not be applicable in relation to litigation in another country.

6. Agreements

A variety of commercial agreements may be in place regarding the assets forming the basis of the transaction. These may include licences, supply or manufacturing agreements, distribution agreements, consultancy or design contracts, employment contracts and technology transfer agreements. All of these are likely to carry IP provisions that may bear on the obligations of the owner of the asset or require consideration if the rights to use rather than ownership are being transferred.

Some of the more likely clauses are discussed below.

6.1 Assignment provisions

Most licence agreements will contain a specific provision around assignment of the licence. Regardless of whether the seller, and by transmission of the rights, the purchaser, are the licensee or licensor, a 'no assignment' clause in a licence will provide an opportunity for the third party to terminate the licence. Naturally, this may eliminate value in the licence itself. Often such clauses may provide for assignment with consent whereby such consent may not be unreasonably withheld. The circumstances that may constitute an unreasonable withholding of consent will vary by jurisdiction and are poorly defined. Hence such a clause should be considered as assignment only on consent. The seller should require all consents to be provided in these circumstances and it is a key part of the diligence process to ensure that all consents for key licences are in place before signing.

6.2 Sub-licensing provisions

Rather than passing on completely ownership or a licence, the transaction may involve the seller passing on the rights to the buyer so that the buyer is the sub-licensee under identical terms. Again, these provisions are subject to the head licence agreement allowing sub-licensing and may still leave the buyer exposed to cancellation of the licence. In particular, provisions around the solvency of the seller or change of control may jeopardise the licence, rendering the sub-licence ineffective. Rather than rely on negotiation of the execution of a step-in deed in favour of the sub-licensee, it is often simpler to negotiate full transfer of the licence to the buyer. Again, diligence is required to identify any potential issues and to ensure that they are resolved before signing.

6.3 Change of control provisions

If the transaction involves maintaining the seller as a legal entity and comprises a purchase of some or all of its equity, all agreements need to be reviewed for change of control provisions that may allow a third party to terminate the agreement. These provisions are common in licensing, supply and manufacturing agreements, where they are used to prevent the potential acquisition of a licensee and hence licensed IP rights for a competitor.

6.4 Ownership of improvements clauses

Technology licence agreements, supply or manufacturing agreements and distribution agreements often include provisions to pass ownership of improvements back to, for example, the licensor. It is important to consider the implications of these clauses on rights being transferred. Does the seller own the rights being transferred? Is the ownership subject to an obligation to be assigned to a licensor? Even if ownership of an improvement does belong to the seller, can it be enjoyed without the rights from the licensor? If not, any product produced is likely to be a product of mixed IP ownership. Such mixed ownership can be very difficult to enforce without the complete cooperation of the co-owner. Hence the value of the rights is seriously impaired. Rights are only of significant value if they can be asserted.

6.5 Use of open source licences

Any transaction in which an open source licence may apply (typically in relation to rights in software although other 'free to use' licences exist in other areas) requires consideration of the particular licence provisions. It is common for software to be developed using open source libraries. Some such licences limit the right to commercialise the end product using such a library. This may have been of little consequence to the seller if the software in question was for in-house use or used under a different business model from that intended by the buyer. However, it may limit the buyer's ability to use the software strategically in the manner they intend.

All open source licences need review in the context of the intended use of the purchaser and where conflict arises, alternative libraries need to be considered for substitution. Many libraries are available, under various terms. For example, while a free version may be available under an open source licence, the same library may be available under an alternative licence for those that do wish to commercialise their end product. These issues need to be identified and resolved prior to signing.

6.6 Co-existence agreements or provisions

Co-existence agreements usually provide that the parties will not assert their rights against each other. Whether in a stand-alone agreement or as part of a more complex third-party agreement, careful consideration needs to be given to the implications co-existence may have on the value of the transaction. Typically co-existence agreements will be in relation to trademarks and contain specific provisions on the use that each party may make of its respective trademarks. The buyer must ensure that any limitations on use, or indeed the grant of such rights, do not conflict with their strategic intent.

7. Conclusion

In summary, due diligence in an IP transaction is not a prescriptive exercise. There is no single solution or process that can cover the myriad transactions possible between businesses. As stated at the outset of this chapter, the budget for due diligence is always constrained and rarely seems enough to limit the risks being undertaken in the transaction. Hence all due diligence must be tailored to the transaction at hand and guided by the strategic intent of the buyer. It is the buyer that will take the greatest risk over the ability to generate a fair value for the rights transferred. The diligence process is the way in which the buyer identifies, considers and provides the information required to inform its decisions regarding its purchase.

Warranties and indemnities

Christoff Pienaar
Cliffe Dekker Hofmeyr Inc

1. Introduction

Intellectual property rights are key assets in most businesses. Recent times have seen the rise of technology enterprises which have claimed titles such as 'the world's most valuable business' as well as enormous transactions hinging on the sale of vital IP assets. Studies show that up to 80% of the value of a typical business is intellectual property, the bulk of which is made up of know-how. In almost every industry, intellectual property is increasing its presence on corporate balance sheets and demonstrating that it has an influence on revenue generation and shareholder value. The identification and evaluation of IP rights in the due diligence process and the evaluation and proper allocation of risk between the parties under contract are, therefore, essential to the success of many commercial transactions.

Warranties are not a substitute for thorough due diligence and should be used to supplement the due diligence exercise, not replace it. The types of warranty required will depend on all of the circumstances, including the specific goods and/or services at issue. From a commercial perspective it is advisable for contracting parties to consider, during the pre-contract stage, which of them is in a better position to manage a particular risk. This chapter will address practical aspects of the due diligence and disclosure process in the context of share and asset purchase transactions, with a focus on how the parties can agree to allocate risk under the contract in the form of IP-specific warranties and indemnities.

2. The interaction between due diligence and warranties

It is an established principle of English law that in ordinary commercial relations, unless there has been a voluntary assumption of responsibility, the parties usually owe no duty of care to one another and are not generally obliged to disclose matters to one another. In order to evaluate a commercial arrangement, therefore, purchasers have always been required to carry out their own preliminary investigations. Thorough due diligence as part of any commercial transaction is essential to understanding the scope of the rights protecting products, services and brands, and the underlying patents, copyrights, trademarks, design rights, confidential processes, and ideas owned or used by the business. This pressure has coincided with a rising awareness of the value and importance of IP rights to most commercial and corporate transactions.

The role of contractual protection is to provide a post-completion price-adjustment mechanism to protect the purchaser. Contractual protection in the form of warranties and indemnities is not an alternative to the due diligence process, and only due diligence can inform the purchaser as to whether they are paying a fair price or getting a good deal. Inadequate due diligence can result in overlooked and incorrectly valued IP rights and can leave undiscovered disputes over the ownership or provenance of critical IP rights. A purchaser who enters an arrangement without due diligence may never be able to recover the full amount of his loss – it can be difficult, expensive and time-consuming to establish a successful warranty claim and in most cases even if the claim is successful, there may be a contractual limit on the amount recoverable. Due diligence, therefore, will help the parties to decide what contractual protections are appropriate.

A warranty is a contractual assurance from one party to another confirming that a certain state of affairs exists.[1] In principle, the beneficiary of the warranty will have a claim against the warrantor for breach of contract (breach of warranty) if the assurances turn out to be untrue. A breach of warranty establishes a right to damages, but will only give rise to a successful claim if the aggrieved party can show that the effect of the breach is to cause that party loss. This is, however, subject to common-law restraints such as the principle of remoteness. Loss which does not flow naturally from the breach of warranty, or which was not fairly and reasonably in the parties' contemplation when they entered into the contract, is in principle irrecoverable. The party who suffers loss must also use reasonable endeavours to minimise (or mitigate) its loss wherever possible.

In the specific context of IP rights, the seller will usually be asked to make certain representations and warranties in connection with the intangible assets to be sold (or licensed) for the benefit of the purchaser. The principal purpose of warranties is to override the common-law principle of *caveat emptor*. The second purpose for warranties is to elicit information relevant to whether to proceed with the proposed transaction. The third (and most important) purpose is to allocate risk between the contracting parties – warranties provide the purchaser with a legal right to commence proceedings against the seller if matters that were not known to the purchaser come to light, or material issues arise after completion.

3. The due diligence process

Warranties cannot be separated from the due diligence process, and we have seen the key issues for due diligence reviews in another chapter in this publication. There is almost always no 'industry standard' which dictates the extent of warranties in any given circumstance – in almost all cases, the nature and strength of the IP rights in issue, as revealed by due diligence, and the relative bargaining position of the parties will dictate the warranties that are reasonable and appropriate. For sector-specific issues, please refer elsewhere in this publication.

All businesses own or use at least some IP rights, even if the only relevant IP rights are comprised in the name of the business. IP rights will be more important to some transactions than to others, but it is always advisable to consider carefully the question of what IP rights the business owns and uses. IP rights are often acquired as

1 Treitel, G, Treitel's *Law of Contract* (13th edition), Sweet & Maxwell Ltd, 2011.

part of a transaction which includes other property such as the assets of a company, tangible property (such as computer hardware) and other plant and equipment. Some IP assets, disclosed in the form of data or documents, might be easily overlooked.

From a buyer's perspective, IP due diligence is meant to ensure that it will acquire all the rights it needs in order to carry on the business after completion. The process allows for informed decision-making on the part of the buyer as to the risks of entering into the transaction. From the seller's perspective, disclosure is important as a means of limiting its liability by only accepting liability under the warranties to the extent that they are not qualified by the information disclosed to the buyer. Together, due diligence and warranties allocate risk between the parties. However perfect the due diligence process, a buyer will usually insist on warranties on important issues in order to balance the risk between the parties post-completion and as a useful way of flushing out further information from the seller.

Proper investigation of IP rights is essential to the success of due diligence when buying a business or asset that includes IP rights. IP rights can sometimes be overlooked in a due diligence exercise because they are not physical assets. Knowledge about IP rights tends to be dispersed and held by different individuals within a business and for this reason it is important that IP warranties in asset-purchase or sale-of-business contracts are 'comprehensible'. Pointed questions during the due diligence process should be designed to elicit specific disclosures, which make it easier to identify information (or gaps in information), so that effective warranty cover can be formulated.

From the seller's point of view, full disclosure can limit potential liability to the purchaser. This means that broadly worded warranties (which can be extremely difficult to negotiate in practice and which will be disclosed against by the seller in similarly broad terms) can be avoided, and short and specific warranties which are more easily digestible (for example, "all renewal and application fees have been paid up to date") can be used. A full review of the due diligence process is set out in another chapter of this publication, and it is the information gleaned and the answers to enquiries given during this process that will condition the scope of warranties that a purchaser will rely on to give it appropriate contractual protection.

In general, the party acquiring the assets and/or property will typically make enquiries under the following headings.

- What IP rights are used by the seller in order to carry out the business?
- What IP rights are owned by the seller?
- Whether the IP rights are owned outright or jointly and whether there are any restrictions on the use of the intellectual property.
- Whether the seller is using any IP rights under a licence granted by a third party and, if so, the terms of the licence.
- Whether the seller has granted any licences in respect of the IP rights to third parties (for example, manufacturing licences) and whether there are any other restrictions on the use by the seller of IP rights which are not contained in licences (for example, restrictions contained in litigation settlement agreements or co-existence agreements).

- With regard to registered IP rights, check:
  - that all previous transactions in respect of the IP rights were registered with the appropriate registries;
  - that all renewal fees in respect of registered IP rights have been paid;
  - that all registered trademarks have been used by the seller within the last five years (a period of more than five years' 'non-use' could make the relevant registered trademarks liable to be revoked);
  - whether there are any current applications for registration filed by a seller (or in respect of IP rights used by the seller) that are in difficulty, by reason of third-party oppositions or because there are official actions in progress by the relevant registration authority; and
  - when the rights expire.
- Have any of the IP rights been infringed by a third party?
- Does the use of the IP rights infringe on the rights of any third parties?

4. Intellectual property warranties

The majority of the due diligence questions set out above can be answered by investigating the seller's IP rights as part of a due diligence exercise, but appropriate warranties that address these and any other applicable issues arising from the due diligence exercise and the disclosure letter should also be included.

Intellectual property warranties should be drafted with the potential problems affecting the value of IP rights being acquired or sold and the potential dependence on third parties in mind. In particular, due diligence enquiries, the way in which a seller amends the warranties during negotiations and the contents of the disclosure letter should all be used as pointers to where there may be issues that require warranty protection – backed, potentially, by an indemnity. Buyers should in particular:

- beware of any IP rights shared within the target's group of companies;
- carefully review any research and development or collaboration agreements and any sale-and-leaseback arrangements;
- investigate IP rights licensed by the business;
- review potential competition law issues; and
- investigate infringements and be wary of litigation already under way which may be expensive and time-consuming.

From the purchaser's point of view, the requisite warranties should always be appropriately drafted to induce information, to provide the protection sought and maximise the chances of success of any eventual claim.

The warranties typically found in contracts dealing with the transfer or licensing of intellectual property relate to the ownership, sufficiency and validity of the IP rights in question. Under such warranties, the seller warrants that:

- asset schedules are complete and accurate;
- it owns or has valid licences for all its IP rights;
- it has taken adequate steps to protect its IP rights;
- it has sufficient intellectual property necessary to conduct its business;

- it is not conducting its business in a manner that infringes the intellectual property of others; and
- no one else is infringing its IP rights.

Each of these six elements is discussed further in sections 4.1 to 4.9 below. Two other important aspects are described in sections 4.10 and 4.11 thereafter.

4.1 Completeness and accuracy of asset schedules

Regardless of the nature of a transaction, asset schedules play a key role in determining the representations and warranties to be included in the contract. At the request of the purchaser, the seller will frequently provide an asset schedule which lists all the IP rights owned or used by the business rather than listing all of the IP rights in the disclosure letter. The purchaser will typically seek warranties to the effect that the schedule of intangible assets is complete and accurate.

This is straightforward in the case of registered IP rights, but may be more complicated where the key IP assets are unregistered IP rights. Therefore, the seller is likely to want to resist any warranty as to the completeness or accuracy of the asset schedule. However, while registered IP rights can be relatively easily identified and checked by the purchaser, the identification of unregistered IP rights is more complicated. Detailed review of unregistered IP rights is only likely to be justified where the rights are important to the transaction, as is likely to be the case in transactions dealing with computer software or trade secrets. Specific issues with regard to computer software are set out in section 4.11 below. In those circumstances, however, the purchaser is likely to want the asset schedule – or at least the disclosure letter – to list all material registered and unregistered IP rights, and the seller to warrant the completeness and accuracy of the schedule, since otherwise it can be difficult to identify unregistered intellectual property and there may be no other way to confirm that the business has disclosed all material IP rights.

4.2 Ownership

Because of their intangible nature and the distinct rule sets applicable to each type of IP right, confirming whether a seller or target company owns or is validly licensed to use relevant intellectual property can be a laborious process. A purchaser may not be able to ensure that all ownership and/or licence rights which are valuable to, or necessary for the operation of, the business are in fact held by the seller or target company and should, therefore, seek assurances from the seller as to its entitlement to the IP rights. In the course of due diligence, the buyer should not only identify IP rights owned by the target but should also address authorship/inventor issues to ensure that the rights identified were created by the seller or its employees and, if not, to review a documented chain of title which evidences the ownership of the rights by the seller. Despite an in-depth due diligence process, a purchaser should still negotiate the provisions of comprehensive warranties by the seller, and target company stakeholders, dealing with the seller's or the target company stakeholders' title and/or usage rights.

Although most sellers in the United Kingdom will offer title guarantees concerning the ownership of IP rights under the Law of Property (Miscellaneous Provisions) Act 1994, express contractual warranties should also be given. The most important warranties are those relating to title and/or authority. A supplier of goods and/or services should be the owner of the goods (or should have the necessary rights to sell the goods in question) and the provider of services should have the necessary rights, licences and consents required for the provision of the services.

Where IP rights are being assigned by the seller, the purchaser should bear in mind that unless the seller is in fact the owner of the IP rights in question or is acting as a duly authorised agent for the owner, it cannot transfer title in the relevant IP rights. It should therefore seek a warranty from the seller that the seller has the necessary title to the IP rights concerned. In the context of a share purchase, where there is no transfer of intellectual property as the transaction entails the purchase of shares in the target which owns or utilises the IP rights in its business, it will still be important for the purchaser to seek appropriate warranty protection that the target owns or has the right to use all relevant intellectual property in order to ensure that the purchaser will acquire title following completion.

4.3 Licensed intellectual property

Many businesses use intellectual property which is licensed from third parties, such as computer software, trademarks, technology, know-how and the like. In most agreements dealing with acquisitions, the seller provides to the buyer details of the IP rights used in conducting the business, and a substantial quantity of such IP rights are owned by third parties and licensed to the seller. As part of its due diligence, the buyer will obtain and review copies of these licences and, most often, such licences are not readily assignable. This is usually not problematic in so far as a share purchase is concerned (unless the licence prohibits a change of control of the licensee), since the identity of the licensee does not change. In an asset sale (or sale of business), the buyer is required to step into the shoes of the seller (as licensee). As a general rule, IP licences are not transferable from one licensee to another without the licensor's consent. Some licences permit transfer, but most do not. The buyer and seller will need to determine whether the obligation to negotiate and obtain such consents falls on the buyer or the seller. The acquisition agreement may even provide that the buyer is not obligated to close the transaction if consents from key licensors cannot be obtained, or cannot be obtained without considerable expense.

The purchaser should seek warranties that the company (and any other licensees or sub-licensees) has not breached the terms of any licences and that there is no outstanding liability in respect of unpaid licence fees or royalties payable under the licence agreements. In the due diligence process, the purchaser should also have checked that the benefit of the licences can be assigned by the seller or that there are no limitations on change of control, depending whether the transaction is an asset or a share purchase.

A warranty that the seller is not using third-party IP rights except under and in accordance with a licence is also tantamount to a warranty that the seller is not infringing third-party IP rights and is likely to be resisted by a seller.

4.4 Validity, protection and maintenance of intellectual property

The buyer is likely to seek warranties with regard to the protection and maintenance of the target's IP rights. Due diligence enquiries should be targeted towards ensuring the seller's key IP rights are protected and that those rights that are capable of registration have been registered. As regards registered IP rights, a search of the records maintained by the relevant national or supranational intellectual property office as part of the due diligence exercise by the buyer will allow it to verify the information provided by the seller as to the proprietorship, geographical coverage, term, payment of renewal fees and subject matter of registered IP rights. In practice, it often happens that changes of ownership of registered trademarks, designs or patents have not been recorded at the appropriate registry. Under such circumstances, the chain of title has to be investigated and the buyer should request appropriate warranties relating to the ownership of such registered trademarks, designs or patents.

The buyer may also seek a warranty that nothing has been done, or not been done, by the seller that could affect the validity of registered IP rights. In relation to registered trademarks, for example, this would include non-use of the trademark for five consecutive years. In the case of trade secrets, it could include non-confidential disclosures.

The buyer will usually seek a broad warranty that the IP rights are valid, subsisting and enforceable. From the seller's perspective, this could be problematic because (for instance) the registration of IP rights is no guarantee as to their validity. For example, in the case of granted patents, there may be prior art of which the seller is not aware that would invalidate the patent. It is likely, therefore, that the seller would seek at the very least an awareness qualification to such a warranty.

4.5 Sufficiency

The IP rights necessary in order to carry out the business may consist of rights owned by the seller or by third parties, or a combination. The distinction between rights that are owned and those that are used is key – the buyer's aim during due diligence is to ascertain that the rights it will acquire are sufficient in order to carry on the business. This is a question of what rights are used by the business as opposed to what rights are owned.

Sellers will usually resist a warranty that the IP rights owned (or identified as licensed) by the company or that are being transferred as part of an asset sale are sufficient to carry on the target's business after completion or sufficient to carry out a specified purpose. Such a warranty can be tantamount to a warranty that the use of the intellectual property does not infringe third-party IP rights. It is unusual, therefore, for a seller to grant such a warranty unless it is subject to an awareness qualification.

4.6 Non-infringement of third-party IP rights

It is common for the buyer to seek a warranty that so far as the seller is aware the normal day-to-day activities of the business, or the use of the IP rights being transferred, do not infringe the rights of third parties. This may also be supported by a warranty that the seller has not received any threats of infringement by third parties.

Where the buyer is aware of a potential issue, it would be more appropriate to seek an indemnity rather than a warranty from the seller in respect of potential claims by third parties for infringement in connection with the use of the relevant intellectual property. Where the intellectual property in question is material to the business, the buyer should assess whether it should obtain a licence from the IP owner.

4.7 No challenges or oppositions

The seller may be asked to warrant that the relevant intellectual property has not been subject to or threatened with any opposition or challenge to its validity. Disclosure under this warranty would include details of any oppositions filed or threatened by third parties in respect of registered IP rights, including any third-party threats to invalidate the intellectual property. The disclosures give the buyer an opportunity to check the validity of the IP rights – for instance, whether the IP rights have withstood a validity challenge that would give comfort to the buyer as to the validity of the rights. If, however, an opposition or challenge is outstanding, the buyer should evaluate the risk that the IP rights may not proceed to registration or could be invalidated or revoked.

Depending on the grounds of any opposition or challenge, the buyer should assess whether the use of the IP rights infringes earlier third-party IP rights and should consider requesting an indemnity in the event that a third party brings a claim for infringement against the buyer or the target company after completion.

4.8 Licences, liens or encumbrances

In addition to warranties that the seller is the rightful owner of the intellectual property, the purchaser should also seek warranties that no liens or encumbrances exist with respect to such intellectual property. To limit its liability under any such warranties, the seller should disclose any existing licences (express or implied) that it has granted over the IP rights, any agreement granting a fixed or floating charge or other security interest in the intellectual property, settlement agreements, consent agreements, ongoing litigation, opposition, interference or other actions which may affect the use of the intellectual property.

4.9 Non-infringement by third parties

A buyer will usually seek a warranty that the IP rights are not being infringed by third parties. If the seller gives the warranty, it is likely to be subject to an awareness qualification (see section 4.10 below). Where the IP rights of a company are being infringed by a third party, the buyer may be forced to take legal action – which can be costly and which might put the IP rights in question in jeopardy if the action provokes a validity challenge. A failure to take action against third-party infringers could also suggest a lack of conviction on the part of the seller as to the strength and validity of the IP rights in question. Finally, if the company has failed to take action against a third-party infringer, there could be risk that the seller would be deemed to have acquiesced in the use of the rights (in the case of trademarks) and can no longer enforce its rights against the infringing party. In some cases, it might be possible to infer from the surrounding circumstances that the third party has an implied licence from the seller to use the rights in question.

4.10 Qualifications

Warranties are usually given subject to limitations or qualifications. With regard to some issues, such as the non-infringement of third-party intellectual property, the seller will refuse to give a warranty unless it is subject to an awareness qualification. Whether the buyer should accept an awareness qualification depends on the particular clause and the level of risk involved, which will depend on the nature of the IP rights in question and how vital they are to the business.

Limitations include time limits within which a breach-of-warranty claim can be brought, *de minimis* thresholds and caps on liability. Where a warranty given by the seller turns out not to be true, therefore, the amount recoverable by the purchaser under a breach-of-warranty claim may be insufficient to make good its loss. Any caps on liability, therefore, should take into account the potential risks that are exposed in the due diligence process and should be based on a careful consideration of the harm likely to the business in the event of a breach of warranty. This will be dictated by many factors, including the value of the IP rights to the business, the extent to which the rights have already been 'tested' on the market by the seller (and any latent risks, such as infringement of third-party rights, would be expected to have materialised in that period) and will also be affected by matters which may not be known to the seller, including the purchaser's plans for expansion after completion.

It should be remembered that warranties and indemnities are only as good as the entity giving them. In the event that a party giving the warranty is insolvent or has no assets, unless resort may be had to an insurer, the warranty or indemnity has no value or benefit. If acting for a 'customer' (as opposed to a supplier), one should make enquiries in respect of the legal entity providing the warranties, whether such legal entity has sufficient assets and whether such entity is of a financial standing that will allow it to satisfy breach-of-contract (breach-of-warranty) claims. Where a customer has concerns in this regard, the supplier can be requested to provide appropriate security or guarantees, such as a bank guarantee, performance bond or parent company guarantee. The provision of security and guarantees comes at a cost and a supplier might request that the customer be responsible for such cost.

Finally, where there are multiple sellers, the buyer will usually want the sellers' obligations under the warranties and indemnities to be 'joint and several'. This means that if the buyer has a claim under the warranties or indemnities, it can bring that claim against all or any of the sellers and can select the seller who is best placed to discharge the liability. Under English Law, a seller who satisfies a warranty or indemnity claim will usually have a right of contribution from the other sellers.[2]

4.11 Computer software warranties

In the course of due diligence it is important to consider the manner of development of the software products listed as forming part of the assets of the seller or target

2 Civil Liability (Contribution) Act 1978.

company. It is often the case that software is developed by specialist independent contractors based on the seller's or target company's specifications. Although the seller or target company may have been the commissioner of the development of the software, where the contract with the contractor is silent on the ownership of the software, it is likely that the software will be owned by the contractor.[3] However, should an employee, in the course of his employment, have created the software, the seller or target company will be the owner of the copyright unless the contrary is specified in the employee's contract of employment.[4]

The purchaser should determine whether any open-source software (OSS) was used in the development of the software forming part of the transaction, as well as the libraries from which the OSS originated. In essence, OSS is software provided under a licence which grants certain freedoms to a licensee. It should properly be seen as a range of associated licensing techniques and there are many different types of OSS licence, varying widely in clarity, length and legal effect. OSS licences can be broadly grouped into two distinct categories, namely 'permissive OSS licences' and 'restrictive OSS licences'. While the exact terms vary between OSS licences, the key difference between the two categories of licence is how subsequent amendments, improvements and adaptations of the OSS (or combinations of the OSS with other software) are licensed or restricted.

Permissive OSS licences usually only require that any distribution of the original OSS be on the same OSS terms as those on which it was provided. Importantly, permissive licences are designed to be compatible with commercial proprietary 'closed source' software licences and therefore permit a licensee to freely amend and adapt OSS code, and/or combine OSS code with proprietary code, without placing significant restrictions on such amendments, adaptations or combinations (usually called 'derivative works') and how these derivative works can be licensed onwards.

Restrictive OSS licences, on the other hand, go one step further than permissive OSS licences, imposing licensing restrictions or requirements where the OSS is amended, adapted or combined with any other software (whether proprietary or OSS) to produce a derivative work. While the provisions vary, restrictive OSS licences will (to a certain extent) apply to both the original OSS and any derivative works based upon it. This can be of key concern to organisations when using restrictive OSS alongside their proprietary closed-source software, as proprietary software could unintentionally be made subject to the OSS licence.

In so far as OSS is concerned, a purchaser should consider including warranties dealing with the seller's compliance with the licence terms of OSS libraries and with the fact that only OSS with permissive licences was used in the development of the relevant software. It is also important to request, during the due diligence process, details about OSS used in the development of the relevant software. An appropriate indemnity to protect a purchaser against any infringement of third-party IP rights should also be included.

3 *Clearsprings Management Ltd v Businesslinx Ltd* [2005] EWHC 1487 (Ch); and *Meridian International Services Limited v Ian Richardson* [2008] EWCA Civ 609.

4 Section 11(2) of the Copyright, Designs and Patents Act 1988.

A warranty of non-infringement provides a buyer/licensee with significantly less protection than if both a warranty and an indemnity are included. The reason for this is that a breach of the warranty only provides for damages and does not force the seller/licensor to remedy the infringement. In fact, it may even involve less cost for the seller/licensor to pay the damages and walk away from the problem. If there is an infringement claim against a buyer/licensee, the buyer/licensee will need to defend itself against the claim, pay the claim (if so ordered by the court) and seek to recover both its costs and any damages paid as a claim for breach of the warranty of non-infringement.

5. The disclosure letter

It is typical in sale-and-purchase transactions that, in response to the warranties, the seller conducts a disclosure exercise, which results in the preparation of a disclosure letter. For the disclosure exercise to be successful, it is necessary for the seller's advisers to understand all material aspects of the business or company being sold. In essence, the disclosure letter has two primary functions: it acts as a collection point for information disclosed to the buyer about the business or company being sold; and it records exceptions or qualifications to the warranties contained in the sale agreement. The courts will look at the language used by the parties in the agreement and the disclosure letter to determine whether a disclosure constitutes an effective disclosure and will not apply a standard qualitative test to determine whether a disclosure is effective.[5]

In all cases, it is important for the buyer to ascertain the fairness or otherwise of disclosures made against the warranties in the disclosure letter. Where there is disagreement between the parties as to the contents of the disclosure letter, it is likely that at least one party will want to change the warranties and any indemnities under the agreement to protect its position. Since the disclosure letter is usually one of the last documents to be settled between the parties, this may involve renegotiating provisions under the agreement that may previously have been the subject of lengthy negotiation and were close to being agreed. In the interests of timely completion of the transaction, therefore, the process should be initiated, usually by the seller, as early as possible.

Warranties may be drafted in wide, general terms and disclosure is the mechanism by which exceptions or qualifications to such warranties can be properly documented and agreed. As each disclosure in a disclosure letter reduces the buyer's rights under the warranties by excluding the matter disclosed from the scope of the general warranty, it effectively increases the buyer's risk. For this reason, the buyer may not accept all disclosures which the seller would like to make in the disclosure letter. Sellers will commonly attempt to include in the disclosure letter 'information obtainable from public registers'. Such a disclosure is extraordinarily broad and should almost always be resisted by the buyer.

From the seller's perspective, the disclosure letter should contain all relevant information which if not disclosed would constitute a breach of warranty, including

---

5 *Infiniteland Ltd v Artisan Contracting Ltd* [2005] All ER (D) 236 (Jun).

information of which the buyer is aware. In contrast, the buyer will wish to limit the disclosure letter only to those specific issues, clearly and unambiguously expressed, that are set out in the disclosure letter. It is in both parties' interests for the disclosure letter to be complete: from the seller's point of view, to limit its liability under the warranties only to those matters not contained in the disclosure letter and, from the buyer's perspective, to give the fullest picture of the target company or business and to flush out the risks of proceeding with the transaction. While it is in the seller's interests to cast the net as broadly as possible under the disclosure letter, there is a balance to be struck. Insufficiently precise disclosures may not effectively preclude a warranty claim.[6]

The buyer will commonly seek wording to the effect that the warranties are only given subject to the matters fully and specifically disclosed in the disclosure letter and will specifically exclude matters on which the buyer may have actual, constructive or imputed knowledge. There is some doubt in legal circles, however, as to whether such an exclusion would be effective. There is a risk, therefore, that a buyer would be precluded from relying on such an exclusion where it has actual knowledge of matters not contained in the disclosure letter. It is advisable, therefore, for the buyer to insist on a specific indemnity in respect of known issues, rather than relying on wording that excludes matters not stated in the disclosure letter but of which the buyer has actual knowledge.

The buyer may also seek a warranty that the disclosure letter is true, accurate and not misleading. To the extent that the disclosure letter does not satisfy these criteria and the information relates to an existing warranty under the agreement, the purchaser would have a breach-of-warranty claim in any event. It is common for the seller to refuse a separate warranty to this effect on that basis. However, depending on the wording of such a warranty, it could give the purchaser additional protection if the disclosures provided by the seller are a fraudulent misrepresentation of the state of affairs of the business, which induces the buyer to enter into the transaction where otherwise it would not have.

6. Indemnities

Depending on the terms of a contract, a buyer that is aware of a breach of warranty might be precluded from bringing a claim on the basis that they were aware of a breach and decided to enter into a contract regardless. Warranties may not, therefore, be appropriate in situations where the buyer becomes aware of an issue. The buyer's actual knowledge of the situation, whether as a result of disclosure by the seller or independent enquiry, may preclude it from bringing a claim for breach of warranty even where the circumstances giving rise to the issue are not contained in the disclosure letter. Where there is a known risk, the buyer should instead evaluate the viability of the transaction – it may choose to terminate or delay the transaction until a particular issue is determined, or it can renegotiate the deal. An alternative option is for the parties to agree that the seller will indemnify the purchaser in respect of the known risk.

---

6 *Levison v Farin* [1978] 2 All ER 1149.

Under an indemnity, the party providing the indemnity agrees, as an original and independent obligation, to indemnify the party in whose favour the indemnity is provided against a loss (ie, to make good the loss in question). Simply put, it's a promise to pay someone an amount if an event occurs. A typical indemnity clause should read something along the following lines (in this case dealing with the infringement of third-party IP rights). It is paramount to make reference to there being 'consideration' for the indemnity; and where there is concern about the adequacy of the consideration, the agreement should be executed as a deed. Thus:

In consideration of the licensee making payment of the licence fees, the licensor shall indemnify, defend and hold the licensee harmless against any liability, damages or loss suffered and/or any costs and expenses incurred (including legal fees and other expenses related to litigation, such as the cost of expert witnesses) by or imposed on the licensee in connection with any claims, suits, actions, demands or judgments (including, but not limited to, actions in the form of contract, tort or strict liability) arising directly or indirectly from or in connection with the infringement of the intellectual property rights of any third party by the licensee resulting from the licensee's possession or use of the intellectual property rights licensed to it by the licensor.

The purpose of an indemnity is to provide guaranteed compensation (on a pound-for-pound basis) in circumstances in which a breach of warranty would not necessarily give rise to a claim for damages or to provide a specific remedy that might not otherwise be available at law. The quantum of recovery will depend on the specific wording of the indemnity – in particular, the circumstances it envisages and the losses, damages or other costs it specifies.

In the context of the infringement of third-party IP rights, most IP rights indemnities will require that the infringing party defend against the third-party claim (thereby assuming the cost of the defence). They will also require the infringing party to pay any damages awarded. There may also be an issue of who controls the defence of the claim.

As a general rule, warranties protect against the unknown and indemnities allocate risk in respect of a known liability or risk. For that very reason, it is unusual for a seller to give a warranty on an indemnity basis. However, from the purchaser's point of view, a warranty given on an indemnity basis can avoid the need to show that the loss arising from the breach is not so remote as to be unrecoverable.

In practice, it is not uncommon for sellers to make last-minute disclosures. Unless it is given sufficient opportunity to evaluate the disclosures, a purchaser should resist any attempt by the seller to include the disclosures under the disclosure letter. Usually, however, because of time constraints, the purchaser will not have the opportunity to review the disclosure documents. In those circumstances, a purchaser would be advised to seek an indemnity in respect of those matters disclosed. Forceful resistance by the seller to an indemnity on that basis may indicate that the disclosure is relevant to the warranties given under the agreement and may justify the purchaser delaying the transaction or negotiating a price reduction to allow the transaction to proceed.

Joint ventures

Neil Coulson
Baker Botts LLP

1. Introduction

Joint ventures are a popular business medium for achieving growth or expansion into new sectors or territories. They maximise the potential for success and profit while spreading capital investment and risk between the parties. Many companies and individuals seek to join forces with others in order to maximise revenues from pre-existing IP assets or to minimise the risk of expansion into new markets or research and development into innovative technologies. This is especially likely to be the case where individually the parties may lack all of the resources required to start up or expand an existing business into a new market or new technology, but together with others have access to greater resources.

The essence of most joint ventures is a pooling of resources. The most valuable of these resources are often IP rights, and frequently the success of the joint venture depends on the effective exploitation of those rights. To a large extent, the issues will depend on the structure and the purpose of the joint venture. In order to consider the issues in their broadest sense, the discussion below focuses on the various stages in the life cycle of a joint venture since different considerations apply on the joint venture's formation, operation and, finally, on its termination through the exit of one of the joint venture partners or otherwise.

Ideally, the parties should determine issues relating to the ownership and exploitation of IP rights before the formation of the joint venture so that appropriate mechanisms can be put in place in the governing agreements. Therefore, while the issues are discussed in relation to the stages of the joint venture, they should be considered and addressed up front. Where the parties fail to address sufficiently the issues at the outset, the default position will apply by operation of the law, which can lead to unintended and less than ideal consequences.

2. Pre-formation

2.1 Structure of the joint venture

There is no precise legal definition for the term 'joint venture'. In its broadest sense it refers to any collaboration between two or more parties who pool their resources (ie, capital, assets or other resources) in order to carry on a particular business with the aim of achieving a mutually beneficial goal.

The most popular joint venture structure is the equity joint venture, whereby the joint venture is carried on through a separate legal entity, usually a limited liability company, in which the joint venture parties will hold shares. This is also referred to as a 'corporate' joint venture and is the focus of this chapter.

Joint ventures can take many forms and another popular structure is the collaboration agreement, under which the parties collaborate in a commercial enterprise without becoming partners or shareholders in a joint venture company. This is generally referred to as a 'contractual' joint venture. A variation on the contractual joint venture is a strategic alliance agreement. The objects and structure of a strategic alliance often vary; they are frequently used in research and development, cross-supply or cross-shareholding agreements.

The main advantages of the contractual joint venture are that it is quick and easy to dismantle, each party retains its own assets (with jointly created assets being jointly owned unless the parties have agreed otherwise), and neither party is generally liable for the debts and liabilities of the other party in relation to the joint venture. As such, it is ideal for short-term or speculative collaborations.

A common example of a contractual joint venture would be a collaboration between a manufacturer and a producer whereby the producer has developed a product but lacks the capacity or know-how to manufacture it and the manufacturer has the required expertise but not the IP rights needed to make the product. In exchange for a price, the manufacturer might agree to manufacture the product for the producer who sells the product on his own account. In most cases, the parties will want to ensure that they each retain their own IP rights, so that the producer owns the IP relating to the product and the manufacturer owns IP relating to the process of manufacture.

A corporate joint venture agreement is a specific type of shareholders' agreement. The main documents involved in a corporate joint venture are, therefore, the shareholders' agreement and the articles of association of the joint company. The shareholders' agreement should reflect the agreement of the parties in relation to the division of ownership of intellectual property and rights of exploitation between the parties. There may also be ancillary agreements confirming or implementing the agreement under the shareholders' agreement, including IP licences, assignments and, depending on the circumstances, joint ownership agreements.

The main difference between the contractual and corporate joint venture structure is what happens on the termination of the joint venture. Under either structure, consideration must be given to the division of assets on termination. With the corporate joint venture, however, control of the joint company means joint control of the IP assets (including licences) belonging to the company unless there is an agreement to the contrary. Therefore careful consideration should be given to the circumstances in which the joint venture terminates and, in particular, involuntary exit mechanisms that might result in one of the joint venture parties losing control of the intellectual property involuntarily.

2.2 IP due diligence

The scope of a joint venture due diligence project, which determines the balance of rights and risks between the IP owner and the joint venture, is similar to that on any acquisition. By its very nature, the joint venture entails an ongoing relationship between the parties, which makes it especially important to ensure that due diligence review is thorough and detailed enough to reveal at the outset any potential issues that might affect the success of the joint venture or the liability of the parties.

The scope of due diligence on IP rights will depend on several factors, the most important of which is the significance of IP rights to the joint venture. It will also depend fundamentally on the IP contributions from the parties and their nature and value, the legal structure of the joint venture – whether a purely contractual relationship or a joint venture company or partnership. The status of the joint venture, which may or may not already be trading when the parties embark on their collaboration, also affects the scope of due diligence. Another consideration is the relationship of the parties and whether they have an existing commercial or legal relationship outside the proposed venture, and their respective market positions. Finally, the duration of the venture, which might be ongoing or may be limited to a specific fixed-term project, is also a determining factor in the scope of a due diligence review.

The first matter to be addressed in any IP review is whether any existing IP rights are being contributed, either by way of assignment or licence, to the venture. Where IP assets are being transferred or licensed to the venture by the parties, a more extensive IP review will be required than in the situation where the venture starts from scratch without any pre-existing intellectual property.

Where IP rights are contributed to the venture, intended to be used by the joint venture, the key information that must be established is as follows:

- *ownership:* whether the contributing party has adequate title to the IP rights being transferred. In the case of registered IP rights, searches can help to ascertain the ownership of the intellectual property and identify any third-party rights, including licences and security interests, recorded over the assets;
- *value:* the value of the IP rights being transferred, which is likely to affect the respective shares in the venture held by the parties (whereby the party that contributes the greater value receives a commensurately greater shareholding or profit share or is entitled to a balancing cash payment);
- *capacity:* whether any third-party consents are required for the transfer of the IP rights to the venture. For example, in the case of IP rights transferred to the joint venture by way of sub-licence, it should be checked that there are no restrictions on the contributing party's right to grant the sub-licence under the head licence (ie, the licence from the ultimate owner of the IP rights);
- *third-party restrictions:* whether there are any restrictions on the use of the IP assets due to conflicting third-party rights. Usually the purchaser in an acquisition will seek warranties protecting against any issues caused by the existence of third-party rights that invalidate the IP rights being transferred, but in a joint venture, where the parties have an ongoing commercial relationship, warranties may not provide adequate protection. Therefore, a detailed landscape review may be warranted;
- *potential omissions:* whether the IP rights being transferred to the joint venture consist of all of the relevant IP rights that are intended to be

transferred or that are required by the joint venture to operate successfully, including any improvements that might be made to the IP rights by the contributing party in the future.

Whether warranties are required will depend on several factors. Where one party contributes all or most of the IP rights required by the joint venture, that party may give warranties as to those IP rights to the joint venture. In some circumstances, for example where the venture is unincorporated, it will be appropriate for those warranties to be given to the other venture partners. In the case of a pre-existing joint venture already holding IP rights, the incumbent shareholders may give warranties in favour of incoming parties.

A breach of warranty will give rise to a damages claim. However, the joint venture agreement could also provide for termination of the joint venture in the event of a material breach of warranty. A breach might also constitute a compulsory transfer event. The potential for the IP owner to lose control of its intellectual property in that scenario and on any termination event should be mitigated under the agreements, as explained further below.

3. Formation

At the formation stage the parties should consider what IP rights the venture requires in order to carry out its purpose. This will dictate what rights should be conferred on the joint venture (or, in the case of a contractual joint venture, on the other parties). This will also determine the scope of the rights conferred. One of the best ways to protect background intellectual property is to ensure that it is limited strictly to those IP rights required by the joint company.

Background IP rights either pre-date the joint venture or were created or acquired by the joint venture parties during the life of, but not for the purposes of, the joint venture. In some cases, background intellectual property will comprise highly valuable IP rights that that IP owner will refuse to licence once the joint venture is terminated.

Where a joint venture has been established with the specific purpose of commercialising certain IP rights, the background intellectual property will necessarily include those rights, since they are likely to represent the crown jewels of the joint venture business. Background intellectual property can also refer to valuable, though not essential, IP rights, which might not be essential for the joint venture's business but which may improve its efficiency and profitability (eg, customer databases).

The parties should decide if and when such rights can be used by the joint venture, how the rights will be identified and the terms on which they will be transferred or licensed to the joint venture to enable their use, and whether their use by the joint venture or the other parties will be allowed to continue after the exit of the party contributing those rights to the joint venture. Often, this will depend on the value of the IP rights and their ability to generate revenue outside the joint venture. It can also depend on whether the owner of the IP rights competes using those IP rights in the same market as the venture or the other venture partners.

A key question is how the rights will be conferred on the joint venture. The joint venture parties will be focused at the outset on how to maximise the potential of the joint venture to deliver value. However, there are inherent risks for an IP owner in compromising its interest in favour of the commercial interest of the joint venture arrangement. The focus should be on reaching a commercially reasonable arrangement, which balances the rights and obligations of the parties in a mutually beneficial way.

Intellectual property rights may be contributed by way of licence or assignment or a combination of both. A consideration that may affect the determination of this question is to what extent the party contributing the IP rights will continue to use those rights in parallel with the venture. Background IP rights are usually contributed to the joint venture by way of direct or indirect licence from the IP owner. It is rare that the IP owner will assign its rights to the joint venture. However, if the rights are used exclusively by the joint venture, the other parties are likely to prefer an assignment of the relevant rights.

The key actions at the outset of a transaction are:

- ensuring the joint venture has all the rights that it needs in order to carry on the business. This requires the background intellectual property to be identified with sufficient particularity to enable the parties to identify any gaps in the IP rights being contributed;
- determining how background IP rights will be contributed to the joint venture;
- deciding on the ownership and exploitation rights in relation to background intellectual property after the termination of the agreement.

3.1 Licence or assignment

Commonly, background intellectual property is licensed by its owner to the joint venture, so that the owner retains continuing control and the intellectual property is still available to the owner if the joint venture terminates. While licensing is generally preferred by the IP owner for the foregoing reasons, for the other joint venture parties it could present a risk due to a lack of security for the joint venture, particularly where the IP rights are vital to the venture. Licences are subject to termination for various reasons, and it is not uncommon for a start-up venture to stumble into a technical default of the licence. The result is that the IP owner is likely to have considerable bargaining power or the venture might terminate prematurely. Effective licence terms will therefore need to balance the concerns of the IP owner and those of the other parties. An acceptable compromise is usually a perpetual licence to the joint company that terminates on the bankruptcy or winding up of the company.

Given the potential commercial insecurity of a licence, the other parties may insist that the IP owner assigns its right to the joint venture. This is not generally practicable where the IP owner needs to use those IP rights in its own business. However, a possible solution is for the IP owner to assign the IP to the joint company and take a licence back from the company on a non-exclusive, royalty-free, perpetual basis. The licence back may limit exploitation of the intellectual property in any areas covered by the scope of the joint venture.

In some cases, it might be appropriate for some background IP rights to be assigned and for others, usually those that are used by the IP owner in the course of its own business, to be licensed to the joint company.

3.2 Assignments

Where background intellectual property is contributed by way of assignment, the agreement may provide for an assignment back to the IP owner on the occurrence of a particular event (for example, breach of the agreement, exit of the IP owner or termination). However, the risk is that if the joint venture becomes insolvent, the automatic transfer of background intellectual property back to the original IP owner is likely to be restricted. In the United Kingdom an agreement that prefers an unsecured creditor by removing assets from the estate on bankruptcy or winding up is likely to be struck down and will not be binding on the liquidator or trustee in bankruptcy.[1]

3.3 Statutory formalities for assignment

Where IP rights are being assigned to the joint company, the assignment should be checked to confirm it complies with the following requirements.

(a) Copyright

An assignment of copyright is not effective unless it is in writing and signed by or on behalf of the assignor.[2] However, an agreement to assign copyright, which might be an express oral agreement or an agreement implied from conduct, does not need to be in writing.[3]

(b) Trademarks

An assignment of a UK registered trademark is not effective unless it is in writing and signed by or on behalf of the assignor or, as the case may be, a personal representative.[4] However, the assignment must be signed by both parties if it includes any European Community trademark applications or registrations.[5]

(c) Patents

Before January 1 2005 an assignment of a patent or patent application was void unless it was in writing and signed by or behalf of both parties to the transaction. The current requirement, effective as of that date, is that an assignment must be in writing and signed by the assignor only.[6] However, an assignment of a European patent application still needs to be signed by both parties.[7]

Patent assignments should expressly include an assignment of the right to bring proceedings for any previous infringements in order to gain the benefit of this right.[8]

---

1 *British Eagle International Airlines Limited v Compagnie Nationale Air France* [1975] 2 All ER 390.
2 Section 90(3), Copyright, Designs and Patents Act 1988.
3 *Lakeview Computers plc v Steadman and others* [1999] All ER (D) 1327.
4 Section 24(3), Trade Marks Act 1994.
5 Article 17(3), Council Regulation (EC) No 207/2009 of 26 February 2009 on the Community trade mark.
6 Section 30(6), Patents Act 1977; as amended by Article 10(2)(a), The Regulatory Reform (Patents) Order 2004.
7 Article 72, European Patent Convention.

3.4 Licences

Usually, the IP owner will license the background intellectual property directly to the joint company. However, in some cases the intellectual property may be licensed directly to the customers of the joint company, rather than the joint venture itself. For example, in a software licensing joint venture where the joint company is established to act as the vendor or agent for the IP owner and does not need rights to use the software itself, the IP owner can either license intellectual property directly to the customers of the joint venture, or license the intellectual property to the joint company for it to sub-license to its customers. The approach will generally depend on the commercial demands of the parties and whether the joint company itself requires the ability to use the background intellectual property to provide services.

In addition to an initial contribution of the background intellectual property at the outset, the parties may agree that future background intellectual property should also be contributed. This may relate to IP rights developed or acquired by the parties after the formation of the joint venture, or it may be subject to the needs of the joint venture. For example, in the process of carrying out its purposes it might become clear that the joint venture needs additional rights in order to progress and those rights can be acquired by the parties or contributed to the joint venture at that stage.

3.5 Statutory formalities for licences

A licence of intellectual property to the joint company (or back to the IP owner where the assets are being assigned to the company and the company is licensing the assets back) should comply with the following formal requirements.

(a) Copyright

The licensing of copyright requires no specific formalities – a licence granted orally or by implication can still be effective. However, in order for the licensee to have the express right to commence and maintain proceedings for copyright infringement in its own name[9] it must meet certain criteria necessary for the licence to be characterised as an exclusive licence. An exclusive licence must be in writing, signed by or on behalf of the copyright owner, and authorise the licensee to the exclusion of all other persons, including the person granting the licence, to exercise a right that would otherwise be exercisable exclusively by the copyright owner.[10]

(b) Trademarks

A licence to use a registered trademark may be general or limited.[11] A limited licence may, in particular, apply in relation to some but not all of the goods or services for which the trademark is registered, or to use of the trademark in a particular manner or a particular locality.[12] A licence of a UK registered trademark is not effective unless

---

8 Section 30(7), Patents Act 1977.
9 Section 101(1), Copyright, Designs and Patents Act 1988.
10 Section 92(1), Copyright, Designs and Patents Act 1988.
11 Section 28(1), Trade Marks Act 1994.
12 Section 28(1), Trade Marks Act 1994.

it is in writing and signed by or on behalf of the grantor.[13] No such formalities apply to the licence of a European Community trademark.

In the United Kingdom both licences and assignments of trademarks are registrable transactions.[14] While there is no formal statutory requirement that they must be registered, there are drawbacks to failing to register. Unless the licensee or assignee registers a transaction within six months he is not entitled to damages or an account of profits in respect of infringement proceedings occurring between the date of transaction and registration, unless the court is satisfied that it was not practicable for such an application to be made before the end of that period and that an application was made as soon as practicable thereafter.[15]

For licensees, registration of a trademark provides a statutory right, in the absence of contrary agreement, to bring infringement proceedings in default of an action by the registered proprietor.[16] Meanwhile it is desirable for an assignee to register an assignment since it will otherwise be ineffective against a third party acquiring a conflicting interest in the mark.

(c) *Patents*

A licence may be granted under any patent or any such application for working the invention that is the subject of the patent or the application.[17] There is no specific requirement for licences to be in writing, but in practice it is desirable that a licence is in writing so that third parties can be put on notice through registration.

As with trademarks, there is no formal statutory requirement that licences and assignments of patents must be registered. However, such transactions should nonetheless be registered as soon as possible to put on notice third parties, which are otherwise not bound unless they actually knew of the transaction.[18] Additionally, a patent owner that does not register a transaction within six months of its taking place cannot claim costs or expenses in infringement proceedings occurring before registration, unless it can satisfy the court that it was not practicable to register it in that period and that the transaction was registered as soon as practicable afterwards.[19]

3.6 Background IP due diligence

If the licensor is a joint venture party, there may be a desire to treat the licence as if it were an inter-group agreement, thereby not insisting on the restrictions that are usually desirable from a licensor's perspective in an arms-length licensing transaction. Consideration should always be given to what happens to the licence if the licensor party exits the joint venture. From the licensor's perspective, unless the licence automatically terminates in those circumstances, the licensor might find itself tied in to an unfavourable licence with a third party. From the perspective of the other joint venture parties, if the joint venture terminates in acrimonious

---

13 Section 28(2), Trade Marks Act 1994.
14 Sections 24(1) and 28(1), Trade Marks Act 1994.
15 Section 25(4), Trade Marks Act 1994.
16 Sections 30(2) and 30(3), Trade Marks Act 1994.
17 Section 30(4), Patents Act 1977.
18 Section 33, Patents Act 1977.
19 Section 68, Patents Act 1977.

circumstances, it may be commercially impossible to agree a licence with the licensor party at that stage. It is important to envisage such issues at the outset and provide for their occurrence in the joint venture agreement.

In the case of cross-border joint ventures, licence terms should reflect the local law requirements of the joint venture.

In relation to licences of the background intellectual property, due diligence on the terms of the licence agreement should always address the following matters.

(a) Identity of the parties

From the perspective of the licensee, it is essential that the licensor has rights in the intellectual property it is purporting to license. As part of the due diligence, the ownership of relevant IP rights should have been verified and the terms of any head licences checked. Where the licensor is in fact only a licensee, and not the owner, of the rights itself, it might be appropriate to seek covenants from the ultimate IP owner that if the head licence is terminated, the owner will enter into a licence agreement with the joint venture party. If the benefit of the licence is expected to extend to other beneficiaries, particular care should be taken to define those beneficiaries. For example, a licence granted to a joint venture company that extends the benefit to the joint venture's affiliates could, depending on the way 'affiliates' is defined, extend the benefit of the licence to unintended third parties such as other joint venture parties and their group companies, who may be competitors of the IP owner.

(b) Scope of licence

The scope of the licence will depend on the purpose of the venture. The rights granted must be sufficiently broad in order to give the joint venture access to the rights it needs in order to carry out its purpose. In the case of licensed technology, the licensor may wish to define the boundaries of the licence by reference to the field of use in which the joint venture operates. This ensures that the technology can be exploited to its fullest potential in other fields of use, enabling the licensor to maximise its income from the intellectual property while still ensuring that the joint venture has the rights it needs to carry out its purpose. To a large extent the scope of the licence may depend on the type of licence granted.

(c) Type of licence

An 'exclusive' licence means that the right to exercise the IP rights subject to the licence is exclusive to the licensee, to the exclusion of everyone else, including the licensor. A 'sole' licence allows the licensor and the licensee to exercise the licensed IP rights at the same time. Effectively, the licensor and the licensee are able to compete with each other. It is not unusual for an agreement to provide for different types of licence depending on the circumstances. For example, a licensee may have a non-exclusive licence to manufacture products using the licensed intellectual property, because the licensor or its other licensees also manufacture in the same territory, but it may have an exclusive licence to offer the products for sale in the territory, because the licensor or its other licensees offer the products for sale only in other territories. Care should be taken when restricting anything other than active sales to a licensed territory within the EEA. Such restrictions can raise competition law issues. These are addressed in more detail in Jonathan Cornthwaite's chapter on IP and competition law.

(d) *Improvements*

The parties should consider how future developments and improvements to the licensed IP rights should be treated under the licence. Relevant considerations include which party developed the improvements. The parties should also consider how future IP rights generated or acquired by one of the joint venture partners, which would have application in the joint venture business, will be contributed to the venture. In the case of improvements and new intellectual property generated or acquired by one or more of the venture partners, a possible solution would be to give the joint venture automatic access to those rights on the same terms as the original licence. It might be more appealing to the licensor to give the licensee a right of first refusal of the intellectual property, which would at least enable the parties to enter into negotiations about the licensing terms.

(e) *Sub-licences*

The right to grant sub-licences is not generally implied into a licence agreement. Therefore, if it is intended that the joint venture should be entitled to sub-licence the right (eg, to its customers), this should be stated in the licence and the circumstances in which the right can be exercised and conditions on its exercise should be specified. Common conditions include requirements that the sub-licensee must be approved by the head licensor, the terms of the sub-licence must be in writing and be consistent with the head licence, and adoption of liability by the head licensee for breaches of the sub-licence by the sub-licensee. The head licence may also make provision for the treatment of sub-licence income. The licensor will want to ensure that the income it will ultimately generate is not less than would have been generated if the rights were exploited by the head licensee.

(f) *Term and termination*

The term of a licence is commonly linked to the life of the joint venture. This is inevitable if the joint venture requires the IP rights in order to operate; without those rights, it cannot carry on its business. Therefore, if the licence terminates, so must the joint venture. Where the licensor does not intend the licensee to have rights post-termination, ideally the licence agreement should contain an express term prohibiting post-termination use. In some cases, the parties may agree that the licence should continue even after the joint venture terminates or on a change of control. This is particularly the case where the sale of the whole venture to a third party is envisaged.

Where the licensor party exits the joint venture (in a voluntary or involuntarily exit) one or more of the joint venture parties is likely to inherit the business of the joint venture. In these circumstances, it is unlikely to be commercially acceptable for a licence to terminate automatically – the joint venture might still need the licence in order to operate. If the licensor is exiting the joint venture at that stage, it may agree to allow the licence to continue but on varied terms, such as increased royalties, a more restricted scope or field of use or on non-exclusive terms to reflect the 'arm's length' nature of the licence. Where the licensor is not prepared to allow the licence to continue after its exit, it may be possible to agree that the licence continues for a transition period, while the party taking over the joint venture business assumes control.

During the life of the joint venture, the licensor may wish to specify a fixed initial term after which the licence will be subject to renewal. There is a balance to be struck between ensuring that any fixed initial term is sufficiently long to enable the joint venture to build up customers, experience and sales, maximise its revenue and give the joint venture partners, including the licensee, the opportunity to recoup their initial investment. Following the expiry of the initial terms, the licensor may want to make further renewals of the licence contingent on the achievement of certain milestones, such as research milestones or revenue targets. This is more likely to be the case if the licensor is a third party or once the licensor has exited the joint venture.

If a licence is intended to be perpetual and irrevocable, even where the licensor exits the joint venture, this should be negotiated at the outset and expressly provided for in the terms of the licence.

The parties other than the IP owner are likely to want to ensure that the licence does not terminate on the insolvency of the venture company in order to ensure that there is as a satisfactory realisation of the business.

(g) Financial provisions

From the perspective of the licensee joint venture, it will want to ensure that any royalties that may be payable under the licence are only payable if the licensed intellectual property is actually used to generate the income that is subject to payment obligations. Particularly in technology licences, the licensee might find that the licensed intellectual property is not relevant or the technology may have moved on, but the terms of the licence may nonetheless provide for payment or performance obligations. Where the joint venture parties are each contributing IP rights that are considered at the outset to have complementary uses, the licences of the IP rights to the joint venture may provide for varying royalties depending on which parties' IP rights transpire as being the most valuable in commercial terms.

(h) Confidentiality

Valuable know-how and confidential information should be kept confidential. This is especially important since in any action brought by the licensor for infringement against the joint venture or joint venture parties, the IP owner may find that the defendant counterclaims for invalidity, using information received under the agreement to support its claim.

(i) Non-compete restrictions

Non-compete restrictions can be used to restrict any rights that the joint venture might have to use the licensed IP rights following termination. Restrictions might include prohibitions on the use of confidential information and know-how; on the ability of the joint venture parties to carry on a particular business within a specified market for a limited period; or on the solicitation of employees of the IP owner or the joint venture company. Restrictions should not go beyond what is reasonably required to protect the legitimate interests of the IP owner.

4. Operation

Every joint venture is set up with a purpose in mind. In the area of technology joint ventures, the purpose is usually to invent, evaluate or exploit technology, or a combination of those purposes.

Foreground intellectual property generally refers to IP rights created in the course of carrying out the joint venture by the joint venture itself or by a third party under a contract with the joint venture. Where the joint venture has been prolific in developing IP rights through innovation or brand investment these rights are likely to be valuable and it is important that issues relating to the division of ownership and exploitation rights are addressed under the joint venture agreement.

Foreground intellectual property might rely on background IP rights and may be unusable without those rights. It might also be essential to the successful exploitation of the background intellectual property. For example, the foreground intellectual property might constitute improvements to the background intellectual property that would enable the background intellectual property to be exploited to the fullest extent during the life of the joint venture and afterwards on its termination or expiry.

In addition to intellectual property created by the joint venture itself, the joint venture parties may themselves develop intellectual property or acquire control of third-party IP rights that would be relevant to the joint venture. Such rights are a hybrid of background and foreground intellectual property. Where that is a possibility, the parties should consider what should happen to these IP rights, how they will be identified, whether they should be conferred on the joint venture and on what terms.

At the exploitation stage, the issues are who will be responsible for protecting and exploiting the intellectual property and how the benefits will be shared between the parties and the joint venture. The structure of licensing and other arrangements will depend to a large extent on whether exploitation is to be undertaken by the joint venture, the joint venture partners themselves or a third party.

4.1 IP ownership

Where the joint venture agreement fails to address the ownership position in relation to foreground intellectual property, the default legal position will apply. In most jurisdictions that means that the creator will own any intellectual property. In the case of creator employees, the IP rights usually vest in the employer. Therefore, where intellectual property is generated by the employees of the joint company, it is likely to be owned by the joint company. However, where the rights are generated by an employee of one of the joint venture parties, even if the work is carried out for the purpose of the joint venture, the legal ownership of the rights will vest in the joint venture party employer.[20] This is of particular concern where employees of the

---

20 Sections 7, 13 and 39, Patents Act 1977. Section 11, Copyright Designs and Patents Act 1988. Section2(1)(b) [CHECK] Registered Designs Act 1949.

joint venture parties are seconded to the joint venture company. It is also likely to be an issue in the case of contractual joint ventures where there is no separate joint venture entity with its own employees.

In the situation where IP rights are created by the employees of the joint venture and by seconded employees of the joint venture parties, the IP rights could be jointly owned by the joint venture and the seconding company.

Clearly, a failure to address the ownership position under the joint venture agreement can lead to a complicated ownership position which can make it difficult to ascertain the correct ownership of relevant IP rights. Given the potential disadvantages of joint ownership of IP rights, agreements usually provide that one party will own all foreground intellectual property and license the rights to the other parties as appropriate.

At the outset of the joint venture agreement, the parties should agree and provide for the following under the agreements:

- who will own and who will have rights to use foreground IP rights; and
- what rights the parties will have to use foreground intellectual property after the termination of the joint venture.

4.2 Ownership and rights to use

As a starting point, the joint venture agreements should stipulate how foreground intellectual property is to be identified. In most cases this is done by reference to a schedule of work and is likely to be supported by technical audits and reporting obligations between the parties. How foreground intellectual property is identified will give an indication of the default ownership position of any IP rights immediately on creation.

Second, the parties should agree whether the rights are to be assigned. This will depend on how the parties have agreed the rights should be owned. In some cases assignment will not be necessary. For example, where foreground intellectual property is defined as all the intellectual property created by the employees of the joint venture and the parties agree that the joint venture shall own the intellectual property, assignment will not be necessary (provided, of course, that the employees of the joint venture are in fact employees and are not employees of one of the joint venture parties). However, if one of the joint venture parties seconds employees to the joint venture, anything created by those employees will be owned by the seconding party. Therefore, if the parties agree that the joint company will own intellectual property, the agreements should provide for an assignment of IP rights to the joint company.

When considering the ownership of foreground IP rights post-termination, related assets such as specialised plant and machinery, employees with their technical expertise, contracts and relationships with third parties such as suppliers and distributors should also be considered. The utility of the foreground intellectual property and hence its value can be tied to these collateral assets, without which the foreground intellectual property may be unusable.

The decision as to which party will own the intellectual property depends to a significant extent on the contributions of the parties to the joint venture, their relative bargaining positions and practical issues such as which of the parties is in a better position to seek protection for, and maintain, foreground intellectual property. The continued exploitation of background intellectual property following termination of the joint venture may depend on having access to the foreground intellectual property, particularly when carrying on a commercial activity in the same market, which can also affect how the parties decide rights should be allocated on termination. Where one party makes a greater initial contribution to the joint venture, it may be able to secure ownership in relation to all foreground intellectual property or foreground intellectual property that consists of improvements to or is dependent on background intellectual property contributed by that party.

4.3 Rights to use post-termination

Finally, the parties should address who will be entitled to exploit foreground intellectual property after termination of the agreement. If it is anticipated that a party other than the owner of the intellectual property should have exploitation rights, the scope and terms of cross licences should be agreed. If the parties are considering whether to restrict the IP owner's right to use freely the intellectual property, competition law analysis will be required.

The key issues under a licence from the IP owner to the other joint venture parties are essentially the same as any other licence arrangement. The licence should address the same issues as regards scope and non-compete restrictions, as follows.

(a) Maintenance and protection

The parties should agree how foreground intellectual property should be protected. This will usually entail filing applications for registration, maintaining registrations, paying renewal fees on time and prosecuting infringers, depending on the IP rights likely to be involved. Maintenance and protection of background intellectual property are usually assumed by the contributing party (unless the background intellectual property is assigned to the joint venture), whereas the joint venture company will usually be responsible for maintenance and protection of foreground intellectual property (where the joint venture is fully functioning), with the parties sharing the cost. The agreement should provide a mechanism that allows the parties to decide which intellectual property is worth protecting. It should also allocate responsibility for protecting intellectual property, including the allocation of costs for doing so; provide for an active monitoring programme to identify third-party infringement at an early stage; and establish which party is responsible for bringing action against third-party infringers.

(b) Termination

If the joint venture company owns foreground intellectual property, it should consider what rights are required for the parties to continue the business post-termination. Usually the owner of relevant background intellectual property will want to ensure that it has sufficient rights to use the foreground intellectual property post-termination. Where the other joint venture parties do not have post-termination access to the background intellectual property and the foreground intellectual property cannot be used without a licence for the background intellectual property, the IP owner is in a strong position as he effectively has exclusive rights in the foreground intellectual property if it is assigned to him. Whether this is a commercially reasonable outcome is likely to depend on the relative bargaining power of the parties and their contributions to the joint venture during its operation. If any party requires access to the background or foreground intellectual property, licence terms should be agreed with the ultimate post-termination owner and provided for under the joint venture agreements.

4.4 Confidential information

A joint venture agreement is likely to entail an exchange of confidential background information between the parties. It is also likely that during its operation the joint venture itself will generate foreground confidential information. The parties should ensure that during the operation of the joint venture best commercial practices are employed to preserve confidentiality and the appropriate contractual restrictions against disclosure are provided for under the joint venture agreements. An IP owner that has contributed background intellectual property or acquires rights to use foreground intellectual property from the joint venture should ensure that its freedom to use those IP rights and information relevant to the joint venture business is not restricted by obligations of confidentiality. From an IP owner's perspective, it will want to ensure that obligations of confidentiality are excluded and that the agreement provides freedom to use such information. Further, when employees seconded to a joint venture return to the seconding company, the other parties may lose access to the skills and know-how acquired by those employees. To the extent possible, therefore, confidential information should be properly documented to ensure that it is accessible post-termination.

5. Termination

The main issues on termination concern the division of the IP assets of the joint venture between the parties. This entails looking at ownership issues as well as ongoing licences between the parties, as discussed above in relation to background and foreground intellectual property.

In the absence of agreement to the contrary, the mode of exit from a joint venture will determine what rights vest in the parties on termination. The structure of the joint venture and, in particular, the exit mechanisms that provide rights for the parties to terminate the joint venture and force the other parties to sell their shares need careful consideration.

Where one party has the right to acquire the shares of the other joint venture parties, unless there is a specific contractual arrangement regulating the ownership of the joint venture's IP assets, the acquiring party will obtain the assets of the joint venture, including intangible assets such as intellectual property as well as tangible assets such as plant and machinery, employees, licences and regulatory approvals.

In addition to ensuring that their IP rights are secure, IP owners will also want to ensure that their ability to exploit IP assets, including third-party licences, regulatory approvals, valuable contracts with customers, suppliers and distributors as well as employees with specialist expertise and know-how are also protected as they may be key to the exploitation of their IP assets. When regulating IP ownership under the agreements, careful attention should be paid to these complimentary assets. This is particularly important if the IP owner wants access to the markets in which the joint venture operates.

From an IP owner's point of view, the best-case scenario would be to have a buy-out right, which would allow it to acquire 100% of the shares and take control of the company. At the very least, the IP owner should have a right to take control of the joint venture in certain circumstances in order to preserve its rights and there should be suitable restrictions on the circumstances in which other parties can take control. Ideally, the overall structure of the joint venture should provide for appropriate licences and assignments that allow the parties to use the IP rights on exit and regulate the ownership position as agreed up front.

6. Competition law constraints

Various competition law constraints have an effect on how the parties can address IP issues. A detailed analysis is contained in Jonathan Cornthwaite's chapter on competition law. However, the most common exemptions for joint venture agreements from the impact of Article 101(1) of the Treaty on the Functioning of the European Union (TFEU) warrant brief discussion in this chapter.

Article 101 of the TFEU prohibits agreements that may affect trade between member states and that have the object or effect of preventing, restricting or distorting competition within the internal market. Agreements falling within Article 101(1) may be exempted under Article 101(3) if they fall within the parameters of a block exemption, or if they are *de minimis* in terms of the Commission's Notice on Agreements of Minor Importance.[21]

6.1 Specialisation Agreements Block Exemption

The block exemption relating to specialisation agreements[22] applies to the following types of agreement provided they do not contain any hardcore restrictions:

- *unilateral specialisation agreements* under which one party agrees to cease production and instead to purchase from a competitor, while the competitor agrees to produce and supply these products;
- *reciprocal specialisation agreements* under which two or more parties on a reciprocal basis agree to cease or refrain from producing different products and to purchase those they cease to produce from the other party, who agrees to supply them;
- *joint production venture agreements* under which two or more parties agree to produce certain products jointly.

---

21 (OJ 2001 C368/13): joint ventures between actual or potential competitors whose combined share of the relevant market does not exceed 10% are generally regarded by the Commission as falling outside Article 101(1). Where the parents are not actual or potential competitors the relevant market share is 15%.

22 Commission Regulation No 1218/2010 on the application of Article 101(3) of the TFEU to categories of specialisation agreements.

The above types of agreement will benefit from automatic exemption from Article 101(1) if the combined share of the relevant market is less than 20%. The justification for the exemption is that it promotes economic benefits such as economies of scale and better production technologies. If the parties' combined market share exceeds 20% of the relevant market the likely effect of the agreement on the market will need to be assessed and the agreement should be individually notified.

6.2 Technology transfer block exemption

The technology transfer block exemption[23] applies to IP licensing agreements between joint venture parties for the manufacture or provision of goods or services incorporating licensed technology and exempts such agreements from Article 101(1) where they fall below certain market share thresholds.

Where the parties are competing undertakings, the exemption will only apply if the combined market share of the parties does not exceed 20%. Where the parties to the technology transfer agreement are not competing, the exemption will only apply if the market share of each of the parties does not exceed 30%.

6.3 Research and development block exemption

The research and development (R&D) block exemption[24] applies to the following types of agreement provided they do not contain any hardcore restrictions:

- joint R&D of products or processes and joint exploitation of the results;
- joint exploitation of the results of R&D of products or processes jointly carried out pursuant to a prior agreement between the same undertakings;
- joint R&D of products or processes excluding joint exploitation of the results;
- paid-for R&D of contract products or contract technologies and joint exploitation of the results;
- joint exploitation of the results of paid-for R&D of contract products or contract technologies pursuant to a prior agreement between the same parties;
- paid-for R&D of contract products or contract technologies excluding joint exploitation of the results.

Where the parties are not competing, the block exemption will apply for the duration of the R&D programme, and for seven years afterwards if the results are to be jointly exploited. If the parties are competing undertakings, the same period will apply only if the parties' combined market share does not exceed 25% of the market for the contract products.

After the seven-year exploitation period, the exemption may apply indefinitely provided the parties' continued production of the contract products does not exceed 25% of the total market for such products.

---

23 Commission Regulation (EU) No 316/2014 on the application of Article 101(3) of the Treaty to categories of technology transfer agreement.

24 Commission Regulation No 1217/2010 on the application of Article 101(3) of the TFEU to categories of research and development agreements.

Life sciences

Colin McCall
Taylor Wessing

1. Introduction

High research costs, complex regulatory requirements and dwindling opportunities for developing small molecule targets: these are some of the factors blamed for the difficulties encountered by some branded pharmaceutical companies in recent years when trying to bolster the number of candidates entering and progressing through their product pipelines. At the other end of the medicinal product life cycle, many of the blockbuster drugs that have dominated the market in the last decade now have generic competition.

The life sciences industry is one of the most highly regulated industry sectors there is and the level of regulatory burden continues to grow. Indeed, one report by the Progressive Policy Institute[1] suggests that the regulatory burden on the life sciences industry, at least in the United States, has risen by 40% since 2000 alone. This increasing burden continually raises the bar for companies trying to bring new medicinal products to market and new medicinal product approvals are more and more difficult to achieve.

This trend shows no sign of letting up. For instance, greater transparency in Europe as regards clinical trials is required under the new Clinical Trials Regulation, which stipulates that the results of a clinical trial must be made available within a year of the trial finishing. With this greater requirement for transparency in the results of clinical trials it is likely that there will be pressure for evidence of superior comparative efficacy of new medicinal products over existing treatments before a marketing approval will be granted. Given that, according to one report, only around 10% of new medicinal products that are granted marketing approval are deemed superior to existing treatments[2] it is likely that new approvals are going to be even thinner on the ground in the future.

There is a similarly increasing regulatory burden on the medical devices industry, especially in the wake of the PIP scandal, with the EU currently in the process of revising the regulatory framework in respect of medical devices and in vitro diagnostic medical devices. In particular it has been suggested that these new regulations should require some form of pre-marketing approval process akin to the clinical trials required for medicinal products. Until there is agreement on the new

1 See www.progressivepolicy.org/wp-content/uploads/2014/10/2014.10-Carew_FDA-Regulation-in-the-Data-Driven-Economy.pdf.

2 JC Van Luijn, FW Gribnau and HG Leufkens, Superior efficacy of new medicines? *European Journal of Clinical Pharmacology* (2010) 66: 445-8.

regulations there is considerable uncertainty regarding the level of regulatory burden in the sector for the future.

Further difficulties have, of course, come from the worst economic downturn in living memory, with ensuing pressures on costs. As a result of these pressures, some companies are moving away from reliance on the traditional small molecule pharmaceutical business model and are attempting to broaden the nature of their product offerings to, among other things, branded generic products, biologicals and medical devices. There have been other developments: the acquisition of small research companies with promising drug candidates has become an attractive alternative to conducting early-stage development in-house. Interest has also turned to divestment of certain business operations and the efficiencies brought by cooperation and collaboration with third parties.

This diversification of the traditional, small molecules industry may have actually sustained it through the downturn. Indeed, this is the view of a major report prepared by Battelle and the Biotechnology Industry Organization in 2012 (the Battelle Report),[3] which attributes the resilience of the bioscience industry in the United States to its diversity. However, innovation in this field is not restricted to the United States and Europe. For example, although it has been known for many years as a centre of generic drug production, India is now seeing a number of novel drug research projects coming to fruition,[4] with more anticipated in the coming years. Also, new levels of deal making within the sector in 2014 are attributed to a desire for efficiency, productivity and the need to reshape businesses after retrenchment over the last few years.[5]

With the time and money that is being invested in the sector and the potential commercial rewards at stake, how do those making that investment and others depending on the success of a life sciences business ensure that the innovations at the centre of their businesses provide a return for them? Furthermore, in such a competitive sector, what is to ensure that the technology being developed by one enterprise is not being appropriated by another? The answer is that where there is innovation, especially when it has a prospect of commercial application, there is intellectual property and, in particular, patents.

2. Important IP rights in the life sciences

2.1 Patents

Patenting a technology provides exclusivity against competitors. Even though patents cannot guarantee that an innovation will be commercially successful, they do ensure, if properly managed, that the rewards of a successful invention flow to the patent owner. Indeed, as the Battelle Report states, the industries in the biosciences sector are among those with the highest levels of patenting and this, says the report, is key to their competitive advantage in the marketplace.

3 Battelle/Bio, *State Biosciences Industry Development 2012*.
4 See Amy Kazmin, Indian pharmaceutical groups shed copycat image, *Financial Times*, July 22 2013.
5 Andrew Ward, Pharma deals reach new level of intensity, *Financial Times*, May 1 2014.

The importance of patents is further explained by another report, published in January 2014 by University College London's School of Pharmacy and co-written with the London School of Economics (the UCL Report).[6] The UCL Report examines patient interests in medicines and biomedical innovation, and the extent to which these are served by IP rights and patents in particular. As the UCL Report points out, the market value placed on medicines is not a reflection of simply the cost of raw materials and manufacture, but of the scientific challenges and material costs of their development. These include the preclinical developments and clinical trial costs not only of successful drugs but also of drug candidates that never make it to market. The UCL Report supports the estimate that the costs of developing an innovative medicine to market are in excess of $1 billion. Hence, as the UCL Report notes, patents do not just enable rewards for innovations that are already available; patents are also important to secure the willingness of investors to continue to put large sums of money towards innovations for the future.

Patents in themselves are key, but there is more to the development of successful products than ensuring exclusivity. As the UCL Report explains, patents are recorded as a property right on a register, allowing the owner to share that information in the patent with the public at large without losing their claim to it. But, importantly for the purpose of commercial activity, this also allows patents to be dealt in as an asset with third parties, as with any other property right, or to enable the proprietor to collaborate with third parties to share the technology for the advancement of the interests of both. The fundamental ways in which this is achieved are by patent assignment, by which rights to a patented technology are transferred from one owner to another, and by licence, in which certain rights to the patent can be granted in a controlled way to one or more third parties without ownership itself being transferred. Both methods allow the proprietor to ask for money by way of exchange; thus the patent is monetised, without a single product having been sold or, necessarily, developed.

Given the importance of patents to the sector, when looking at a commercial transaction, it is important to identify whether or not the patent portfolio is secure, whether pending applications (if an early stage investment or acquisition) will proceed to grant and underlying issues that may affect patentability and as a result exclusivity. The following are examples of such issues that are specific to the life science sector, with comment also on enforceability, as the way to protect exclusivity granted by patents is through litigation in the courts.

2.2 Patentability of gene-based inventions

Ever since the adoption of Directive 98/44/EC (the Biotechnology Directive) in 1998, which was then incorporated into the Implementing Regulations of the European Patent Convention (EPC), the position as to whether biological inventions are capable of being patented in Europe has been settled. In particular Article 3(2) of the Biotechnology Directive and Rule 27 of the EPC confirms that patents for isolated

6 Mari Lundeby-Grepstad and David Tordrup (LSE), and Tinas Craig and David Taylor (UCL School of Pharmacy), *Patients' needs, medicines innovation and the global public's interests*, January 2014.

biological material, even if occurring previously in nature and plants and animals, are available per se provided that the technical feasibility of the invention is not limited to a particular plant or animal variety. Further, Article 5 of the Biotechnology Directive and Rule 29 of the EPC confirm that gene sequences can be patented so long as the industrial applicability of the sequence is disclosed in the application for a patent.

However, as a result of recent case law in the United States, there is a very different approach in the United States to the patentability of gene sequences. The cases are, firstly, *Association for Molecular Pathology v Myriad Genetics, Inc.*[7] regarding Myriad Genetics' patents in respect of the BRCA1 and BRCA2 genes (specific mutations that indicate an increased risk of breast and ovarian cancer), in which the US Supreme Court ruled that patents are not available for inventions that claim isolated but naturally occurring DNA. Furthermore, the even more recent Federal Circuit Court of Appeals case of *University of Utah Research Foundation et al. v Ambry Genetics Corp.*,[8] again in relation to Myriad's BRCA1 and BRCA2 patents, has gone further and clarified that man-made versions of naturally occurring DNA are also ineligible for patentability.

2.3 Patentability of stem cell-based inventions

In the United States, patents in respect of stem cells and in particular human embryonic stem cells have long been available. However, this position may be in doubt following the Supreme Court decision in *Myriad*, since if naturally occurring DNA is exempted from patentability then the same may be said to be true for naturally occurring stem cells as well.

On the other hand, in Europe, uses of human embryos for industrial or commercial purposes are expressly not patentable, as provided by Article 6(2)(c) of the Biotechnology Directive and Rule 28 of the EPC. Furthermore, a landmark European Patent Office ruling on the patentability of stem cells was issued in the *WARF/Thomson* case,[9] stating that an invention that necessarily involves the use and destruction of human embryos is not patentable. At that time, the only source of human embryonic stem cells was the destruction of a blastocyst (a pre-implantation embryo), precluding patentability for all stem cell-based inventions. The judgment of the Court of Justice of the European Union (CJEU) in its *Brüstle* decision[10] stated that stem cells obtained from the destruction of human embryos directly, or indirectly (ie, from publicly available cell lines), are unpatentable, thus making the patenting of stem cell-based inventions in Europe problematic.

Since then, however, stem cell technology has moved on such that other non-embryo destructive methods of generating human stem cells are available. This means that patents for stem cell-based inventions should now be available in Europe. This is so especially in light of the recent ruling by the CJEU[11] on a referral from the

---

7 133 S. Ct. 2107 (2013).
8 No. 2014-1361 (Fed. Cir. Dec. 17, 2014).
9 EPO G 0002/06 (Use of embryos/WARF) of 25.11.2008.
10 C-34/10.
11 C364/13

United Kingdom in the case of *International Stem Cell Corporation v Comptroller General of Patents*,[12] which stated:

in order to be classified as a "human embryo", a non-fertilised human ovum must necessarily have the inherent capacity of developing into a human being. Consequently, the mere fact that a parthenogenetically-activated human ovum commences a process of development is not sufficient for it to be regarded as a "human embryo".

Accordingly, cells and inventions that require human embryonic stem cells should no longer be barred from patentability on the basis of Article 6(2)(c)of the Biotechnology Directive. However, the date from which applications for such patents will be allowable is likely to be the date on which stem cells derived from such technology were publicly available, with applications filed prior to that date likely to continue to be unallowable.

2.4 Second medical use patents

A claim to a known substance or composition for a second or subsequent medical use is patentable in principle in Europe if the substance or composition has not previously been used for that specific purpose. However, actually enforcing second medical use patents in Europe has proven problematic, especially with the increase in off-label prescribing in Europe. Some argue that the carve-outs that generic firms use in the summary of product characteristics labels submitted in the marketing authorisation process to avoid second medical use patents ignore market realities and that even if a generic drug is formally approved only for unpatented uses, doctors may still prescribe for the patented indication, and pharmacists may nonetheless substitute the generic for all indications once it becomes available.[13] However, in the United Kingdom[14] and in Germany[15] the courts have taken the approach that such skinny labelling is enough to avoid infringement of second medical use patents. Indeed, the courts require that there is an intention by the generic manufacturer that their product is used for the patented indication. But a recent case in the Netherlands[16] held, in finding infringement of a second medical use patent, that a generic firm supplying product far in excess of the amount required to treat the condition for which it is approved indicates knowledge that the product would be used for the infringing second medical use.

Accordingly, there is no widespread harmony in Europe on the issue of infringement of second medical use patents. Even with convergence of interpretation on the law between the member states, there are still the widely differing healthcare systems in Europe to consider. Where the intention and/or knowledge of the manufacturer is concerned, a finding of infringement in any

---

12 [2013] EWHC 807 (Ch).

13 'Off-label' use usually means the use of a drug for an unapproved indication, age group, dosage or way of administration while 'cross-label' use means the use of a drug for an approved and patented indication, age group, dosage or way of administration that is not mentioned on the label instructions. In this regard, the often-used term 'skinny labelling' refers to label instructions that do not mention the patented use, but only the uses that are already off-patent.

14 *Warner-Lambert Company LLC v Actavis Group PTC EHF & Ors* [2015] EWHC 72 (Pat).

15 Düsseldorf Court of Appeal, docket number 2 U 54/11, 31 January 2013 – Cistus Incanus; Düsseldorf District Court, docket number 4a O 145/12, 14 March 2013 – Chronic Hepatitis C.

16 *Novartis AG v Sun Pharmaceutical Industries (Europe) BV* C/09/460540 / KG ZA.

European member state may depend on factors such as procurement and prescribing practices, in particular the frequency and known acceptability of off-label prescribing, together with policies on substitution and interchangeability. However, as a means of protecting Pfizer's second medical use patent rights in respect of the use of pregabalin for pain relief, the UK High Court has recently[17] ordered the UK National Health Service to issue central guidance that when the drug pregabalin is prescribed for pain relief the prescription must indicate LYRICA (the brand name) and not the generic pregabalin.

2.5 Freedom to operate

Given that the cost of developing new life sciences technologies or developing new products to the point of authorisation is prohibitively high without an absolute monopoly on the right to exploit the technologies or products, it is hard to underestimate the value of acquiring strong IP rights in order to protect investments and to ensure ongoing returns. Furthermore, as a result of the huge sums involved and the disastrous consequences of early competition the life sciences industry is a highly litigious one in the field of intellectual property with a high degree of willingness among IP asset owners to litigate in order to protect them. Accordingly, before acquiring a company in this sector on the basis of its IP assets it is extremely important as part of the due diligence process to ensure that the target company has freedom to operate in respect of its present business activities as well as those it intends to pursue in the future, or at least to assess its scope of freedom to operate by assessing the relevant IP landscape. Failure to conduct a freedom to operate search could lead to wasting resources on an enterprise that may later be adversely affected as a result of infringing third party intellectual property and, in some cases, in respect of which there could be payment of significant damages. Conducting such a search early in the transaction process may identify third-party rights that may prove problematic, thereby identifying rights that either need to be licensed or worked around. This helps to further gauge the cost of acquiring the company and can also prevent wasted transactional costs, both in terms of time and money, if any third-party rights prove insurmountable.

2.6 Supplementary protection certificates

The system of supplementary protection certificates (SPCs) was introduced in 1993 under Council Regulation (EEC) No 1768/92 (now Regulation 469/2009/EC) (SPC Regulation) as a means to effectively extend the patent term of protection for particular medicinal products.

The purpose of this legislation is to remedy the common problem that the term of patent monopoly for many medicinal products can be significantly eroded by the time the patentee or their licensee has to wait for the grant of a marketing authorisation. The result can be that there is little or no patent monopoly left on the product by the time it reaches the market, limiting the commercial return on the product and thus undermining the investment made in it.

---

17 HC-2014-001795 *Warner-Lambert Company LLC v National Health Service.*

(a) *Calculation of duration of SPC*

The SPC Regulation seeks to address this problem by providing up to five years' further monopoly protection for specific patented products. The precise period of extension is the period between the date on which the application for a basic patent was lodged and the date of the first authorisation to place the product on the market in the Community, less 5 years, and subject to a cap of a maximum of 5 years' duration.

The formula provides that a patentee does not obtain an extension of its patent monopoly if it has only been eroded by five years or less by the wait for the grant of marketing authorisation. For example:

- A patent filed on November 1 2005 and marketing authorisation granted on November 1 2010: the patent expires on October 31 2025 with no further SPC protection.
- A patent filed on November 1 2000 and marketing authorisation granted on November 1 2010: five years' SPC protection commencing on November 1 2020.[18]
- A patent filed on November 1 1995 and marketing authorisation granted on November 1 2010: five years' SPC protection commencing on November 1 2015.

(b) *Eligibility for SPC*

In order to obtain an SPC, there are three key conditions that must first be satisfied. The conditions are found in Article 3 of the SPC Regulation:

- Protection by a basic patent in force
  The product must be protected by a basic patent in force (Article 3(a)). The purpose of this provision is to reflect the intention of the SPC legislation to prolong monopoly protection for products that are already patented;
- A first authorisation
  A valid authorisation to place the product on the market as a medicinal product must have been granted (Article 3(b)). This must be the first authorisation to place the product on the market as a medicinal product; and
- No pre-existing SPC
  The product must not have already been the subject of an SPC (Article 3(c)). The purpose of this provision is to prevent further SPCs for modifications of the same product. For example, it is unlikely that a new formulation of an active ingredient that is already the subject of an SPC can be subject to a further SPC, because a "combination of active ingredients of a medicinal product" used in the definition of 'product' in Article 1(b) excludes situations in which only one ingredient has therapeutic effects and the other, such as an excipient, only improves the therapeutic efficacy of the first substance.

---

18 Whether the period of SPC protection ends at 23:59 on October 31 or 23:59 on November 1 depends on the country whose patent office granted the SPC (eg, the United Kingdom, Switzerland, Spain and the Netherlands adhere to the former, and Germany, Poland, Austria and Sweden adhere to the latter expiry dates).

If these conditions are satisfied, the legislation provides SPC protection for specific patented products. It does not prolong the patent protection itself, so that many other potential products that fall within the scope of protection of the patent are not covered by the additional SPC protection.

However, it has proved difficult to interpret the SPC Regulation, especially as to the degree to which the underlying patent must identify the product to be protected and as regards combination drugs. This is widely thought to be because the SPC Regulation was drafted to deal only with those drugs comprising single, small molecule active ingredients and patents that covered them alone. Indeed, a number of issues under the SPC Regulation have been, and continue to be, referred to the CJEU. This reflects the problems that are being encountered with applying the SPC Regulation to modern pharmaceutical developments and the regime implemented by the SPC Regulation has been the subject of judicial criticism for this reason.

(c) Availability of SPCs for combinations

Many drugs, including vaccines, oncology therapies, anti-asthmatics and hypertensives are administered as combinations of active ingredients. This is due to a number of different reasons ranging from policy to synergistic interaction. Combination drugs may also require substantial investment, even when one or both components have themselves been available as separate treatments for many years. In many circumstances, this has led those that manufacture and sell such drugs to seek SPCs to preserve protection and thus protect the investment in the drug from generic competition.

It has proved very difficult to interpret the SPC Regulation as regards combination drugs. The key questions that have arisen for combination products under Article 3 are whether a marketing authorisation for a hypothetical product A+B+C is capable of constituting a "valid authorisation" of product A alone, for the purposes of Article 3(b)? Or can it serve only as an authorisation for A+B+C?

Alternatively, an applicant might seek an SPC to protect product A+B+C, so that its SPC application reflects the marketing authorisation instead of the patent. In this situation, does a hypothetical patent covering A alone protect the combination product A+B+C for the purpose of Article 3(a)?

To answer these questions, a large number of cases were referred by national courts to the CJEU.

Principal among these references was the case of *Medeva BV's SPC Applications*,[19] which concerned five SPC applications for a variety of combination vaccines, all of which had been refused.

Under Article 3(a) of the SPC Regulation the CJEU ruled that an SPC cannot be granted for a combination product that is not "specified" in the wording of the claims of the basic patent. Hence, an application for an SPC on product A+B+C must be supported by a patent claim that specifies A+B+C.

Under Article 3(b), the CJEU ruled in *Medeva* that the SPC need only be sought for one or more of the products for which the marketing authorisation has been

---

19 C-322/10, 24 November 2011.

granted. In other words, an SPC can be sought for product A only, based on a marketing authorisation for A+B+C.

If an SPC can only be obtained for product A alone, because it is only A that is specified in the basic patent, how does this affect the SPC proprietor's ability to enforce its SPC for A against third-party use of a combination product such as A+B+C? This question has also been resolved by the CJEU, in *Novartis v Actavis*.[20]

As a result of the CJEU ruling in *Novartis v Actavis*, the owner of an SPC for A would be able to enforce that SPC against a product comprising A in combination with other active ingredients.

This is important for proprietors of combination drugs, given the *Medeva* ruling. It confirms a wide scope of enforcement of an SPC for A (against A+B+C, etc), compensating for the fact that the SPC may need to be limited to one active ingredient if that is all that is covered by the basic patent.

(d) *Availability of more than one SPC under the same basic patent*

In the case of *Georgetown University v Octrooicentrum Nederland*,[21] the key question was whether several products covered by one patent (eg, active ingredient A alone, the combination of active ingredients A+B, the combination of active ingredients A+B+C, etc) were each capable of SPC protection.

According to the CJEU's ruling, it is possible, in principle, on the basis of a patent that protects several different products, to obtain several SPCs in relation to each of those different products. Each of those products should, however, be protected as such by that basic patent in accordance with Article 3(a) and be contained in a medicinal product and subject to an MA.

(e) *Paediatric extensions*

A further six-month extension to the SPC is available if an agreed research and development (R&D) programme aimed at ensuring that the necessary data is generated determining the conditions in which a medicinal product may be authorised to treat the paediatric population, known as a paediatric investigation plan (PIP), is executed, with the results of the PIP included in the summary of product characteristics.

Since 2007, following the Paediatric Regulation (Regulation (EC) 1901/2006), agreement to the PIP by the Paediatrics Committee of the European Medicines Agency has been compulsory for all applications for a marketing authorisation, whether for new medicinal products or for new indications for medicinal products already authorised for other indications. However, the Paediatrics Committee may agree a waiver of the requirement to submit the results of the PIP if the medicine is likely to be ineffective or unsafe in the paediatric population, if the disease to be treated only occurs in the adult population or if the medicine does not represent a significant therapeutic benefit over the existing treatments for paediatric patients. It is also possible for the measures set out in the PIP to be deferred; for instance, if it is appropriate for studies to be carried out only on adults first.

---

20 C-442/11, 9 February 2012.
21 C-484/12, 12 December 2013.

It is not necessary for the product actually to be indicated for use in the paediatric population (if, for example, the results show that that would not be appropriate) for the six-month extension to be applied – this six-month extension to the SPC applies to all indications for the product. Furthermore, the existence of this six-month paediatric extension to an SPC has meant that applying for zero-term or even negative-term SPCs (ie, for products that receive marketing approval within the period of four-and-a-half to five years after filing the basic patent) can be worthwhile since while the SPC itself for such zero-term or negative-term periods will confer no additional monopoly protection, the six-month paediatric extension that can be added to these zero-term or negative-term periods will do (provided any negative-term SPC is less than six months of course).

3. Confidential information

A life sciences company will, in the course of developing its technology or products, generate information that has a commercial value. This information for as long as it remains secret is known as confidential information or a trade secret. Keeping the information confidential will be valuable as a means of maintaining a competitive advantage over others operating in the field for a number of reasons, including:

- In order to obtain a patent in respect of a new invention, that new invention must not be disclosed to the public (even if the disclosure is made by the inventor himself) prior to the filing date of the patent application.
- Much developed know-how will not be of itself patentable, such as formulae and other technical data, but may be of technical importance.
- Methods developed may show best practice, for example, in terms of efficiency or cost effectiveness, as to how to work a particular technology or manufacture a particular product.
- The information can show that a particular method of trying to do something is in fact an "evolutionary dead-end". Other researchers in the field would benefit from this knowledge since they could avoid expending resources in pursuing such methods.

Clearly, the value of confidential information to the innovator will diminish as soon as that information ceases to be confidential or secret and becomes publicly available to all. However, in order to exploit confidential information and trade secrets it is sometimes necessary to disclose it to others. Such disclosure can be protected by the law of confidence, enabling a person to disclose secret information to a recipient in confidence, thereby imposing an obligation on the recipient to maintain the secrecy of the information.

While the patent system provides a time-limited monopoly right in return for a public disclosure of the invention, confidential information can remain secret indefinitely. Accordingly, it can be tempting to rely on the confidential nature of the invention rather than applying for patents. However, most inventions, once marketed, are capable of being reverse engineered and in the absence of patent protection such reverse engineering by a competitor is perfectly permissible.

Nevertheless, confidential information is a vital asset for a life science company and needs to be approached carefully both in transaction diligence and in the transaction documents.

4. Data and market exclusivity in Europe

Regulatory approval for medicinal products requires applicants to provide information about the efficacy and safety of their product to regulatory authorities. The first applicant for approval of a new medicinal product must provide a substantial body of data relating to the product (including the results of preclinical tests and clinical trials).

The regulatory regime permits generic companies, who subsequently wish to gain their own approval for the same drug substance, to rely on information filed by the innovator company that made the first application. In order to be able to benefit from the data provided by the innovator in their regulatory filings for that medicinal product – the 'reference medicinal product' – a generic company must show that their product has the same qualitative and quantitative composition as that product and that it is bioequivalent.

Accordingly, data exclusivity is a form of product exclusivity in Europe with a subsequent period of market exclusivity being allied to that period of data exclusivity. The rationale for granting data and market exclusivity is to compensate the innovator company for the investment it has put into developing the new medicinal product and generating the data required to obtain a marketing authorisation, and is separate to patent and SPC protection.

For marketing authorisation applications made from November 2005 onwards, the period of data exclusivity in Europe has been harmonised as eight years from the date of first authorisation in Europe. For marketing authorisation applications made before November 2005, the period of data exclusivity varies between EU member states and is either 6 or 10 years. During the period of data exclusivity the innovator's preclinical and clinical trials data may not be referenced in the regulatory filings of any other company for the same drug substance.

For marketing authorisation applications made from November 2005 onwards, there is an additional period of two years of market exclusivity. This is the period of time during which a generic company may not market an equivalent generic version of the originator's medicinal product (although their application for authorisation may be processed during this period, such that they are in a position to market their product on the expiry of this additional two-year period). An additional one year of market exclusivity may be obtained if, within the eight-year data exclusivity period, the innovator company is granted another marketing authorisation for a new indication for the relevant medicinal product that brings significant clinical benefit over existing therapies.

In this way the regime ensures that generic competition can be prevented for up to 11 years following the first grant of a marketing authorisation regardless of the patent position in respect of the relevant medicinal product.

5. Trademarks and designs

While perhaps not so immediately obviously valuable in the life sciences industry, both trademark rights and design rights can assist in maintaining market share after patent expiry. For instance, Pfizer has numerous trademark and design rights in respect of its Viagra product, in each of the name, the colour and the shape of the product. Design rights are even more important in the medical devices industry, where they can protect features that are not purely functional in nature.

6. The development cycle and the patent cliff

Intellectual property protection is vital to maximising the benefit of R&D in the life sciences. Technological improvements, especially when embodied in commercial products, tend to be fairly transparent and therefore available to potential competitors. Such competitors can therefore acquire knowledge about new medicinal products within a reasonably short period of time and with a relatively modest R&D effort of their own.

In order to understand the benefit of IP protection and the effect of the 'patent cliff', an understanding of the development cycle of a successful medicinal product is important. Early phases in the development cycle, such as discovery and preclinical and clinical phases are typically characterised by initially low but rapidly increasing improvements in the medicinal product (eg, preferred formulations, efficient manufacturing processes, new indications, dosing regimen, etc) as development issues are ironed out, but accompanied by negative total revenue given the huge costs associated with discovery and clinical development. During the intermediate phases of post-marketing approval and then peak sales, improvements become increasingly hard to achieve but revenues rapidly increase. In the later stages of generic competition and commoditisation little or no performance improvements are possible and revenues in respect of the product diminish.

In Figures 1 and 2 the columns each represent a phase during the development cycle: A = research (ie, discovery); B = preclinical and clinical phase; C = post-marketing approval; D = peak sales; E = generic competition/product substitution; and F = fully commoditised/obsolescence.

The time at which competition occurs is known as the patent cliff and will depend entirely on the strength of the IP portfolio the initial developer has managed to acquire. When the patent cliff is reached, the revenues available to all market entrants in respect of the product rapidly collapse. But it is the patent holder that loses most. By way of example, the best-selling drug in history, Pfizer's Lipitor, had peak sales of around $11 billion per annum in 2009 and 2010 before going off patent in 2011. Since then Pfizer's sales of Lipitor collapsed to $2 billion for 2013. Indeed, in the last five years according to an IMS report[22] the patent cliff has caused losses in revenue to innovator pharmaceutical companies of $154 billion.

The costs/revenues shown in the development cycle curve in Figure 1 represent the costs/revenues spent or achieved by all market entrants in respect of a given medicinal product as a whole and not just the costs/revenue of the first life sciences company to develop the new medicinal product. It will be the first developer that

22 Report by the IMS Institute for Healthcare Informatics, *Global Outlook for Medicines Through 2018*, November 2014.

Figure 1: Revenue at different stages of the development cycle

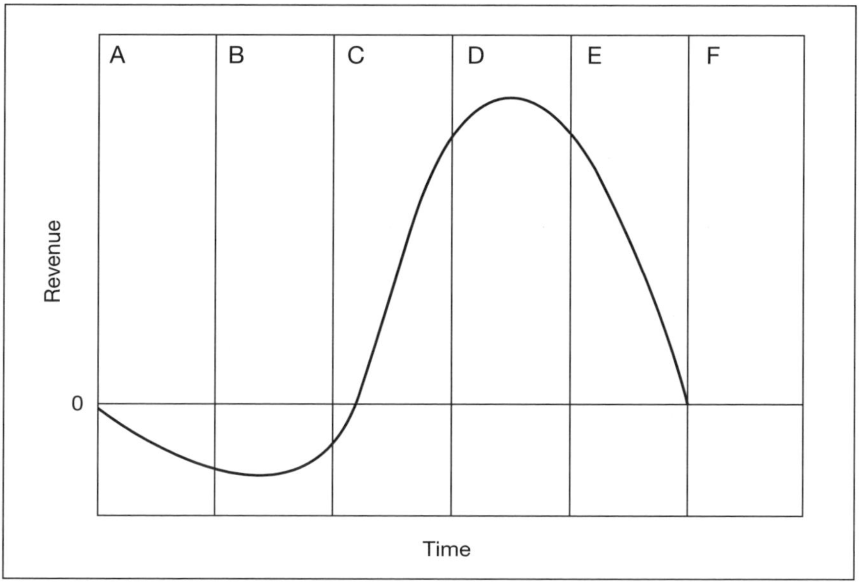

Figure 2: Technology improvements during the development cycle

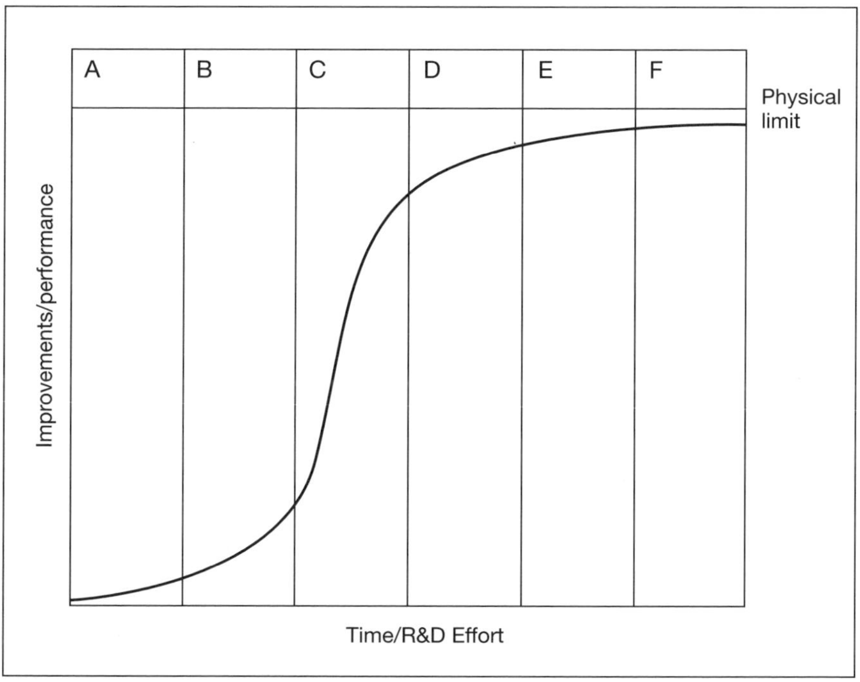

incurs almost all of the cost and derives almost all of the revenue up until the patent cliff. Thereafter, the revenues are shared by all market entrants.

The longer a life sciences company can prevent competition and delay the patent cliff, the longer it can prevent price erosion and the greater the proportion of the available revenues from a particular product it can keep for itself. In order for life sciences companies to weather the storm of patent cliff faces they must continually bring new medicinal products to market through a development pipeline. Historically these pipelines have been derived through internal R&D efforts, but increasingly, larger life sciences companies are seeking to bolster their development pipeline with the acquisition of smaller-cap life sciences companies with late-stage development products through corporate transactions or through in-licensing deals. Accordingly, early-stage life sciences companies that have broad IP protection in respect of their core technologies are much more attractive investment propositions.

7. Other matters of importance in the life science sector

7.1 Biosimilars

Improvements in technology and pressures to diversify business models away from small molecule drugs are just two of the factors that are focusing attention on biological medicinal products (ie, medicinal products that are made by a living organism such as a bacterium or yeast and can consist of relatively small molecules such as human insulin or erythropoietin, or complex molecules such as monoclonal antibodies). This has led to a rise in biosimilars.

Biosimilars are biological medicinal products that are similar to another biological product that has already been authorised and that do not differ significantly from the original product in terms of quality, safety and efficacy. As such, biosimilars are copies of biological medicines that are already approved.

There is no formal definition of 'biosimilar' in European legislation and the term biosimilar should not be confused with the terms 'biobetter' and 'me-too biologic'.

A biobetter is a biological product that has been altered structurally or functionally to improve its performance. A me-too biologic is a biological medicine that targets the same pathway but is developed independently of a reference biological and is not compared to it. Neither a biobetter nor a me-too biologic can be authorised using the biosimilar route.

An applicant for approval of a biosimilar product under the biosimilar route is required to demonstrate that its product is similar to a previously authorised product. The application for approval can reference data submitted for the previously authorised product after the expiry of the data exclusivity period.

However, the use of the term 'similar' reflects the scientific reality that biological products cannot be copied precisely. Biological products are much larger and more complex than chemical pharmaceutical compounds and are produced in sensitive biological systems that can be affected by small changes in process conditions. Controlling the production of biological products, in particular any post-translational modifications, is therefore challenging. So, while it is possible to control precisely the production of generic chemical pharmaceutical compounds and to authorise them using an abridged procedure on the basis of bioequivalence data, this is not possible with biological products.

Data over and above the standard tests required for small molecule generics will therefore normally be required in order to demonstrate that a biosimilar is comparable to the reference biologic product. As a general rule, the biosimilar route requires more extensive testing and, most likely, clinical trials (which are not needed for small molecule generic drugs).

7.2 Orphan medicines

Since the pharmaceutical industry has fewer incentives, under normal market conditions, to develop and market medicinal products intended for rare diseases that by definition will only be used to treat small numbers of patients, the EU offers a range of incentives to encourage the development of these medicinal products – known as orphan medicines.

For a medicinal product to be classed as an orphan medicine, it must be intended for the diagnosis, prevention or treatment of either:

- a life-threatening or chronically debilitating condition affecting no more than 5 in 10,000 people in the EU at the time of submission of the application for orphan designation; or
- a life-threatening, seriously debilitating or serious and chronic condition where, without incentives, it would be unlikely that the revenue after marketing of the medicinal product would cover the investment in its development.

There must also be either no satisfactory method of diagnosis, prevention or treatment of the condition concerned, or, if there is such a method, the new medicine must be of significant benefit to those affected by the condition.

The principal benefit for medicinal products designated as orphan medicines is that they benefit from more generous treatment as regards market exclusivity, namely:

- a period of 10 years from the date of marketing authorisation, which may run in parallel with the basic marketing exclusivity if the drug is also authorised (via a separate marketing authorisation) for other indications;
- any additional orphan indications for the same product will also benefit from their own separate 10-year period of market exclusivity; and
- where an application for a marketing authorisation for an orphan product includes the results of studies conducted in accordance with an agreed PIP, the 10-year period is extended to a period of 12 years.

7.3 Parallel imports

(a) Parallel import regime in Europe

Parallel importation of medicinal products in the EEA relies on the principle of patent exhaustion, which itself arises from the EU's and also the EEA's treaty commitments to the free movement of goods. These freedom of movement of goods rules as regards patented medicinal products were first established in 1974 in the case of *Centrafarm BV v Sterling Drug Inc*[23] and dictate that when a patent/SPC holder puts (or consents to the putting of) a medicinal product on the market anywhere in the EEA, the patent/SPC holder cannot object to a purchaser of those products subsequently putting them on the market in a different EEA member state, regardless of whether such import into a subsequent EEA member state would infringe the patent/SPC holder's national patent/SPC rights in the member state of destination. As a result of the differences in prices set by national governments and also by the patent/SPC owners themselves in the various different EEA states there is now a significant volume of parallel import activity.

The parallel import of medicinal products is, however, subject to significant regulation. The importer still requires a licence to import and market the product in the member state of destination, and the product packaging must meet the requirements of the member state of destination.

(b) Parallel import licences

A parallel imported medicinal product may be distributed under an authorisation obtained through a simpler procedure than that for the initial marketing authorisation for the product. To qualify for the simplified procedure, the parallel imported medicinal product must satisfy two conditions. It must:

- have been granted a marketing authorisation in the member state of origin; and
- be sufficiently similar to a product that has already received marketing authorisation in the member state of destination.

The similarity between two medicinal products is considered to be sufficient when the two products have been manufactured according to the same formulation, using the same active ingredient, and have the same therapeutic effects. A parallel imported medicinal product can also be distributed under the simplified procedure even if the similar product upon which its licence is based is no longer available on the market, provided that public health requirements are met.

(c) Repackaging of parallel imports

Repackaging will be necessary if the packaging sizes in use in the member state of origin are not permitted in the member state of destination. In principle, however, this is precluded by the trademark right of the manufacturer since all changes to the packaging or the product itself will constitute an infringement of the manufacturer's trademark. But this rule conflicts with the principle of the free movement of goods within the EEA. The case of *Bristol-Myers Squibb*[24] has therefore established that certain necessary and appropriate changes are permitted, if they are made in order to eliminate obstacles in the distribution process. The so-called BMS Conditions are:

- the use of the trademark right by the owner contributes to the artificial partitioning of the internal market;

---

23 15/74.
24 Joined cases C-427/93, C-429/93 and C-436/93.

- the repackaging does not adversely affect the original condition of the product;
- it is stated on the new packaging by whom the product has been manufactured and by whom it has been repackaged;
- the presentation of the repackaged product is not such as to damage the reputation of the trademark or of its proprietor; and
- the proprietor of the trademark receives written notice of the repackaging before the new product is put on sale and in addition, if he requests it, is supplied with a specimen of the repackaged product upon demand.

The repackaging must be necessary, and not just motivated by commercial interests. For example, repackaging is not justified for a parallel imported product that may be put on sale in the member state of destination simply by changing the labelling of the outer packaging (eg, language matters).

7.4 Compulsory licences

The availability of compulsory licences in respect of patents, especially in relation to pharmaceutical patents, has been the subject of considerable attention lately. This is mainly as a result of the Indian courts showing their willingness to grant compulsory licences in respect of pharmaceutical patents. In particular, the Indian courts recently granted a compulsory licence to an Indian generic pharmaceutical company under Bayer's patent for its cancer drug Nexavar, determining that in essence Bayer's price for Nexavar was too high. This, together with Bayer's failed challenge that India's patent legislation under which the compulsory licence was granted was not compliant with the Agreement on Trade-Related Aspects of Intellectual Property Rights (the TRIPS agreement puts restrictions on the ability of World Trade Organization members (of which India is one) to restrict the exclusive rights of patentees through – among other things – compulsory licences), has led to significant media interest in the power under national patent legislation to grant compulsory patent licences.

Article 31 of the TRIPS agreement provides that where patent legislation of World Trade Organization member states allows compulsory licences to be granted the following provisions must be included:

- Each case must be decided on its own merits.
- The applicant for the compulsory licence must have made efforts to take a licence from the patentee on reasonable commercial terms.
- The scope and duration of the compulsory licence must be limited to the purpose for which it was granted, such that it may be terminated or amended if the circumstances that led to the grant of the compulsory licence change or cease to exist.
- The patentee must be paid adequate remuneration for use under the compulsory licence.
- The decision to grant a compulsory licence and the determination of what is adequate remuneration shall be subject to judicial review.
- Where a compulsory licence is granted in order to enable a second patent to

be exploited, the invention claimed in the second patent must involve an important technical advance of considerable economic significance in relation to the invention claimed in the first patent and the patentee of the first patent must be entitled (on reasonable terms) to a cross-licence in respect of the second patent.

Fast-moving consumer goods

Zarah Rasool
Baker Botts LLP

---

1. Introduction

Fast-moving consumer goods (FMCG), also sometimes referred to as consumer packaged goods (CPG), is an umbrella term that refers generally to consumer goods that are sold quickly and at relatively low cost. The sector encompasses perishable and non-perishable consumables such as fruit and vegetables, dairy products, meat and drinks. It also encompasses many other sectors, including household cleaning products, medicines, medical devices, cosmetics, toys, fashion clothing, handbags and accessories, consumer electronics, and motor vehicles.

The various products classified as FMCG are extremely diverse. However, they all share certain commercial characteristics:

- extremely high turnover rates either as the result of having a short replacement cycle due to perishability (in the case of food products), transience or built-in obsolescence (in the case of fashion items and certain consumer electronics) or as a result of extremely high consumer demand;
- sold at relatively low cost but in large volumes;
- distributed under extensive distribution networks; and
- subject to generic and/or sector-specific regulatory controls.

The FMCG industry is one of the world's most crowded and competitive. As a result, many industry players face the same challenges: namely, how to differentiate themselves from their competitors and how to maintain a competitive advantage once it is won. These are achieved through research and development (R&D), innovation and brand equity investment, which are key strategies for commercial success and growth in this sector. In order to maximise the strategic advantage of investment in these key areas, IP rights are essential: investment through new product activity or advertising relies on pre-existing IP rights and has the potential to generate new IP rights. IP rights often secure the success of a company and insulate it, as far as possible, from competition and market forces. Consequently, an effective IP strategy should protect new product introductions and marketing efforts.

This chapter will consider IP issues that are relevant in a business or asset purchase involving the acquisition of a company or business in the FMCG sector.

As part of the valuation of the IP assets and in any assessment in the course of due diligence as to the viability of the target's business, the IP issues likely to be relevant can be broadly outlined as follows:

- investigating what IP rights are owned or used by the target company or target business;
- checking (a) whether owned IP assets are adequately protected and (b) the terms on which the company or business uses third-party IP assets, if any;
- investigating whether there is freedom to operate on the market; and
- ascertaining whether any circumstances exist that might harm the market share or the reputation and goodwill of the company or business.

It is not possible in the scope of this chapter to cover IP issues comprehensively across every sector within FMCG. This chapter, therefore, provides a non-sector-specific overview of IP considerations. The materiality of the issues may depend on whether the company or business undertakes particular activities, such as new product development or advertising to consumers. However, the issues covered are potentially relevant to the FMCG sector as a whole.

The initial step in a due diligence review into a company or business in the FMCG sector is to identify what IP rights the target company or business owns in respect of its products. As well as checking whether the target has in place protection for its most valuable and essential IP assets, including registered protection where registration is available and appropriate, a purchaser will want to check whether the target's IP portfolio provides access to all of the rights necessary in order to carry on the business of the target following acquisition. If the target does not own all of the relevant rights, but relies on licensed third-party IP rights, the purchaser may need to negotiate and agree terms with third-party IP owners in order to secure access to those rights, unless the target has the ability to sub-license or assign its rights under those licences to the purchaser.

2. Identifying IP rights owned by the target

As we have seen in Paul Davies' chapter on due diligence, the preliminary stage of an IP due diligence project is to identify what assets are owned by the target and will be subject to the transaction. Once this is established, it leads to consideration of whether the assets are sufficient to carry on the business and whether their exploitation is subject to any restrictions.

It is convenient to consider IP assets in terms of IP assets generated at or relevant to the product development stage and IP assets that are generated at or relevant to the product naming and marketing stages. Those relating to the product development stage (in particular, copyright, design rights and patents) are more likely to be relevant when the target company or business is a supplier or manufacturer of FMCG. Those IP assets relating to product naming and marketing (in particular, copyright and trademarks), although relevant also to manufacturers, are most likely to be relevant when the target is involved in marketing and selling FMCG to consumers.

The purposes of identifying the IP assets owned by the target are primarily:

- to ensure that key elements of the product and business are protected against third-party use; and
- to enable the purchaser to investigate whether the seller has good title to the IP assets being transferred.

2.1 Trademarks

In the FMCG sector, brands play a vital role in distinguishing the source of origin of goods or services from those offered by others, enabling consumers to differentiate between products in a crowded market. Trademarks are an important component of any brand and are likely to be found in the IP portfolio of most FMCG businesses. As IP assets, trademarks represent the goodwill of a business and are the product of sometimes significant investment in promoting and establishing a brand on the market; they are highly valuable assets that can represent a significant portion of the value of a business. For the purchaser, the primary purpose of due diligence in the target's trademark portfolio is to ascertain whether the value of the brand, in terms of its market share and longevity, is appropriately protected.

(a) Registered trademarks

Trademarks protect the brand under which products or services are offered to the public. A trademark can be any sign capable of graphical representation that is capable of distinguishing the goods or services of one undertaking from the goods or services of other undertakings. Accordingly, they can consist of words, numbers, symbols, shapes, including the appearance of a product or its packaging, colours, sounds, smells or any combination thereof.

The first step in trademark due diligence is to identify what trademarks the target company uses. Since trademark protection is on a country-by-country basis, a purchaser should also identify where the trademarks are protected.

The jurisdictional coverage of the target company's trademark portfolio should reflect the geographical distribution of its product sales. Therefore, a purchaser should identify what trademarks the target company is using in relation to its products and where those products are or are intended to be sold. Using that information, the purchaser can then check what steps have been taken nationally and internationally to protect the trademarks through trademark registration applications in order to check whether the target's trademark strategy aligns with its product sales and its product development plans. The purpose of the exercise is to identify any gaps in the target's trademark protection and to assess what, if any, corrective steps are necessary.

The target would normally be expected to provide a list of all trademarks owned or exploited or planned to be owned or exploited by the target business, as well as information (country, application and registration number and date of filing and registration, international and local classes and the specification of goods and services under each application or registration) of all registrations and pending applications. Where the information provided by the target on its trademark portfolio is incomplete, searches of national and supranational registers (the majority of which are accessible online) can identify trademark registrations owned by the target company.

A purchaser can verify the information provided by the target using available online resources or local counsel and should pay particular attention to registration status, ownership, extent of coverage of the target's trademark portfolio, payment of renewal fees and whether any third-party rights have been registered in relation to the trademark.

To identify any gaps in the coverage of the target's trademark portfolio, the purchaser should always have reference to the target's business and/or product development plans and copies of its promotional and marketing materials, all of which provide an indication of what trademarks ought to have been protected or may in future need to be protected. Due diligence should also identify other companies within the seller's group that may be using the same or similar trademarks or company names to those being acquired. Where the purchaser identifies any entities with a name or selling product under a name that incorporates or is similar to the trademarks of the seller, the purchaser should seek appropriate assurances from the seller under the acquisition agreements that it will procure that those entities will change their names or stop selling product under the trademark without the purchaser's permission.

A purchaser should also check what internal procedures the brand owner has in place for dealing with potential infringements and clearing product packaging and physical marketing materials, as these issues may affect the validity of the mark. Landscape searches can also reveal potentially infringing third-party marks or, alternatively, prior rights that could affect the validity of the trademark in the event of challenge by a third party. A useful indicator as to the relative strength of a mark is whether the mark has been challenged in litigation. Therefore, as with all IP rights, purchasers should seek disclosure of any litigation and its outcome relating to trademarks.

Where the purchaser is acquiring the target's assets or business, but is not acquiring the target's trademarks, the purchaser should consider whether it requires a licence to use the seller's trademarks for a period after the acquisition. In such circumstances, the parties can agree to enter into a transitional trademark licence, giving the purchaser the right to make limited use of the trademark for a wind-down period. It is important for a purchaser to establish what rights are required and how long a transitional period is needed in order to operate the business or for the target company to continue operating after the acquisition.

In addition to checking whether any third party has acquired an interest over any registered trademarks, either under the terms of a licence agreement from the seller or under an agreement granting a security interest in the relevant trademarks, a purchaser should check whether there are any coexistence agreements in relation to the seller's trademarks. Coexistence agreements are usually entered into by brand owners on the resolution of a trademark dispute or to avoid the potential for dispute further down the line. Most coexistence agreements will limit to some extent the manner in which a trademark owner may use, register and enforce its brand. It is important, therefore, for the seller to be aware of any restrictions on the use of the trademark that may affect its ability to expand the use of the trademark into new products or markets.

(b) Unregistered trademarks

In the FMCG sector, where brand reputation and market share can be affected by the prevalence of copycat branding and lookalike products, trademark registration provides the most robust protection against infringement. However, while registered protection is more attractive, certain features of a brand may qualify for protection under the law of passing off without the need for registration. Unregistered trademark protection extends to all of the features of a brand that identify the products sold under the brand as originating from their source, and is not confined to features that meet the criteria for trademark registration. Therefore, where it might be difficult to obtain registered protection for certain aspects of the presentation of a product (for example, the colour or the shape of the product or packaging), the law of passing off or, outside the United Kingdom and Ireland, the law of unfair competition can provide useful protection against lookalikes.

The law of passing off involves a three-part test:[1]

- there must be goodwill or reputation attached to the goods or services;
- there must be a misrepresentation by the defendant to the public leading or likely to lead the public to believe that the goods or services offered by them are the goods or services of the claimant; and
- there must be damage to the claimant by reasons of the erroneous belief engendered by the defendant's misrepresentation that the source of the defendant's goods or services is the same as the source of those offered by the claimant.

Registered trademark infringement is easier and less expensive to establish than passing off as it avoids the difficulties in establishing goodwill and reputation required under the first limb of the tripartite test for passing off. It is also much harder to value unregistered rights due to the difficulties in proving ownership and subsistence of those rights. Important brands, particularly well-established brands or brands that are key to the seller's product development goals should ideally, therefore, be registered, and unregistered rights should only be relied on for those elements in the overall look and feel of the product and its packing for which registration may be more difficult to obtain.

On the transfer by the seller of its trademarks, trade names, rights in get-up, or rights to sue for passing off, the goodwill owned by the target must also be assigned. Goodwill is defined as "the benefit and advantage of the good name, reputation, and connection of a business. It is the attractive force which brings in custom".[2] It is personal property and can be assigned and/or jointly owned. Where a business is carried on in more than one country, there is separate goodwill in each country. In the United Kingdom, goodwill is established by providing proof of use of the relevant mark or sign in the marketplace in relation to goods or services.

A common error is to assume that unregistered trademarks are assets in their own right; the only right in relation to unregistered trademarks is to sue for passing off, which only the holder of the goodwill in an unregistered trademark is entitled to do. Therefore, in the case of unregistered trademarks, it is essential to obtain an assignment of the goodwill of the company.

It is sometimes unclear who owns goodwill in a particular product if more than

---

1 *Reckitt & Colman Products Ltd v Borden Inc* [1990] RPC 341. The analysis is based on the English law of passing off, rather than unfair competition, which applies generally outside the United Kingdom and Ireland.

2 *Inland Revenue Commissioners v Muller & Co's Margarine Ltd* [1901] AC 217 at page 223.

one company is involved in the supply chain. In those situations, the following questions can help to establish who owns the goodwill in a line of products:[3]

- Are the goods brought on the strength of the reputation of an identifiable trader?
- Who does the public perceive as responsible for the character or quality of the goods?
- Who is, in fact, responsible for the character or quality of the goods?
- What circumstances support the claim of any particular trader to be the owner of the goodwill?

If the target company or business does not own goodwill in the products, the purchaser should ensure that the goodwill is assigned to the target prior to the sale since otherwise it might find it impossible to sue third-party infringers in respect of passing off.

2.2 Design rights

Design rights protect the appearance of industrially reproduced products and can play an essential role in the FMCG sector. In design-led sectors, such as toys, fashion clothing and fashion accessories, design right protection can be very valuable. However, the relevance of designs is not limited to those sectors; almost all commercial goods, from drinks bottles to packaging for household cleaning products, are designed to appeal or communicate a message to consumers and to differentiate competing products. Therefore, design rights are potentially applicable to products and their packaging across the entire range of consumer goods.

Both registered and unregistered protection is available for functional designs. Unregistered design right arises automatically without the expense and delay of applying for registration. In sectors with a rapid design turnaround, for example the fashion sector where a producer might market hundreds of designs each season that are withdrawn from the market within months, unregistered protection is a cost-effective form of protection against copying.

The registration of design rights is a relatively quick and simple process. When compared to other forms of IP protection, the lack of any formal examination procedure (other than a review of basic formalities) in the procedure for registering UK registered designs and registered Community designs (see the introductory chapter) means that the registration process is relatively quick. Unlike most other registered IP rights, the simplicity and speed of the registration process for design rights means that they are suited even to those sectors where product ranges have a short turnaround. The availability of rapid relief against infringement and the enhanced term of protection offered by registration means that generally purchasers should expect the target company to have registered important designs. In addition to the appearance of novel aspects of a product and its packaging, design protection may be sought for digital images (particularly relevant if the target business is a game developer or uses computer applications in the course of its business) and can

3 C Wadlow, *The Law of Passing-Off* (Sweet & Maxwell, 3rd edn, 2004), pp 183–184.

complement trademark protection for the stylistic elements of a brand design, provided that they have sufficient novelty.

A purchaser should review the document trail relating to the creation process of the design. Ideally, the creator of the work, the date of first creation and any subsequent amendments should be identified. For the purpose of ascertaining whether design right protection subsists or has expired, the date of the first marketing of a product made to the design should also be recorded. Purchasers should note that in relation to UK design right, during the last five years of the term of the design right, any person is entitled to a licence under the design right[4] subject to the payment of a reasonable royalty.

In relation to both UK registered design and registered Community design, a purchaser should check the registration on the records maintained by the Intellectual Property Office and the Office for Harmonization in the Internal Market, respectively, in order to ascertain:

- the scope of the design right;
- the status of the registration to check whether it is in force;
- the date of application and registration in order to calculate the term of monopoly that applies;
- the identity of the registered proprietor;
- whether any third-party rights have been recorded in relation to the registration; and
- whether any third parties have applied to challenge the validity of the registered design (there is no provision for opposition to an application before grant).

As with UK design right and unregistered Community design right, the author is treated as the original proprietor of the design, with the exception of designs produced by an employee in the course of his employment, in which case the employer will be the proprietor of the design.[5]

With respect to UK registered design right only, in the case of designs commissioned for money or money's worth, the commissioner is the owner of the registered design provided that it was created before October 1 2014, or created on or after October 1 2014 provided it was created pursuant to a contract between the designer and the commissioner entered into before October 1 2014. For all designs created after October 1 2014, the author of the design will be the owner of the registered design, not the person who commissioned it.[6]

For registered Community design right, designs created by independent contractors and commissionees will be owned by the author, not the commissioner.[7] Therefore, for designs created otherwise than by employees in the course of their employment, purchasers should check that the rights have been assigned by the author (or the author's employer if the author created the work in the course of his employment).

4 Section 237(1), Copyright, Designs and Patents Act 1988.
5 Section 2(1)B, Registered Designs Act 1949; Article 14 Council Regulation No 6/2002/EC.
6 Section 2, Registered Designs Act 1949, as amended by section 6(1), Intellectual Property Act 2014.
7 *FEIA v Cul de Sac Espacio Creativo SL*, ECJ Case C-32/08.

2.3 Copyright

Most product development begins with an idea and the expression of the idea in the form of words or design drawings and diagrams. The final product is likely to be an accumulation of considerable time, effort and creativity. Copyright[8] protects the form of expression of a particular idea, provided that the work in which the idea is expressed is original, that is, not itself a copy, and involves independent skill and labour.

In the context of FMCG, copyright is most likely to be relevant in relation to logos and images used on product packaging or in advertising campaigns. Accordingly, it can be a valuable component in brand protection. Copyright may also apply to the contents of product information leaflets, user manuals and written marketing materials.

As copyright arises automatically, without the need for registration, it is more difficult to ascertain its ownership: there is no official register on which a purchaser can rely.[9] However, there are steps that a purchaser can take to assess whether the target owns any relevant copyright. Essentially, this involves identifying who created the copyright work, their relationship (employee or otherwise) with the company and, in the case of contractors, the terms of the contract under which the work was carried out. Ideally, the document trail should identify the creator of the work, the date of first creation and any subsequent amendments (for the purpose of ascertaining whether the rights may have expired).

A purchaser will want to investigate title to the copyright. As a general rule, copyright is owned by the individual who creates the work.[10] A statutory exception to this rule is that where a work is created by an employee in the course of his employment, the employer will be the first owner of copyright in the work, subject to any agreement to the contrary.[11] In the case of employee-created works, therefore, the purchaser should check IP clauses under terms of employment or should seek assurances from the seller that it has not entered into any agreement with its employees under which copyright created by employees in the course of their employment does not automatically vest in the employer.

Where the work is created by a third party under a contract for services, the contractor, not the commissioner of the work, will own the copyright. This is likely to arise where, for example, a business commissions a third party such as an advertising agency to design a logo or product artwork on its behalf. It is essential that the IP position is dealt with under contract between the business and the third-party contractor. Otherwise, the contractor (or his employer if the contractor is an employee and the work is created in the course of his employment) will own any copyright created under that commission. Ideally, the target business should take an assignment of any copyright from the contractor (or his employer, as appropriate). It is possible to assign copyright in works not yet in existence, which can be extremely

---

8 For a complete overview of copyright, see chapter one.

9 The United States (in particular) does have a system of copyright registration and maintains a register of copyright works.

10 Section 11(1), Copyright, Designs and Patents Act 1988.

11 Section 11(2), Copyright, Designs and Patents Act 1988.

useful when making contractual arrangements with third-party contractors and it means that an assignment of the copyright can be arranged up front in the contract for services.

Since proof of title can be an issue when it comes to the enforcement of copyright, a purchaser is likely to want warranties from the seller that it owns the copyright and a further warranty that, in respect of all relevant copyright, either the seller is the original owner of the copyright proper or assignments of the copyright have been made to the seller. In the latter case, a purchaser should ask to see copies of those assignments as it may need to rely on the documents to establish chain of title.

2.4 Patents

Within the FMCG sector, patents[12] are most likely to be relevant in high-tech industries, such as pharmaceuticals, medical devices and consumer electronics, but are also relevant to any business which uses innovative technology. In an industry where new products are constantly developed and businesses are continuously searching for efficiencies in methods of manufacturing, packaging and transporting products, patent protection is not only relevant to new products, but also to innovations in the manufacturing process for existing products or innovative improvements in an aspect of an existing product.

Although patent protection can be costly and time-consuming to obtain, it is extremely valuable to a business since it confers an exclusive right on the owner for the duration of the term to manufacture, sell or import the patented invention, giving the patent owner a significant advantage over its competitors and protecting substantial investment in R&D and innovation.

A purchaser's main concern in the FMCG arena is to ensure that inventions capable of protection that are relevant to the products in question or the processes by which they are manufactured have been patented by the target and, since patent protection must be sought on a country-by-country basis, that the coverage extends to key jurisdictions and reflects the target's product development plan.

When evaluating the target's patent portfolio, the purchaser should address the ownership position in order to establish that the target owns the patents and to ascertain whether there are any prior rights registered over the patent that might affect whether the patent can be transferred to the purchaser. Purchasers should also check the status of the patent. Checks include whether it has been granted (and, if so, the term of monopoly that still applies as well as the grant date of the patent to ascertain whether the opposition period has expired) or is still in the application stage. For pending patent applications, there is no guarantee that the patent will be granted and, until grant, there is no right to sue for infringement. In the case of pending patent applications, therefore, a purchaser may wish to commission a landscape search which can identify conflicting prior art in order to assess the strength of the patent application and the likelihood of it proceeding to grant.

Where a patent is of fundamental importance to a business, the purchaser should take professional advice as to its validity. There can never be a guarantee as to the

12 For a complete overview of patents, see chapter one.

validity of any patent. However, reviewing the prosecution history of a patent and, where the invention has been commercialised, information as to whether there has been any litigation in relation to the patent or whether the target is aware of any third-party infringement, can also provide useful indicators as to the patent's relative strength.

3. Evaluating licensed IP rights

Where the target company or business relies on IP rights owned by third parties in order to carry on the business, a purchaser should identify the licence agreements under which the target acquired the right to use the intellectual property. In addition to licence agreements, the target may be entitled to use third-party IP rights under R&D or collaboration agreements or joint venture agreements.

A purchaser is likely to seek assurances from the seller that the target owns or has the right to use all IP rights that are necessary to conduct its business, backed up by assurances that nothing has been done that would amount to a breach of the terms under any IP licence.

In the case of licences of important IP rights to the target, the purchaser will want to check the rights and obligations of the parties under the licence as well as the following:

- the scope of the grant:
  - whether the licence includes the right to sub-license to others;
  - whether the licence is sole (permits use of the licensed IP rights by the licensor and the licensee only), exclusive (permits use of the licensed IP rights by the licensee to the exclusion of the licensor and all others), or non-exclusive (permits the licensor to grant further licences of the licensed IP rights);
  - whether there are any limitations on field of use, and if so, the purchaser will want to ensure that the field is sufficiently wide to encompass the target's activities, taking into account any planned future diversification; and
  - the territorial scope of the licence;
- term and termination:
  - whether the licence is in force and the remaining term;
  - post-termination restrictions;
  - restrictions on the licensee's right to terminate and protection for the licensee against early termination by the licensor; and
  - whether the licensee can assign its right under the licence (which will be necessary in the event of an asset sale to the purchaser) or whether a change of control of the licensee entitles the licensor to terminate (which would mean the licence would be terminable as a result of a share sale);
- payment terms.

In the context of a share purchase it will not usually be necessary for IP licences to be assigned to the purchaser. However, IP rights are frequently licensed to companies as a group (for example a licence to the top company which extends rights to the top company's affiliates). In those circumstances, if the target is not a party to the licence agreement, its rights to use the licensed intellectual property are likely to fall away once it is no longer an affiliate of the top company. In those circumstances, the main options for the purchaser are:

- to take a sub-licence from a company within the target's group. This will only be possible if the licence includes the right to sub-license; or
- to obtain a separate licence from the licensor to take effect from the date of completion.

Where the target company has a licensed right to use certain trademarks, the purchaser should evaluate whether the use is subject to special trademark usage guidelines that would affect the manner in which the trademarks could be used by the purchaser following the acquisition. Brand usage guidelines are commonly used in licence situations to ensure correct usage of a trademark. Indeed, where the target has granted licences to third parties to use the target's trademarks, the purchaser should check that the licence agreement sets out rules concerning proper trademark use.

4. Infringement by third parties of rights owned

IP infringement by third parties can have potentially disastrous consequences for the commercial success of a company. The impact of lookalike products that 'free-ride' on the reputation or goodwill of an established product is a significant issue for the FMCG sector. Unauthorised third-party use of a company's IP rights in relation to lookalike products undermines that company's competitive position, eating into market share, causing losses in sales, profits, and licence and royalty fees. In the area of consumer goods, infringement can have a detrimental and long-term damaging effect on the reputation and value of the company's brand. As a result, a purchaser in any transaction that relates to an FMCG business or product should investigate whether there has been any material litigation relating to the target's IP rights or whether the target is aware of infringement by third parties, and should assess whether there are any issues that could affect the target's ability to conduct its business. The threat of third-party infringement in the FMCG sector commonly arises in the context of counterfeit goods, lookalike products and grey market goods.

4.1 Counterfeit goods

Counterfeit goods are fake or unauthorised imitations or replicas of real, usually well-known and popular products. Counterfeits are often of inferior quality and are produced with the intention of taking advantage of the reputation or value of the imitated product. In most countries, counterfeiting is illegal and is punishable under criminal as well as civil laws.

The prevalence of counterfeit goods presents a particularly difficult challenge for rights holders. Tackling counterfeiting requires vigilance and a concerted anti-counterfeiting strategy. Counterfeit goods are particularly likely to present a challenge for owners of well-known brands. In general, counterfeit goods are sold under trademarks that are identical, or almost indistinguishable, from the brand owner's trademark.

In order to assess the likelihood of damage caused by counterfeit goods to the target, a purchaser will want to know whether the target's products have been counterfeited in the past and, if so, what action was taken as well as what current anti-counterfeiting strategies the company has in place to prevent the potentially disastrous and far-reaching effects of counterfeiting. Where the target company is not a brand owner but is a distributor of FMCG, a purchaser will want to make sure that the target distributor has obtained warranties from its suppliers that the goods being supplied are genuine, licensed products and comply with all applicable laws.

A purchaser should review what anti-counterfeiting strategies the target has in place to limit the threat of counterfeit goods on the market. An effective anti-counterfeiting strategy involves legal, technological and commercial strategies to prevent or minimise counterfeiting, including the following:

- obtaining trademark registrations in jurisdictions where the brand owner's products are sold or manufactured;
- recording trademarks with customs offices and updating customs on product upgrades and changes so that they are aware of its features. Refreshing product labels and packaging from time to time should make it easier for customs to identify counterfeit products. Regulation (EU) No 608/2013 provides procedural rules for customs authorities to enforce IP rights with regard to goods liable to customs supervision or customs control. The Regulation enables information to be provided to customs so as to enable better risk management and includes measures to ensure that the interests of legitimate traders are protected;
- using professional market investigators and trademark watching services to monitor market activity;
- carefully monitoring online websites, particularly online business platforms such as eBay, Amazon and Alibaba;
- updating retailers, distributors and wholesalers with detailed information on product characteristics to prevent inadvertent sales by them of counterfeit goods.

4.2 Lookalikes

Copycat or lookalike products are products sold by a third party that look similar to a branded product, and by reason of that similarity consumers perceive the lookalike to share a greater number of features with the branded product than would be expected simply because the products are in the same product category.

As a result of the similarity, consumers often make purchases mistaking the lookalike for the imitated product, resulting in a loss of sales and profits for the brand owner. Consumers tend also to perceive lookalikes as sharing the same quality as the imitated product, which can cause consumers to switch from the brand owner's product to the lookalike, which also leads to a loss of sales for the brand owner.[13]

Lookalikes can also cause consumers to associate the lookalike product with the

13 *The Impact of lookalikes: similar packaging and fast-moving consumer goods,* Intellectual Property Office report, April 1 2013.

imitated product, believing them to have a common origin. This is potentially dangerous for the brand owner, who has no control over the quality of the lookalike product, which if associated with his product could tarnish the reputation of his brand.

There is no outright prohibition in the United Kingdom against lookalike products. Unlike many overseas jurisdictions, the United Kingdom does not have a law of unfair competition that allows brand owners to prevent competitors from producing copycat or lookalike products. The Consumer Protection from Unfair Trading Regulations 2008 (CPRs)[14] prohibit unfair commercial practices in business-to-consumer cases. Misleading acts and omissions and aggressive practices that have an effect on the consumer are all prohibited. It is likely that misleadingly similar packaging that affects consumers' transactional behavior is unlawful under the CPRs. Brand owners seeking to rely on the CPRs to prevent lookalikes do not have a private right of action and would need to approach Trading Standards Authorities to take action.

The Intellectual Property Office's report dated April 1 2013, *The impact of lookalikes: similar packaging and fast-moving consumer goods*, raises the possibility of introducing a private right of action under the CPRs. Until the law is reformed, however, brand owners will need to rely on claims for IP infringement in order to have a private right of action. Accordingly, they should ensure that distinguishing features of popular products are adequately protected by IP rights.

4.3 Parallel imports and grey market goods

Parallel import or grey-market goods are genuine branded goods that are imported into a market and sold there without the consent of the brand owner. Unlike counterfeits and lookalikes, the goods are 'genuine' because they have been manufactured by or with the consent of the brand owner. However, the brand owner may not consent to the goods being imported into a certain market because the goods were packaged and presented for sale in a particular jurisdiction.

Under the principle of exhaustion, a brand owner cannot object to the use of its trademark in relation to goods that were put on the market in the EEA by or with its consent. A brand owner cannot, therefore, object to the import of genuine goods into a market in the EEA if the goods were originally put on the market in the EEA by the brand owner or its licensee. However, if the parallel import concerns goods that were put on the market by the trademark owner outside the EEA, the brand owner can object to the import of the goods into the United Kingdom because the principle of exhaustion will not apply.

For domestic distributors, grey market diversion undercuts market prices through the sale of goods at lower price points. From the brand owner's perspective, a fundamental concern is that grey market goods can affect consumer experiences, particularly when consumers are confronted with a product designed to appeal to a different national target market. In the FMCG sector, negative user experiences can affect the reputation of a product or the brand under which is sold. Therefore, while

14 SI 2008/1277, implementing the Unfair Commercial Practices Directive 2005.

a manufacturer brand owner can do very little to prevent parallel imports from within the EU, it can take steps (which should be reviewed by a purchaser on the acquisition of a business) to mitigate the importation and sale of grey market goods. Steps a brand owner may take include the following:

- reviewing business supply chains, including licence and distributor agreements, to ensure that conditions for marketing the goods are expressly stipulated;
- drafting manufacturers' warranties to limit the ability of purchasers of grey market goods to rely on those warranties;
- monitoring the source of grey market activity; and
- notifying customs of registered trademarks and IP rights so that imports from outside the EEA can be detained.

5. Reputation management

A strong brand is advantageous because it allows marketers to charge a premium price for products sold under the brand. Having a strong brand can also insulate a business from the harsher effects of heavy competition. For example, with the high level of competition between products, retail shelf-space is scarce. Generally retailers will prefer items with a loyal customer base, preferring high-equity brands over low-equity brands. The rise in recent years in the popularity of private-label and stores' own-brand products, has demonstrated this problem acutely. The change in consumer habits – switching to private-label products – has led retailers carrying own-label stock to restrict the number of brands that they carry. Brands with a strong base of loyal customers are far more likely to be stocked than brands without a reputation. The brands with a strong reputation have thus been insulated from the full effect of the market trend that has seen customers migrating to less expensive, private-label products. This, in turn, has contributed to a practice known as 'slotting' or 'fixed trade spending', by which retailers charge producers or manufacturers a fee simply in order to stock their product.

This section looks at the following factors that can affect a brand's reputation and prestige and can give rise to material liabilities that can affect the value of a company:

- advertising and promotion;
- the quality of the goods sold under the brand, and compliance with policy and regulation.

5.1 Advertising and promotion

Brand success is strongly associated with proactive marketing strategies that provide the means to develop strong customer brand awareness and commitment. Among marketing communication tools, advertising and price promotions (temporary price reductions) play a pivotal role. Reviewing a target business or company's promotional strategy and physical marketing materials can help to identify the value of a company's brand and its goodwill on the market, it enables the purchaser to check whether the IP coverage of the company extends to all of the company's commercial offerings, and it can also identify potential infringement or compliance issues that may give rise to liabilities.

(a) ***Price promotions***

Price promotions are regulated in the United Kingdom. A failure to comply with the applicable regulatory rules can lead to regulatory enforcement; may have a negative impact on a brand's reputation; can lead to legal action by consumers or competitors; and can prove costly if marketing or advertising material needs to be recalled and redesigned.

In addition to general regulatory rules, applicable to all consumer goods, there are sector-specific regulations concerning price promotions for food, alcohol and tobacco.

(b) ***Advertising***

The primary legislation in this area is the CPRs, which implement the EU Unfair Commercial Practices Directive and prohibit commercial practices that are unfair to consumers, including the following practices likely to be relevant to promotional activity and prohibited in all circumstances:

- bait advertising, or 'bait and switch' – advertising products at a specified price when the trader is aware that he does not have reasonable stock available or is not able to supply at that price, or attempts to upsell, persuading consumers to purchase a higher priced product;
- falsely stating that a product is only available for a very limited time in order to persuade the consumer to make an immediate decision;
- falsely stating that a trader is going to cease trading or move premises;
- passing on materially inaccurate market information;
- describing a product as free if the consumer has to pay anything other than the unavoidable cost of responding, collecting or paying for delivery of the item.

Under the Committee of Advertising Practice's UK Code of Non-broadcast Advertising, Sales Promotions and Direct Marketing (CAP Code), marketing communications must:

- be legal, decent, honest and truthful (rule 1.2); and
- be prepared with a sense of responsibility to consumers and to society (rule 1.3).

(c) ***Comparative advertising***

Comparative advertising can be particularly problematic unless brand owners are aware of the legal parameters set out under applicable legislation. Comparative advertising is advertising that explicitly or implicitly identifies the goods or services offered by a competitor. The law on comparative advertising has been harmonised throughout the EU under Directive 2006/114/EC concerning misleading and comparative advertising (Comparative Advertising Directive), which was implemented in the United Kingdom under the Business Protection from Misleading Marketing Regulations 2008 (SI 2008/1276) (BPRs).

Comparative advertising that is misleading under the CPRs will also breach the BPRs. The penalty under regulation 7 of the BPRs for traders engaging in misleading advertising could be a fine, a term of imprisonment of up to two years, or both.

Under regulation 8 of the BPRs, a corporate body can be found guilty of an offence if an offence is proved to have been committed with the consent or the connivance of an officer of the body or to be attributable to any neglect on that officer's part.

Where a company engages in comparative advertising, it should ensure that it meets the following conditions contained in Article 4 of the Comparative Advertising Directive, which are required for the advertising to be lawful:

- The advertisement must not be "misleading". Misleading means any advertising which in any way, including its presentation, deceives or is likely to deceive the persons to whom it is addressed or whom it reaches and which, by reason of its deceptive nature, is likely to affect their economic behaviour or which, for those reasons, injures or is likely to injure a competitor;.
- The advertisement must not constitute a misleading act or omission within the meanings of Articles 6 and 7 of the Unfair Commercial Practices Directive.
- The advertisement must compare goods or services meeting the same needs or intended for the same purpose.
- The advertisement must objectively compare one or more material, relevant, verifiable and representative features, which may include price, of those goods and services.
- The advertisement must not discredit or denigrate the trademarks, trade names, other distinguishing marks, goods, services, activities or circumstances of a competitor.
- For products with designation of origin, the advertisement must relate in each case to products with the same designation.
- The advertisement must not take unfair advantage of the reputation of a trademark, trade name or other distinguishing marks of a competitor or of the designation of origin of competing products.
- The advertisement must not present goods or services as imitations or replicas of goods or services bearing a protected trademark or trade name.
- The advertisement must not create confusion among traders, between the advertiser and a competitor or between the advertiser's trademarks, trade names, other distinguishing marks, goods or services and those of a competitor.

A purchaser is likely to want to see any correspondence between the target business or company and the Office of Fair Trading or local trading standards services, which enforce compliance with the CPRs and BPRs, and the Advertising Standards Authority, which regulates compliance with the CAP Code. In light of the complicated and strict regulation in this area, a purchaser is likely to want warranties from the seller that no breaches of the regulations applicable to advertising and promotions or any infringement of third-party IP rights have occurred in the course of the advertising or promoting of the goods of the seller.

5.2 Product standards and product liability

Generally, a product might be defective or unsafe, giving rise to product liability, where the product itself is inherently dangerous or where the product contains a manufacturing defect, or where the product information, warnings and labelling information supplied with the product are inadequate. Product liability can also arise through marketing materials and statements made by sales representatives.

Brand value can drop dramatically with adverse publicity. Further, since the reputation of a brand hinges on the quality of its products, companies must ensure that their products are safe. Failure to comply with product safety legislation can endanger customers, exposing a company to litigation. It can also damage a company's commercial reputation, causing potentially enormous financial loss, and exposing its officers to prosecution or regulatory action.

In order to guarantee product safety, companies must constantly assess the effectiveness of their operating systems. Safety standards can change. Therefore, it is important to be aware of regulatory or legislative changes and to be flexible enough to adapt operating systems appropriately. In addition to complying with all relevant health and safety regulation requirements, companies should implement a system that allows corrective action to be taken as quickly and effectively as possible, including the option of recalling products found to be unsatisfactory post-marketing. If necessary, appropriate measures should be put in place under agreements with suppliers and distributors.

Purchasers should be aware of the product standards applicable to the target's industry in order to assess the likelihood of harm caused by non-compliance and in order to evaluate the procedures that the target has in place to ensure quality standards are met.

A company should identify and comply with all relevant product safety legislation, remembering that certain product regulations apply to all consumer products and others are specific to a product type. It should also identify and observe any codes of practice or industry standards.

(a) *General Product Safety Directive*

The General Product Safety Directive 2001/95/EC (GPSD) applies to producers and distributors (including retailers) of consumer goods. It sets generic health and safety requirements for all consumer products (other than food products) that are marketed in the EU. As such, the GSPD applies to all non-food consumer goods, whether or not they are also covered by specific sector legislation.

For the purpose of the GPSD, a producer is:[15]

- the manufacturer of the product, when he is established in the EC;
- any other person presenting himself as the manufacturer by affixing to the product his name, trademark or other distinctive mark;
- the person who reconditions the product;
- the manufacturer's representative, when the manufacturer is not established in the EC or, if there is no representative established in the Community, the importer of the product; or
- any other professional in the supply chain, in so far as their activities may affect the safety properties of a product.

15 Article 2(e).

A 'distributor' is any professional in the supply chain whose activity does not affect the safety properties of a product.

The GPSD requires that all products put on the market must be safe and provides what should happen in the event that a product is not safe as well as prescribing corrective action depending on the level of risk.

Companies are expected to determine the risks associated with their products and, based on that assessment, must take certain steps in order to comply with the GPSD. Commission Decision 2010/15/EU sets out a framework for assessing the level of risk posed by non-food products for the purposes of the GPSD. Although the guidelines were intended for the regulatory bodies of member states, they are also useful for those in the industry. It is prudent for industry players to carry out their own risk assessments using the same methodology as that used by relevant regulatory bodies. Complying with the risk assessment methodology and keeping relevant documentary evidence also shows that a company has exercised due diligence in complying with its obligations.

The risks associated with any product will dictate what further action producers and/or distributors must take under the GPSD. Producers and distributors must notify the authorities "immediately" if they become aware of a safety issue. For products that pose a serious risk to health and safety, the GPSD provides for a rapid alert system between member states and the Commission, which alerts relevant national authorities in the EU and partner countries such as the United States and China. The European Commission has also adopted measures that enable it to ban the marketing of goods posing a serious risk, particularly where member states have different approaches to dealing with the risk posed by the product or where urgent or Community-wide measures are necessary.

(b) Sector-specific legislation

In general, the GPSD applies to products and risks that are also covered by sector-specific product safety legislation.

A list of European legislation that applies to specific sectors is published by the Directorate-General for Enterprise and Industry of the European Commission and is updated annually to incorporate legislative developments. The list is known as the Pink Book. It is divided by chapter into specific sectors, including motor vehicles, chemicals, pharmaceuticals, cosmetics and telecommunications. The Commission has also drafted a guide explaining the practical application of the GPSD in areas where sector-specific legislation also exists.

It is important for purchasers to identify the applicable legislation within a given sector at the due diligence stage. Doing so can help to assess the likely areas of liability exposure and to understand the implications of regulatory offences in that sector.

(c) Product labels

For any product that carries a risk based on the product's foreseeable uses, appropriate product information may be essential to guarantee the safe use of the product. Product information may be supplied on product information leaflets or manuals supplied with the product, or may be supplied on the product itself or on its label or packaging. In other cases, it may be more appropriate to give product information to third parties involved in the product's maintenance and repair.

The extent of product information consumers can reasonably expect depends largely on the type of product and risk posed. For a producer, there are often commercial decisions to be made that affect the extent of any warnings or instructions. It is important to remember that appropriate product labelling can avoid the risk of liability in some situations.

Product labels will usually identify the product batch number and its manufacturer, as well as setting out directions for safe use and warnings about conditions for unsafe use and particular hazards. Depending on the nature of the product, it may also need to carry a statutory marking such as the CE marking, which is used to indicate that the product conforms to EU Directives. The IOS/IEC Guide[16] on instructions for use of products by consumers establishes principles and gives recommendations on the design and formulation of instructions for use of products by consumers. The guide suggests that warning notices should be placed conspicuously and the content should be limited to the essential information on what to do and what to avoid, expressed clearly and unambiguously.

(d) ***Post-marketing issues***

As part of their quality management, most companies will continue to monitor the safety of a product after it has been marketed. Certain safety issues may only come to light once the product has been marketed, and producers and distributors need to be in a position to comply with regulatory notification requirements and corrective measures.

In order to trace goods once they have been marketed, products should be batch-marked and should give the name and contact details of the producer or the importer. In certain sectors, this information is mandatory. For example, sector-specific regulations for pharmaceuticals and medical devices provide measures relating to the traceability of products post-marketing.

Safety issues may be revealed post-marketing in a number of ways. The most frequent of these are customer complaints and enquiries and returned goods. There should be communication along the whole length of the supply chain when a consumer returns or makes a claim in respect of a defective product. Throughout most of the EU, the consumer can only claim under breach of contract against the retailer from whom they purchased the product. Therefore, if a customer returns defective goods to the retailer in order to obtain a refund or replacement, unless the retailer communicates this to the producer, the producer may not be aware of a potential safety issue.

(e) ***Damage limitation***

When a consumer product is identified as unsafe, GPSD requires producers and distributors to take appropriate action. In all cases, the relevant regulatory authorities

16 37:2012.

must be informed. For some products, the regulatory authorities must be notified in the event of an adverse product or injury caused by the product. The UK government has published guidance on notification requirements for producers and distributors (The General Product Safety Regulations 2005: Notification guidance for producers and distributors). For certain regulated products, for example medicines, medical devices and motor vehicles, specific notification requirements may exist.

Companies will need to take a view on the appropriate course of action, which should be agreed by the regulatory body in charge. The response should be proportionate to the level of risk to consumers, the threat of damage to reputation caused by a defective product and the likelihood of consumers bringing claims against the company for injury. In some cases recall of the goods from consumers will be the appropriate course of action, depending on the seriousness and extent of the risk and how effectively the product can be recalled. In less serious cases, the appropriate course of action might entail recall limited to a particular defective batch, or it may be that the risk can be addressed simply by amending product warnings or user directions for future sales.

Whatever corrective action is taken, it is important to act quickly and to have procedures in place that ensure that defective or unsafe products can be identified quickly. This will usually require producers and distributors to cooperate in the exchange of information on defective products and for companies to have internal procedures in place so that the process can be managed expeditiously with minimal reputational damage.

Highly regulated products are generally controlled by a dedicated regulatory body. For example, medicines fall under the auspices of the Medicines and Healthcare Products Agency, while the Food Standards Agency is the regulator for food products. In relation to less heavily regulated consumer products, the local trading standards office will usually enforce the applicable consumer protection legislation.

Regulators generally have wide-ranging powers of enforcement over defective products, which include suspending sales of certain products found to be unsafe, requiring producers to alert consumers to risks or to provide adequate warnings, or in serious cases to mandate recall of the products in question. Regulators may also initiate proceedings against a company and its agents or officers. The supply of unsafe products or the failure to take appropriate corrective action is a criminal offence in the United Kingdom.

(f) ***Product liability***

When carrying out due diligence on a producer or distributor in the FMCG sector it is important to identify to the fullest possible extent any ongoing matters that could affect the reputation or goodwill of the company or business. Introducing a defective or unsafe product to the market is likely to harm the reputation of a company and, in turn, the value and goodwill attached to its brand unless adequate corrective measures are taken.

For the purposes of due diligence, therefore, it is important to be aware of the procedures that producers and distributors have in place to manage any safety issues, whether they arise at the production or other pre-sale stage, or whether they come to light only after the product has been marketed. The aim is to identify what measures a company has taken in order to mitigate any product liability risks.

Claims for product liability are generally founded on either breach of contract on the basis of breach of a condition or warranty under the contract between the purchaser and the retailer; negligence, under which a claim may be brought against anyone in the supply chain who may have owed a duty of care to the consumer; or under the Product Liability Directive 85/374/EEC, which creates a regime of strict liability of the producer for defective products.

The purchaser should seek disclosure of any claims against the company, including warranty or repair claims, or claims for personal injury and property or reputational damage. In some cases disclosure is limited to claims over a particular value threshold. A claim under this threshold may nevertheless pre-empt a mass of similar claims based on a defect in the product or its safety instructions. While the amount of a single claim may not meet the liability threshold, liability under multiple claims for the same issue can be significant not only in terms of the amount for which the company is liable, but also potentially exposure of the company to negative publicity and reputational harm.

In order to assess the product liability risk and the resulting risk of reputational damage attached to a company or a business relating to a particular product, a purchaser should ascertain whether the company has received product liability claims generally and whether there has been any increase in claims. It should also ascertain whether the company has had to take corrective action in the past to deal with a defective product. The purchaser will also want to identify who in the company is responsible for managing product safety issues and what internal procedures the company has in place to ensure that the rest of the business cooperates in exchanging information with that person or committee.

Contracts between a producer and its suppliers should give the producer a right of reclaim in the event of the supply of a product that does not comply with quality and safety standards. A producer may also seek a right of reclaim against its distributors for any harm resulting from a distributor's activities, particularly in relation to any sales or marketing materials or statements made by the distributor and its sales force. Distributors are likely to seek a right of reclaim against the producer of the product. From the producer's point of view, it may wish to limit its liability towards its distributors, though clauses attempting to exclude liability for personal injury or death where the producer or supplier is negligent are usually unenforceable. Exclusion of liability in contracts with consumers for personal injury or death or unfair terms generally are prohibited under Directive 93/13/EC.

Technology and telecoms

Mark Heaney
Amy Williams
Baker Botts LLP

---

1. Introduction

The technology and telecoms industries include some of the most innovative and fast-moving companies in the world today. As the various technologies converge, devices are becoming increasingly portable and with ever-growing functionality. Multimedia can now be created and accessed on the go, and transferred quickly and easily between devices over wireless communications links.

For companies looking to grow and succeed in these industries, continuing to make technical advances over their competitors is vital. As a result, companies operating in the technology and telecoms industries are both big creators and big users of IP rights. The IP portfolio of a company is intrinsic to its value and it is important to maximise the commercialisation of these rights.

2. Overview of key issues for technology and telecoms companies

2.1 IP law considerations

As any business in the technology or telecoms sector is built on its intellectual property, it must ensure that the intellectual property that it generates is well protected. Protection allows companies to maintain their technical advantage and ensure that the resources put into research and development are not used by competitors in the market to their own advantage. Companies must consider the types of IP protection that are available and most suitable for their products or services. The recent developments of the law (both statutory and case law) relating to patent and copyright protection for software and computer programs is an area of particular interest to companies in the technology and telecoms sectors.

2.2 Standardisation

One aspect of the technology and telecoms sector that brings unique considerations is the involvement of many, often competing, companies in the development of new technologies and the requirement for their products to be able to interact (ie, to work according to a 'standard'). Technologies that are standardised, for example in order to allow interoperability between devices communicating over central communications networks (such as the telecommunications network or the Internet), give rise to important commercial considerations, particularly in respect of licensing provisions. The current case law concerning licensing patents within the standardisation context and the competition law issues surrounding fair, reasonable and non-discriminatory (FRAND) licensing is reviewed below.

2.3 Commercialisation

Once intellectual property has been generated, a company must consider its options in relation to commercialisation. As part of their involvement in standards bodies, competing entities in the technology and telecoms sectors commonly license rights between themselves. However, beyond 'standard-essential' patent portfolios (ie, patents that must be used if the standard is used), companies expend a great deal of time, effort and money negotiating commercial licence agreements to allow them to use other non-essential technological advances for their benefit and to exploit their own intellectual property. Some key considerations for companies negotiating licences for intellectual property in the technology and telecoms fields are highlighted below, including the importance of considering the competition law position. In addition, purchases within the technology and telecoms sectors can lead to considerable IP due diligence exercises to ensure that the required intellectual property is available and free to use after the purchase is complete.

3. Specific IP law considerations in the technology and telecoms industries

Many technology and telecoms companies are innovators as well as manufacturers, with substantial teams of researchers responsible for driving their businesses forward and giving the companies a commercial advantage within their constantly evolving industries. Such competition to advance technology and corner a market can give rise to large portfolios of intellectual property. The principal areas of focus for technology and telecoms companies are patents, copyright and confidential information, although design rights also become relevant in respect of the physical design of a finished product.

3.1 Patentable inventions

The primary method of protecting a technical advance is to obtain patent protection. Once granted, a patent confers an exclusive right to exploit the invention and prevents competitors using it without permission.

A patent will be granted only where the invention is novel and contributes to the state of the art in a particular area of technology in an inventive way. The invention therefore must not have been known already and also must not have been obvious to the representative 'skilled person' who is said to have been working in that area of technology at the date the application was made for the patent. Inventions can be patented in the form of claims to a product, a process or products of a particular process. The patent must disclose the invention sufficiently that it can be implemented by others in the field.

(a) Competition and the patent system

There has always been an underlying tension between the laws surrounding the protection of intellectual property and those relating to anti-competitive behaviour.

Patents give their owners a monopoly right, which, it could be said, puts them in a dominant position that could be abused. However, proponents of the patent system argue that it is important to incentivise investment in research and development (R&D) by allowing a successful developer a monopoly for a fixed amount of time in return. Companies can justify investing the necessary money to research new technologies in the knowledge that they will be granted exclusive rights to use the technology and so can capitalise on their investment and recover the research and development costs.

(b) Key considerations for due diligence reviews of patents

When reviewing patents as part of a due diligence process, it is necessary to consider who owns the patent. While employees are generally employed to invent and their rights may therefore be automatically assigned to their employer, the buyer must check this position and ensure that ownership has been transferred, if necessary, to the seller from any previous owner. All assignments of patents and applications should be in writing and signed by both parties. If not, the assignment may be void. In the United States, the first owner of a patent application is often an employed inventor, and the application will be made in the inventor's name, together with an assignment of the rights to the employer. It is important to check that the assignment has been made, but also that it was made before any further applications were made in reliance on that initial filing (ie, relying on the initial filing as a priority document). If the assignments are not made at the correct time, it could lead to the patents being invalid or, at the very least, susceptible to a validity attack.

It is also necessary to consider where the patent applications have been filed and, therefore, in which jurisdictions the patents provide a monopoly. As a buyer, it is important to be aware of the countries in which the invention will be relevant, and in which markets it wishes to have its interests protected. In practice, technology and telecoms are worldwide industries, and the potential remit required for protection will be vast.

3.2 Rights in software: patent or copyright protection

(a) Patents and software

One unique issue that arises in protecting inventions in the technology and telecoms industries is where the invention is, or may be, in the form of software, such as a new application for use on a smartphone.

Under Article 52 of the European Patent Convention, a patent may be granted in "all fields of technology" as long as the invention is new, involves an inventive step and is capable of industrial application. However, there are also some specific exclusions to this rule:

> *discoveries, scientific theories, mathematical methods, aesthetic creations, schemes, rules and methods for performing mental acts, playing games or during business and programs for computers, presentations of information.*

Article 52 says that these exclusions will only apply where the application "relates to such [above listed] subject matter or activities as such".

As a result of the ambiguous meaning of this clause, the understanding of whether a patent is applicable for a "computer program as such" has been the subject of numerous court cases in Europe. The conclusion of these cases demonstrates that the courts will find that the invention relates to more than just a computer program "as such" where a so-called "technical effect" can be identified. However, defining the requirements to prove that a computer program has a technical effect has also been the subject of much debate.

It is important to note here that issues relating to the patentability of computer programs are complex and detailed and a thorough analysis is beyond the scope of this chapter. The treatment of such patents or applications for patents differs between courts to some degree. Notably, there is a difference of approach between the UK courts (and hence the UK patent offices, which follow UK court guidelines) and the European Patent Office (EPO).

The UK Court of Appeal has interpreted the provisions of Article 52 (and the UK legislation implemented in the Patents Act 1977, s 1(2)) in two key judgments in the *Aerotel/Macrossan*[1] and *Symbian*[2] cases. The *Symbian* case developed the UK position set out already in *Aerotel*, giving a clearer indication of what is necessary to demonstrate a technical contribution that is more than merely a computer program as such. The UK courts will consider the functionality of the computer program. It is therefore possible to patent an invention that either solves a technical problem external to the computer or solves a technical problem within the computer.

The position in the EPO is set out in *Computer Program Product/IBM*,[3] which allows patents for computer programs which create a technical effect by controlling the computer in some way. This is a lower hurdle than has been set in the UK courts. Therefore, while a patent for a computer program may be allowed in the EPO, there is a significant possibility that the patent will not be subsequently upheld by a UK court if challenged.

As a result of the development of the law in this area, the current position in both the European and UK courts appears to allow for patenting of computer programs to some degree, but this remains limited. Special care should be taken if the value of any commercial transaction lies in patents or applications relating to computer programs and a validity opinion from a specialist in the area may be of assistance.

(b) Copyright and software

Under s 3(1)(b) of the Copyright, Designs and Patents Act 1988, computer programs are specifically designated as literary works in which copyright can subsist. However, it is important to remember that only the expression of a computer program is protected (ie, the code itself) and not the ideas, principles and methods that underlie the program. One of the leading cases in the European courts in this area is *SAS v WPL*[4] in which the Court of Justice of the European Union (CJEU) confirmed that

1 *Aerotel v Telco*; Macrossan's Application [2007] R.P.C. 7.
2 *Symbian Limited v Comptroller General of Patents* [2008] EWCA Civ 1066.
3 T-1173/97.
4 C-406/10.

functionality, programming language and formatting of data files (such as application programming interfaces) would not fall within the scope of copyright protection.

Copyright is an automatic right which arises on the creation of a copyright work, without need for registration. It adds an additional layer of protection for companies operating in the software development area by allowing the owner to prevent others from copying the whole or a substantial portion of the code of a computer program. However, it does not protect the owner from a competitor who creates a similar program without copying the original.

Therefore, if the computer program to be protected is of high value, but can be recreated without the need to copy the code, it may not be sufficient to rely on copyright to prevent the functionality of the software or the overall look and feel of the application from being taken by a third party. However, for general applications, in which there is not necessarily any great technical advancement over the prior art and proving a technical effect may be difficult, there is benefit in having the protection of copyright instead of attempting to obtain patent protection.

(c) Key considerations for due diligence of rights in software

Having parallel protection under copyright and patent rights can provide a good deal of benefit to the rights holder, as the different provisions allow different aspects of the computer program to be covered. The main benefit of copyright in the underlying source code and any design documents or manuals relating to the computer program is that any small changes and updates to the software will be covered, which allows the most up-to-date version of the application to be protected as soon as it is created (but in relation to copying only, as discussed above).

A buyer will want to ensure that it obtains title to the copyright in the computer programs developed by a business that it is purchasing, together with any patents relating to the technology. One particular difficulty with copyright, since it is an unregistered right, it making sure that all of the copyright material is identified and transferred. As there is no register of copyright works for the buyer to check (copyright not being registrable, unlike in the United States), the due diligence process will require cooperation and disclosure by the seller.

As with patents, during the due diligence process it will be necessary to ensure that the ownership of the copyright has been transferred from the authors of the code (who may be employees) to the seller. It is important to check whether the programmers are employees (which means that the employer is the first owner of the copyright) or whether they are freelance workers, in which case the buyer will need to see the existence of, or otherwise obtain, copies of signed agreements transferring the rights in the copyright works to the seller. In any event, contracts of employment may include clauses to transfer IP rights even if they would otherwise vest in the employer. As part of the assessment of the ownership of the copyright, it will also be necessary to consider whether the due diligence should investigate the extent to which computer programs were created independently, or whether the work may have been copied in whole or in part from a third party's work.

3.3 Know-how and other IP considerations

(a) Protecting and transferring know-how and confidential information

Important know-how is often found in companies with a heavy focus on R&D and may therefore be key for companies in the technology and telecoms sector, often in conjunction with patents and copyright works. However, know-how is not considered 'property' under English law as it is an intangible and unregistrable entity and may be difficult to record. This can make it difficult to deal with during a commercial transaction.

Know-how and confidential information are generally held by key individuals in the company who are under an obligation to keep that knowledge confidential. This gives the company a mechanism of protecting its valuable know-how, as it can bring a breach of confidence and breach of contract action against employees attempting to make off with vital information and reuse it to their own advantage – for example, by taking it to a competitor company. This is particularly important with software, where code could be physically taken and reused or a programmer could rewrite the code for a new employer.

Although know-how cannot simply be assigned as a document or right from the seller to the buyer, agreements may be put in place to allow the transfer of know-how within a commercial transaction. As discussed in more detail below, this could be by acquiring the relevant employees, keeping them involved in the business going forward, or by transferring written records. The seller and its employees would then be contractually obliged not to use or disclose the information further.

(b) Trademarks, design rights and reputation

Branding is particularly relevant to technology and telecoms companies for whom the image and reputation of their business and products is vital, particularly given the speed of change of the market. Commercially, the brand is extremely important and is very closely linked in consumers' minds with the iconic logos and designs of the products in these fields.

The company name is important for all companies to register as a trade mark, and companies in the technology and telecoms sector usually register the name of their product ranges. In addition, where innovative and recognisable designs may become synonymous with a brand's products, the company will wish to consider design rights. Design rights can be registered in a similar way to patents, in which case the design must have novelty and individual character. Design rights can also arise without the need for registration, much like copyright. In developing new technology and new packaging for each new product, companies tread a fine line, sometimes getting very close to competitors' successful designs. This can lead to significant legal battles between companies, jostling for commercial advantage and to maintain their position in consumers' minds. There have been a number of design rights cases in Europe and in the United States over the last few years, often running in parallel with patent litigation relating to the technology underlying the products.

4. Standardisation in the technology and telecoms industries

One significant issue for companies within the technology and telecoms industries is the requirement for their products to be interoperable with products manufactured by other, often competing, companies. A prime example is the need for a mobile telephone to send signals that can be recognised and processed by the receiving base station and network.

In addition, within a single device, there may be a number of different components, often produced by separate manufacturers, which must work together to allow the device to function (eg, the hardware, software, processor and memory elements within a computer). Therefore, while companies are driven to patent and protect their own inventions, they are also often reliant on other companies' technologies, which may include earlier patented features on which the new inventions are built.

4.1 The history of standardisation

In order for devices to interoperate, developers of specific technologies create a set of rules, recommendations and requirements that define how a device must function. As each technology develops, interested organisations and individuals will join together as members of a standards body and will take on the responsibility for developing documents, known as technical specifications, which describe the functionality of the devices operating in that field. The members of a standards body can include a diverse mix of organisations from device manufacturers, network operators, service and content providers, national administrations, universities, research bodies, consultancies and user organisations, each bringing different resources and skills, and with different outlooks and priorities for the development of the technology.

Standards organisations have developed over time to cover key areas of technology and are often defined by their technological focus or their geographical coverage. For example, two of the key standards organisations in the technology and telecoms field are the Internet Engineering Task Force and the European Telecommunications Standards Institute. Within a standards body there may be many different areas covered, with specific working groups set up to focus on the development of the standard in a certain area. The standardisation organisations themselves provide a central point for checking and recording any changes proposed by the working groups, as well as integrating the developments across all areas of the technology.

4.2 Patents relating to standardised technology – FRAND licences

Members of a standardisation organisation will often file a patent application for their contribution before it is provided for inclusion in the standard. If, as a result of the patented mechanism being adopted, the standard cannot be implemented without necessarily infringing the patent, the patent is described as being essential to the standard.

On joining the standardisation organisation, members agree to make their standard-essential patents available to other members on the licence terms set by the organisation. In return, the member will have access to other standard-essential patents on the same basis. The terms on which the standard-essential patents are licensed must be fair, reasonable and non-discriminatory (known as FRAND terms, sometimes referred to as RAND, particularly in the United States). This enables a patent owner to be rewarded for the use of its patents by anyone implementing the standard but, in theory at least, without the patentee being able to block the use of the standard.

4.3 The European courts' interpretation of FRAND licences – competition law issues

Determining the terms of a licence that satisfy the FRAND requirements can prove difficult. Firstly, the parties must agree on whether a patent is essential. In some cases, one party may seek a declaration of essentiality or non-essentiality from the courts to determine whether a licence must be offered on FRAND terms or on commercial terms (assuming the patented invention is still used, even though it is not essential to implementation of the standard). Secondly, there have been a number of disputes over whether the terms of licences offered by patent holders comply with the FRAND requirements. Over the years, the European courts have been asked to adjudicate on a number of standards-related disagreements and have developed a body of case law to assist parties' interpretation of the requirements for FRAND licences.

The German courts have developed the majority of the case law in this area, with the assistance of references to the CJEU. An early German case is *In re Orange-Book-Standard*[5] from 2009. This case related to the set of standardisation documents for CD-R technology which were known as the Orange Book. The patents in question were standard essential and it was held that the patentee was therefore required to grant a licence to these patents on FRAND terms. Applying EU competition law, the German court held that the patentee could not claim that the other party had infringed its patents and simultaneously refuse to grant a FRAND licence as this would be an abuse of its dominant position in the market. Therefore, if the licensee raised this defence, it was taken to have agreed to take a licence of the patents on FRAND terms and, accordingly, was prohibited from asserting that it did not infringe the patent as part of its defence.

Since the Orange Book case, the German courts have referred further questions to the CJEU concerning FRAND licences relating to whether a patentee is abusing its dominant position by asserting infringement of a standard-essential patent and how willing the licensee has to be to negotiate the FRAND licence. In *Motorola v Apple*,[6] Apple argued that Motorola was abusing its dominant position by refusing to license its patents on FRAND terms. The CJEU found that Apple was not an unwilling licensee (although did not specify that Apple was, in fact, willing). As a result of Apple's position and Motorola's reticence in agreeing the terms of a licence, Motorola's approach was found to be an abuse of a dominant position.

5 German Supreme Court, May 2009.
6 *Motorola v Apple* (Regional Court Mannheim), Dec 2011, upheld by higher Regional Court Karlsruhe, Jan 2012.
7 *Huawei v ZTE*, Case C-170/13.

In *Huawei v ZTE*, the CJEU issued a decision in July 2015[7] which clarified the steps that each party must take. A patentee bringing an infringement action and seeking an injunction or recall/delivery up of a product will not have abused its dominant position if it has first alerted the alleged infringer to the infringement complained about, and then provided the alleged infringer with a specific, written offer on FRAND terms, setting out, among other things, the royalty to be paid. If the alleged infringer does not accept the offer, it must submit, promptly and in writing, a counter-offer that complies with FRAND terms. It must also provide appropriate security (eg, by giving a bank guarantee) in order to prove its position in relation to the counter-offer. If the alleged infringer has satisfied these requirements, and the patentee continues to allege infringement, the alleged infringer can argue that the patentee's actions are an abuse of its dominant position.

However, the CJEU made clear that there will not be an abuse of a dominant position if the patentee only claims a rendering of accounts or an award of damages in respect of a past infringement, and therefore such steps would not be required if an action is limited to such relief.

4.4 What is a FRAND rate?

Part of the problem for parties entering into licence agreements and for a court being asked to adjudicate on the proposed licence terms is that there is little case law on which to rely for guidance on what might be considered a fair, reasonable and non-discriminatory licence fee or royalty rate. The situation may depend on a great many features, including, for example, the technology in question, how important that standard is and whether there are any alternatives. Where there are multiple patents in a portfolio, the court may assess the overall importance of the portfolio to a standard and also consider other comparable licence rates, where this information is available.

Licence fees and royalty rates are often calculated on the basis of a percentage of the value of each unit or a fixed fee per unit, so that they can be factored up based on the number of units sold (ie, the number of times the licensed patent or patents have been implemented). In the technology and telecoms sectors, the few royalty rates that have been granted have generally been a few cents per unit (in those FRAND licences in which the courts have been required to intervene). However, with the large number of units manufactured by companies in these sectors, the licence fee can become a significant revenue for the patent owners, even where they are required to license on a regulated, FRAND basis. While a few cents on the price of a unit retailing for several hundred Euros may seem insignificant, it does provide for a potentially substantial risk for manufacturers without their own patent portfolio to cross-license. While one patent of a few cents may not matter, it would be a different matter for, say, 1,000 patents.

As discussed in section 5 below, once the parties are free to negotiate on a commercial basis on the open market (where the patents are useful to competitors but not essential) the rates can vary more widely and will depend heavily on the bargaining power of the parties and their commercial relationships. The patent owners will be keen to keep their commercially negotiated licence rates confidential, so that they do not lose their bargaining power when it comes to the next negotiation with another licensee.

4.5 Other competition law issues for standardised technologies

In addition to the FRAND issues, standardisation can be seen as a mechanism for giving patent holders a position of power over other companies in the same field, and can also be a cause of competition law arguments. Some concerns have been expressed when holders of standard-essential patents have made access to their standard-essential portfolios conditional upon also taking a licence of their non-essential patents, for which the licensees may have no use.

Furthermore, when companies collaborate on developing standards and patenting any new features, it can result in a select few companies owning the key patents for a specific technology, which they then cross-license between themselves, creating a so-called 'patent pool'. If those companies do not allow third parties to join in the development of the standard, but others are then required to use standardised technology, this may lead to the possibility of anti-competitive behaviour.

Overall the benefits of standardisation to the development of technologies and giving access to those technologies is well recognised and competition issues can be avoided or dealt with in the general schema of standardisation. Benefits of standardisation also include providing a central starting point for R&D in a specific area and a faster rate of innovation. The purpose of FRAND licences is to prevent the patent holders from overcharging third parties, applying pressure and abusing their position as holders of standard-essential patents. In addition, the system has benefits for consumers, such as increased competition between companies and the efficiency effects of product interoperability.

4.6 Key considerations for due diligence reviews of standard-essential patents

When reviewing a potential target's patent portfolio during a commercial transaction, it is important to consider whether any of the patents (or applications for patents) have been declared to be essential or might be essential even if not declared so. For such patents, the potential revenue stream that may be generated is likely to be affected by the requirements to offer licences on FRAND terms. Also, injunctive relief may be more difficult to obtain and, therefore, the usual approach of securing revenue from patents as a result of successful litigation may not be available. These difficulties are to be set off against the increased possibility of obtaining licences owing to the essential nature of the patents.

5. Commercial licence agreements in the technology and telecoms industries

In addition to FRAND licences there are many other situations in which companies in the technology and telecoms industries may wish to negotiate commercial agreements including licences to intellectual property. For example, companies may wish to exploit their intellectual property through licensing to developers or manufacturers instead of using the rights themselves. Alternatively, they may put the rights into a joint venture vehicle (JVV). In a joint venture care needs to be taken to keep control of intellectual property that is put into the JVV and intellectual property that is subsequently generated. Often, complex terms of ownership can be required in joint venture agreements. When considering a company involved in a joint venture, due diligence should be directed to ensuring that the company's existing intellectual property has not been fettered by its licensing into the JVV and, if the company requires any intellectual property generated by the JVV, an assignment or licence has been put in place.

5.1 Considerations for negotiating IP licences

Companies are, in general, free to negotiate any terms in a commercial licence agreement. The general considerations for a licensor and licensee of intellectual property during such negotiations are discussed elsewhere. However, two key considerations for companies in the technology and telecoms sectors are:

- the valuation of a patent portfolio; and
- ensuring that issues with competition laws are avoided or dealt with.

(a) Valuation of patent portfolios

As an intangible asset, intellectual property is notoriously difficult to value. On occasion, parties may cross-license their portfolios, often as a result of litigation. This of course may mean that valuation is unnecessary. However, if the licence is in one direction only, or one party believes its intellectual property to have a greater value than that of the other, there can be lengthy negotiations to finalise the amounts owed under a licence agreement. In the technology and telecoms industries, the difficult task of valuing portfolios often occurs when one party owns a patent portfolio, but does not itself have a manufacturing business and therefore has no requirement for a licence in return. In this case, that party may be able to use the strength of its negotiating position to put pressure on others requiring a licence to pay a higher royalty rate. These types of company (known as non-practising entities) may have a business model based on acquiring patent portfolios solely to obtain an income by licensing to other companies. For manufacturers in the technology and telecoms industries, there is therefore a risk that a non-practising entity will bring a claim for infringement of its patents, and will seek an injunction to prevent further use. The injunction or threat of an injunction can be removed by agreeing a licence fee acceptable to the patentee.

An agreed valuation for a licence (whether in the form of a paid-up fee or a royalty payment) can be kept confidential between the parties. This ensures that other potential licensees come to a negotiation over royalty rates with the same licensor without prior knowledge of the rates agreed with competitors.

If the parties cannot agree the licence fee or royalty rates and end up bringing court proceedings, it may be harder to keep the figures confidential if they are analysed during litigation and ultimately determined by a court. For this reason, if parties cannot agree on the valuation of a patent portfolio for the purpose of a licence agreement, they may elect to have the issue decided privately by an arbitration panel, rather than in open court proceedings.

Where disputes arise in this area, the valuation processes can be very lengthy and expensive for both parties. Independent experts or forensic accountants will be required to give their view on the financial positions of the parties and make a decision on the value of the portfolio. During this process, the experts may take into consideration many factors which might otherwise not have been commercial drivers for the parties when they originally entered into the licence.

Litigation always poses a serious risk to the parties involved. A potential infringer risks having an injunction ordered against it such that it may be required to take its product off the market. A patentee risks having patents revoked. Therefore, it is usual for litigation to settle at some point, with both parties accepting less than they would if they had total success. The balance will depend on obvious factors, such as the strength of the patents, the strength of the infringement case and the relative bargaining power of the parties.

(b) Competition law considerations for commercial IP licences

The terms of Article 101 of the Treaty on the Functioning of the European Union (TFEU) and the Technology Transfer Block Exemption[8] apply to certain terms in patent licences. The Guidelines to the Technology Transfer Block Exemption[9] set out the conditions under which an exemption to Article 101 may apply, and also give examples of other terms that would or would not be expected to fall within Article 101.

Under Article 101, a licence agreement must not result in, or have as its object, the "prevention, restriction or distortion" of competition within the EU. The prohibition covers price fixing, applying dissimilar conditions to equivalent transactions and limiting or controlling production, markets, technical developments or investment. For technology and telecoms companies concerned with licensing patents, it is important to consider whether the licence terms may have an effect on downstream pricing by the licensee or affect the territory in which goods can be manufactured or sold. Such agreements may, under certain circumstances, be deemed void and unenforceable in the EU member states.

The Technology Transfer Block Exemption provides an exemption from Article 101 for technology transfer agreements in which rights relating to technology, such as patents, know-how, designs and copyright are licensed "for the purpose of the production of contract products by the licensee". A contract product is "produced, directly or indirectly, on the basis of the licensed technology rights". This is likely to apply to patent licences entered into by technology and telecoms companies.

This useful exemption will only apply where the joint market share of the companies involved is below 30% (if the contracting parties are non-competitors) or 20% (if they are competitors). If the joint market share is even smaller (10% and 15% respectively), Article 101 does not apply at all. Above these thresholds, the requirements of Article 101 must be taken into consideration when negotiating commercial IP licences. In the technology and telecoms industries, where there are

---

8 Commission Regulation 316/2014 OJ 2014 L93/17.

9 Commission Notice, Guidelines on the application of Article 101 of the TFEU to technology transfer agreements (the Guidelines) (OJ 2014 C89/3).

small numbers of companies competing in the same field (ie, the major players all control significant shares of the market) this limitation will need to be considered, to ensure that the block exemption can be relied upon for licences in these sectors. Of course, the thresholds and whether or not they are exceeded will depend on the definition of the 'market'.

6. Asset purchase agreements involving intellectual property in the technology and telecoms industries

While many technology and telecoms companies will want to retain ownership of their intellectual property and license it out to generate revenue from an ongoing royalty fee, a company may also be in a position to sell its intellectual property. This may be because it is divesting a portion of its business and no longer requires the intellectual property in that field, or because it needs to generate income. The buyer may therefore be purchasing a part of a business as a going concern, including valuable intellectual property, or purchasing only the intellectual property. In either case, the buyer will need to be assigned the intellectual property from the selling company (which must be in writing and signed by both parties) and these assignments perfected, where necessary, by way of registration. Some of the major points in IP due diligence for an asset sale are considered below.

6.1 What intellectual property is being sold?

One of the key things to establish in an acquisition of a business or its assets is the extent of the intellectual property that the seller currently owns and uses. For example, which rights has it registered (such as patents, trademarks and registered design rights) and which unregistered rights does it own (eg, copyright in computer programs)? In relation to the unregistered rights, does the company have sufficient evidence that it is the owner of the rights so that the buyer can be certain of what is being bought and the rights can be enforced in future, if required?

As technology and telecoms businesses are very reliant on patents, checking the worldwide patent registers will be of primary importance during the due diligence stage. Any patents listed as part of the sale can be checked on the registers to ensure that the company is listed as the registered owner of the patents it is assigning, that the patents have not been allowed to lapse (eg, for lack of payment of maintenance fees), and that they are not fettered by a licence to a third party or other commercial dealing such as a mortgage.

If the seller is selling only some of its portfolio, it is important to check the intellectual property that is not being included to ensure that nothing that is required is being left behind. It may be necessary to request any connected or other useful intellectual property to be added to the sale. If the seller is not prepared to sell some key intellectual property, the buyer may need to negotiate a licence to any further rights it will require.

For technology and telecoms companies, confidential information, trade secrets and know-how may also be important. For these and other unregistered rights the buyer needs to know how the information is documented and protected. Important information may be residing in the inventors' lab books and minds, or in emails or other electronic documents, rather than printed material that can be physically transferred after the sale. In some cases, the ability to carry on a business or use the intellectual property after the sale has occurred may be dependent on having not just the documents but the individuals themselves, if the documents cannot be used without the knowledge of how to use them and put the ideas into effect.

It will therefore be important to carry out extensive and thorough due diligence on the company, including a consideration of how it operates and which assets, including key individuals and/or electronic records, are required to be transferred to the buyer.

6.2 Are there any restrictions on the use of intellectual property?

The various IP registers can be a useful starting point to check whether any registered rights are fettered, perhaps by charges or a licence. However, not all limitations are required to be registered. Accordingly information about any undisclosed restrictions on the intellectual property such as disclaimers or co-existence agreements should also be requested from the seller and reviewed.

In some cases, where the seller is intending to continue to carry on part of its business in parallel, there may also need to be co-existence agreements in place, which allow the seller to license some of its retained intellectual property going forward, or to license back some rights. For example, the buyer may be assigned all of the intellectual property that is used exclusively in the business that has been purchased, but will only have a licence to the intellectual property that will continue to be used by the seller. A combination of assignments and licences may also be used where there are already licences in place with third parties, and non-assignment provisions exist in those licences.

6.3 What other intellectual property is being used by the business?

The seller may be using and require the benefit of rights in third parties' intellectual property to implement its own intellectual property or otherwise to carry on its business. The terms of any licences benefiting the seller will therefore also need to be considered to ensure that the rights under these licences can be transferred to the buyer. In order to transfer any burdens on the seller as well as the benefits of such licences, a novation of the agreements may be necessary to ensure a third party's agreement to the transfer. In addition, the third-party agreements may contain restrictions on the transfer of certain burdens on the seller in the form of specific non-assignment provisions. In such cases, it may be appropriate to obtain an agreement from the third party not to enforce such provisions.

6.4 Does the intellectual property include any standard-essential patents?

For patents relating to standardised technology, it is important to consider whether any of the patents to be transferred have been declared to be essential to any standards or may be essential even if not declared. This will affect how the buyer can use the patents in the future, as a result of the FRAND requirements for licensing, and the potential revenue that could be earned in royalties from those patents. The buyer should therefore always ask whether any of the patents relate to and are essential to technical standards for the relevant technology and perform checks on the relevant websites of the standard setting body or bodies. If the seller has not made the relevant declaration but patents are indeed essential, this may still affect the future value of the patent. Additionally, the terms of membership of the standards organisation may have specific requirements, for example, that when transferring any essential intellectual property, the seller is obliged to seek agreement that the buyer agrees to be bound by the terms of the standards.

6.5 Is there a risk to the value of the intellectual property?

If the value of the intellectual property is high, as is often the case with technology and telecoms companies, it may be worth considering carrying out some degree of validity analysis as part of the due diligence process. Although it would not be possible to improve the validity of the patents, a negative report may affect the potential value and allow the buyer to renegotiate a lower purchase price, or even withdraw from the deal.

In all circumstances, the discussion of the indemnities and warranties that the seller is prepared to give in relation to the intellectual property will be key to providing the buyer with some protection against future issues, while also limiting the seller's liability.

6.6 Is there any ongoing or threat of litigation relating to the intellectual property?

When intellectual property is transferred, the right to bring infringement proceedings is also transferred, together, usually, with a right to sue for past infringements. The buyer should request information about any ongoing litigation or threats of litigation which involve the intellectual property. This may include infringement actions by the seller, claims for invalidity of the intellectual property, opposition before any patent or trade mark offices, and claims for ownership of the rights by employees or consultants. Where intellectual property is licensed, the licence agreements should be reviewed to ensure which party is obliged to or has the right to bring litigation if required.

While the buyer will want the right to sue on its IP portfolio to protect its rights, any ongoing or potential litigation which may damage or devalue the intellectual property will be a liability. All forms of litigation can be costly (both in terms of the financial drain to fight often lengthy legal battles and the cost of having key members of staff distracted from running the actual business) and they can also give rise to substantial risk, as there is a chance that the valuable intellectual property that has just been purchased may be revoked. In addition to litigation to determine the validity of intellectual property, technology and telecoms companies may also be involved in actions in which declarations are sought from the court, such as a declaration that a patent is essential or not essential or that it is infringed or not infringed. All types of litigation can require considerable internal effort and external legal support to ensure that the company's rights remain adequately protected if threatened.

6.7 How will the transfer of the intellectual property be effected on completion?

The purchase agreement includes an agreement to assign or transfer the IP rights to the buyer. The parties will be obliged to complete further documentation following signature of the purchase agreement to perfect the assignments. This may include the execution of documents for the novation of any contracts, as well as the assignment of the legal title in the intellectual property, the updating of official registers and the physical transfer of know-how documentation.

For confidential information and trade secrets there may need to be complex provisions to enable the information to be transferred. As well as the options to transfer the individuals with the relevant knowledge or to keep them on retainer contracts after the sale, there may be extensive handovers required to transfer knowledge, which should be set out clearly, in an ancillary document if necessary (eg, in a transitional services agreement). Once the know-how and confidential information has been transferred to the buyer, it will also require the seller and the individuals still aware of this information to sign confidentiality agreements, to ensure that this information is not disclosed further to third parties or used by the seller after the sale. Since there is often a substantial value to this information, the buyer needs to be certain that it has been obtained on an exclusive basis.

7. Summary

For technology and telecoms companies it is extremely important to put in place mechanisms to protect any intellectual property generated internally, but it is how this intellectual property is commercialised that is particularly key within these industries. In this chapter we have considered the types of intellectual property that are of particular relevance to the technology and telecoms industries, and focused on the specific issues that arise as a result of the requirements to share these rights among competitors. We have also considered the key aspects of commercial transactions in relation to a purchase of intellectual property by a technology or telecoms business.

Media and entertainment sectors: further copyright considerations

Tim Davison
Baker Botts (UK) LLP

1. Introduction

As with any form of due diligence enquiries by a prospective purchaser of specific assets or corporate entities, the purchaser of a business in the media sector will want to gain an in-depth knowledge of the target asset and to highlight particular areas of concern which may influence a purchaser's wish to continue with the purchase or otherwise affect the price it will pay. The media sector is a diverse one and the intention of this chapter is not to cover all the issues that a purchaser faces when looking at an acquisition but to focus on key intellectual property (IP) assets and issues that are particularly relevant to the media sector in the United Kingdom. Except where indicated, the IP issues considered in this chapter will generally apply across the media sector as a whole – for example, rights to content will apply whether a purchaser is looking at film, broadcasting or indeed any other media business.

The chapter focuses on issues relating to copyright and related rights. In particular, in order to ensure that the purchaser receives the full value and can exploit all rights in the manner desired, the three areas of particular importance when undertaking due diligence on the acquisition of a company, business or other specific asset in the media sector will be:

- the ownership, status and control of the fundamental intellectual property assets;
- the strength and economic value of each of the intellectual property assets; and
- the potential liability of the target entity for infringement.

1.1 Creation of media content

The creation and exploitation of content in the media sector generally follows three principal stages: development, production and distribution.

The development and production stages usually give rise to the creation of intellectual property rights. At the development stage, the key issues will be those relating to ownership and protection of intellectual property assets, including whether any third-party rights are required. For example, in the film sector the key issue in the development stage will be the creation of works required in the production itself, such as costume design, set design and the screenplay, as well as the acquisition of rights (in the form of a licence from the owner) in any underlying works such as books or plays, a screenplay, or a story outline on which the screenplay may be based.

During the production process, it is likely that new works will be generated in which intellectual property rights will subsist. For the buyer, the key issues will again be ownership of those assets, their duration and what steps have been taken by the vendor to protect and maintain those assets.

In the final stage, when the content is distributed or made available to the public, issues relating to the commercial exploitation and economic value of the created IP assets are likely to be of particular concern. Physical and digital content distribution plays a key role in the media sector. In the publishing, television and film industries in particular, the content creator will usually seek a distributor in order to attract the widest possible market. The distributor will usually acquire a licence on exclusive terms in order to exploit the work in the relevant territory and in the relevant format.

At each stage it is important to be aware of the interplay between statutory rights, which dictate the default position, and rights under contract, which will govern important issues relating to the exploitation of IP assets and may affect or vary the default position. Due diligence in transactions concerning valuable IP rights is considered in detail in another chapter, and the same principles apply to acquisitions in the media sector. This chapter, therefore, will concentrate in particular on copyright and related rights arising under statute, as these rights are likely to be of particular relevance to the creation and exploitation of media content.

As most media content is automatically protected by copyright in the United Kingdom, copyright and related rights are of particular importance to the media sector. That is not to say that other IP rights may not also be relevant. For example, any word, symbol, distinctive phrase, design or sound that identifies and distinguishes the target business would be registrable as a trademark. Important aspects of a concept or idea that may not be protected by copyright and that will not qualify for protection under the law of confidence once the information is released to the public may also be protectable under trademark law. For example, copyright is unlikely to subsist in names of films, websites, character names, etc but those features may qualify for trademark protection. Therefore, while the following discussion relates in particular to copyright and related rights in media content, other IP rights may be relevant to the asset or business being acquired. A purchaser investigating the target's IP portfolio should review whether aspects of the target business that have gathered (or are capable of gathering) strength through public recognition have been registered as trademarks, and also make appropriate checks at to the ownership and validity of those rights.[1]

2. Copyright

2.1 Works protected by copyright

A due diligence investigation will centre on establishing what rights exist to exploit the assets or carry on the business of the company being acquired. The purpose of this exercise is to identify what rights are being acquired, to investigate the chain of

1 Please see the chapter on due diligence for details on conducting due diligence in relation to trademarks.

title of any rights owned and to identify the risk of infringement of third-party IP rights and any deficiencies in the target company's IP protection.

When evaluation of a transaction involving a media asset or company occurs, the core intellectual property rights are copyright and related rights. The main piece of legislation in the United Kingdom is the Copyright, Designs and Patents Act 1988. To understand the detail of when copyright subsists, please refer to a separate chapter in this publication. In summary, however, copyright subsists in any of the categories of works defined in the Copyright, Designs and Patents Act and such copyright will subsist automatically provided that the relevant territorial factors are satisfied.[2]

Certain additional comments are worthy of note here in relation to some of the specified categories of works:

- *Original literary, dramatic, musical or artistic works (LDMA works)*[3] *that have been recorded in writing or otherwise:*[4] A 'literary work' is any work, other than a dramatic or musical work, which is written, spoken or sung, and accordingly includes tables, compilations, computer programs and databases.[5] 'Dramatic work' includes a work of dance or mime and 'musical work' means a work consisting of music, exclusive of any words or action intended to be sung, spoken or performed with the music.[6] The UK Court of Appeal has held that a dramatic work is a "work of action, with or without words or music, which was capable of performance".[7] Accordingly, a screenplay would be protected as a dramatic work; and if the screenplay is an adaptation of a book or play, the underlying book or play would be protected as literary and dramatic works respectively. 'Artistic works' include graphic works (including paintings, drawings, diagrams, charts and plans),[8] photographs, sculpture or collages, irrespective of artistic quality.[9]
- *Sound recordings, and films or broadcasts:*[10] A 'sound recording' is defined as a recording of sounds from which the sounds may be reproduced, or all or part of a literary, dramatic or musical work from which sounds reproducing that working or any part may be produced.[11] 'Films' are defined as "a recording on any medium from which a moving image may be produced, whatever the means of doing so".[12] As such, a film in this context can include a feature film, a television programme or a video (shot on a mobile device, for example); however, copyright does not exist in a film in the event that it is a copy taken from another film.[13] A 'broadcast' is defined as an electronic transmission of visual images, sounds or other information which is

---

2 See sections 153–160 of the Copyright, Designs and Patents Act 1988.
3 Section 1(1)(a) of the Copyright, Designs and Patents Act 1988.
4 Section 3(2) of the Copyright, Designs and Patents Act 1988.
5 Section 3(1) of the Copyright, Designs and Patents Act 1988
6 *Ibid.*
7 *Norowzian v Arks Ltd (No 2)* [2000] FSR 363
8 Section 4(2)(a) of the Copyright, Designs and Patents Act 1988.
9 Section 4(1) of the Copyright, Designs and Patents Act 1988.
10 Section 1(1)(b) of the Copyright, Designs and Patents Act 1988.
11 Section 5A(1) of the Copyright, Designs and Patents Act 1988.
12 Section 5B(1) of the Copyright, Designs and Patents Act 1988.
13 Section 5B(4) of the Copyright, Designs and Patents Act 1988.

transmitted for simultaneous reception by members of the public and is capable of being lawfully received by them or is transmitted at a time determined solely by the person making the transmission for presentation to members of the public (other than certain internet transmissions).[14]

- *Typographical arrangements of published editions:* This category of works protects the style, composition, layout and general appearance of a page of a published work.

A mere idea is not capable of copyright protection of itself, but copyright does subsist in the form of expression of an idea. Where the law draws a line between copying ideas and copying the expression of the idea is not always clear. Therefore, it is not always clear whether copyright law will protect, for example, television show formats or the themes of a novel or film. Where that is the case, of particular importance is protecting the distinctive elements of the work, which may then be exploited by the rights holder in a similar form in other territories. Therefore, while TV formats are regarded in the broadcasting industry as licensable commodities there is no specific category of protection and, as such, producers are best advised to take pre-emptive action to protect a TV format by, for example, implementing non-disclosure agreements with potential collaborators (at the development and production stages, particularly where third parties are engaged to carry out work in relation to the concept or idea, and also at the distribution stage before content is released to the public), registering trademarks and creating brands that may be protected and indirectly protect the show format.

Finally, it should be noted that there is no requirement of originality in relation to non-LDMA works. Other categories of works (sound recordings, films, broadcasts and typographical arrangements) can be derivative works.

2.2 Ownership of copyright

One of the key tasks when acquiring media assets is identifying who owns the copyright in a work. First, it will be necessary to identify who was the first owner of the legal title in the work. Secondly, investigations should be undertaken to establish whether the legal title has been transmitted to some other person or entity (whether by assignment or otherwise by operation of law) and, even then, whether some other person has any form of equitable right to the work.

The overarching principle of copyright law is that the first owner of the copyright in a work is the author, unless two or more persons acted as joint authors in which circumstances the copyright will be owned by such persons as joint authors. The notable exception to the stated principle is that an employer is *prima facie* entitled to copyright produced by its employees, other than in certain limited circumstances.

Accordingly, it will be important to establish whether, at the time that the copyright was created, the author was subject to a contract of employment with the target company. If so:

- What were the provisions of that contract in relation to assignment of rights?

14 Section 6 of the Copyright, Designs and Patents Act 1988.

- Did the author create the work while performing his duties as an employee of the target company?
- Was there any other agreement (written or otherwise) between the author and the target company agreeing something to the contrary of the employer owning such copyright?

Copyright can be transferred by assignment, testamentary disposition or operation of law.[15] The key issue for a purchaser will be to identify what assets the target business or company holds, to identify the copyright works comprising those assets and to investigate the chain of title. Given that copyright arises automatically, without the need for registration and irrespective of the quality of a work, an investigation into chain of title will only be proportionate in relation to those assets that are important to the business. Where the copyright assets of business are key to the purchaser's business plans following completion, the purchaser is likely to insist on warranties as to the ownership of the relevant assets to protect it in the event that there is a break in the chain of title of which the purchaser only becomes aware following completion.

For a copyrighted work in any format, a licence is required by a third party if that third party wishes to:

- copy the work;
- issue copies of the work to the public;
- rent or lend the work to the public;
- perform, show or play the work in public;
- communicate the work to the public; or
- make an adaptation of the work or do any of the above in relation to the adaptation.

Therefore, where the chain of title does not indicate that the target company (in the case of a share acquisition) or the vendor (in the case of an asset acquisition) is the owner of the work (and any underlying works), the purchaser would need to review the terms of the licences under which the target acquired the right to use the works and would need appropriate assurances from the seller with regards to those licences – for example, that there are no outstanding liabilities under payment terms or that nothing that been done which would render the licences unenforceable.

Finally, a purchaser should be careful to ensure that no reversionary interest (for works created under the Copyright Act 1911) exists. Under that act, an author could not assign copyright for any period beyond 25 years after his death, following which period it reverted to his personal representatives.

(a) *Authorship*

The primary task for a purchaser will be to identify material assets and to identify which IP rights are involved. In the case of copyright this can be a difficult task, since there is a greater likelihood that a work consists of 'layers' of works, each with a

15 Section 90(1) of the Copyright, Designs and Patents Act 1988.

different owner. For example, with regard to music, there are three potential copyrights that will need to be considered (the lyrics, the musical composition and, if there has been one, the sound recording) and the type of licensing required will be governed by how the music will be used within the content and the method by which it will be exploited.

The ownership of copyright is dictated by the Copyright, Designs and Patents Act. As discussed in another chapter of this publication, the person who creates the work (ie, the 'author')[16] will be the first owner of copyright in the work. In relation to categories of media works in which copyright can subsist, the author in each case is defined under the Copyright, Designs and Patents Act as set out in Table 1.[17]

Table 1: Definition of 'author' in various categories of copyrighted works

Category	Definition of 'author'
Sound recording	Producer. A 'producer' (in relation to both sound recordings and (see next category) films) is defined as the person by whom the arrangements necessary for the making of the sound recording or film are undertaken.[18]
Film	Producer and principal director. Films made on or after July 1 1994 are treated as works of joint authorship (unless the producer and principal director are the same person).[19] For films made prior to that date, the principal director is not deemed to have any authorship rights.
Broadcast	The person making the broadcast (or, in the case of a broadcast which relays another broadcast by reception and immediate retransmission, the person making that other broadcast). 'Making' the broadcast means: (a) transmitting the programme where the person transmitting has responsibility to any extent for the content of the broadcast; and (b) providing the programme and making arrangements necessary for its transmission with the person transmitting it.[20] Where more than one person is making the broadcast, it will be a work of joint authorship. Where the place from which programme-carrying signals are transmitted to a satellite (the 'uplink station') is in the

continued on next page

16 Section 9(1) of the Copyright, Designs and Patents Act 1988.
17 Section 9(2) of the Copyright, Designs and Patents Act 1988.
18 Section 178 of the Copyright, Designs and Patents Act 1988.
19 Section 10(1A) of the Copyright, Designs and Patents Act 1988.
20 Section 6(3) of the Copyright, Designs and Patents Act 1988.

Category	Definition of 'author'
Broadcast *continued*	European Economic Area (EEA), the person operating the uplink station is treated as the person making the broadcast.[21] However, where the uplink station is not located in the EEA, but a person who is established in the EEA has commissioned the making of the broadcast, that person is treated as the person making the broadcast.[22]
Typographical arrangement	Publisher
Computer-generated LDMA works	Person by whom the arrangements necessary for the creation of the work are undertaken.

Identifying the authors of relevant works enables the purchaser to ascertain the first owner of copyright and to make due enquiries as to the chain of title in relation to the copyright.

In relation to LDMA works and films, where the work is made by an employee in the course of his employment, the employer will be the first owner of any copyright in the work, subject to any agreement to the contrary.[23]

In relation to works of joint authorship, it should be noted that each joint author can prevent the exploitation of the work by the other joint authors and could be entitled to royalties in the event that the work is exploited by the other joint authors.

(b) *Underlying rights*

Depending on the overall complexity of a work, it may contain several other works. These other works can be considered to have associated underlying rights that could be infringed if used without permission. Examples of underlying works can include:

- Individual songs or other musical work in a soundtrack. The sound recording used in the soundtrack would be a distinct underlying copyright work and may itself contain further underlying rights. The recording would be protected as a sound recording, while the song's lyrics may be protected as a literary work and the music would be protected as a musical work.
- Where a screenplay has been adapted from a book or play, such book or play would be protected as a literary or a dramatic work respectively and therefore a licence would be required to exploit them in the screenplay. (Note that where an author of a literary, dramatic, musical or artistic work enters into an agreement concerning film production with a producer, the author is

21 Section 6A(2) of the Copyright, Designs and Patents Act 1988.
22 Section 6A(3) of the Copyright, Designs and Patents Act 1988.
23 Section 11(2) of the Copyright, Designs and Patents Act 1988.

presumed to have transferred any rental rights to the producer in relation to the film arising by inclusion of the author's work in the film.[24] The author retains the right in those circumstances to equitable remuneration for the transfer of those rental rights).[25]

- Unscripted words or actions performed by actors (eg, live interviews on television or a film actor's improvisation) may be protected as copyright works in the form of original literary or dramatic works once recorded and, as such, suitable assignment provisions would need to be included. These are discussed in more detail below.
- Additional works of art that appear in the overall content may also be protected – for example, quoting speeches or poetry (although it should be noted that the Copyright, Designs and Patents Act 1988 allows for the 'incidental' inclusion of artistic works,[26] including filming works of architecture and sculpture on public display[27]).

Where a work contains multiple underlying works, it can be difficult to establish a chain of title that shows that the target company or business has the right to exploit the work. In those circumstances, it is common for the purchaser to rely on warranties as to non-infringement of third-party intellectual property rights. Nevertheless, a purchaser should still seek disclosure of all agreements entered into by the target relating to the underlying IP rights. Depending on the circumstances, it would usually be more appropriate for the purchaser to seek an indemnity rather than a warranty in relation to a known risk. Agreements between the content creator and its distributors will frequently contain warranties to the same effect (ie, that dealing with the work in the proposed manner does not infringe the rights of third parties). Where the purchaser will assume the liability under any such warranty, either automatically on a share purchase or via assignment on an asset sale, it is desirable to obtain equivalent warranty protection from the seller that reflects the liability assumed by the purchaser under existing agreements with third parties.

2.3 Collecting societies and collective bargaining agreements

Collecting societies, also referred to as 'licensing bodies', are associations which are set up to represent the collective interests of various sources of works. The purpose of these organisations is to safeguard the rights of the creative talent when contracting with organisations wishing to commercially exploit the work and to facilitate commercial exploitation by avoiding the need for copyright holders (often represented by trade associations) participating in the scheme from having to grant individual licences in respect of each exploitation of the relevant works. Collecting societies will usually require a copyright holder signing up to the scheme to appoint the society as their agent or alternatively to assign their rights to the society. The society then exploits the work on the creator's behalf.

---

24 Section 93A(1) of the Copyright, Designs and Patents Act 1988.
25 Section 93B(1) of the Copyright, Designs and Patents Act 1988.
26 Section 31 of the Copyright, Designs and Patents Act 1988.
27 Section 62 of the Copyright, Designs and Patents Act 1988.

A purchaser evaluating whether the assets or business being acquired do not infringe any third-party rights will need to ensure that the target company (in the case of a share acquisition) or the vendor (in the case of an asset acquisition) has obtained rights clearances in the event that any third-party works protected by copyright have been used. In some cases, the purchaser will need to review the arrangements between the target company (in the case of a share acquisition) or the vendor (in the case of an asset acquisition) and collecting societies, and may also need to evaluate what rights clearances will be required after completion in order to exploit the assets being acquired in the manner intended by the purchaser.

In the publishing industry there are a number of collecting societies acting as associations responsible for administering the rights of authors. The relevant agency for licensing purposes will depend on what rights the licensee wishes to acquire in the published work. From the point of view of the purchaser, it will want to check that appropriate permissions have been obtained with regard to any third-party rights used in the assets being acquired from the seller. In some cases, therefore, this will entail checking that the target company (in the case of a share acquisition) or the vendor (in the case of an asset acquisition) has sought licences from the appropriate collecting societies. Major collecting societies include:

- The Copyright Licensing Agency (CLA), which collectively licenses on behalf of the Authors Licensing and Collecting Society (ALCS) and the Publishers' Licensing Society Ltd (PLS). Income received by the CLA is distributed among publishers and authors participating in the ALCS and PLS schemes. ALCS also administers certain rights (including rental rights and cable and satellite transmission rights) on behalf of its members. In general, the CLA administers reproduction rights and implements blanket licensing schemes through a rapid clearing system.
- The Society of Authors, which operates as a collecting society as well as a trade union. Unlike the CLA, which gives rights to copy or scan works, the Society of Authors grants licenses to use quotes from protected works.
- The Design and Artists' Copyright Society (DACS), which licenses reproduction rights in artistic works.
- The Newspaper Licensing Agency (NLA), which administers the licensing of material from newspapers (in print and online).[28]

In addition to collecting societies, trade association agreements are also relevant in certain industries to the process of obtaining rights clearances. These associations administer collective bargaining agreements which preserve the rights of creators. In the United Kingdom, examples of such bodies include:

- Producers Alliance for Cinema and Television (PACT), a trade association established to represent UK independent television, film, digital, children's and animation media companies;
- Writers' Guild of Great Britain (WGGB), a trade union representing professional writers in TV, film, theatre, radio, books, poetry, animation and videogames;

28 See *Newspaper Licensing Agency Ltd v Meltwater Holding BV* [2011] EWCA Civ 890 (27 July 2011)

- Equity, the UK trade union for professional performers and creative practitioners;
- PRS for Music, which represents members' performing rights whenever a piece of music is performed or played in any public space or place outside the home;
- Mechanical-Copyright Protection Society (MCPS), which represents members' mechanical rights whenever a piece of music is reproduced as a physical product (and, as such, is different to the work of PRS for Music since mechanical rights royalties are different from performance rights being paid to the songwriter, composer or publisher when music is reproduced as a physical product or for broadcast or online); and
- Musicians' Union (MU), a trade union seeking to ensure that musicians are paid for any original recordings (whether by way of session fee, future royalty share or otherwise) and represent the rights of musicians, including negotiating with employers in the industry, as well as offering insurance cover, legal advice and union representation for issues in the workplace.

Depending on the type of work or performance for which rights clearances are sought, therefore, there may be a requirement to obtain clearance (and make payments) under a collective licensing scheme. In particular, this is likely to be the case where literary works are used as source material or where there is use of a screenplay, script, existing music, sound recordings, artistic works or film footage. Where the work is subject to a collective licensing scheme, provided that clearances are made under the scheme it will not usually be necessary to make clearances individually. However, it may still be necessary to ensure that individual consent is obtained for certain types of exploitation which are not covered by the terms of any blanket agreements, including collective licensing or collective bargaining agreements.

2.4 Duration of copyright

The length of protection afforded to the various categories of copyrighted works is set out in Table 2. The duration of copyright protection has been the subject of changes to the UK law and, in relation to older works, a purchaser should always check the term of copyright protection carefully.

Whereas warranty and indemnity claims are often subject to a time limit within which a claim must be brought following completion of an acquisition, the relevance of copyright protection to the media sector means that the purchaser should consider the potentially lengthy duration of copyright protection when agreeing any limit under a warranty or indemnity in relation to infringement of third-party IP rights.

Table 2: Length of UK copyright protection in various categories of copyrighted works

Category	Length of UK copyright protection
Literary, dramatic, musical or artistic work	Seventy years from the end of the calendar year in which the author dies.[29] Where authorship is unknown, 70 years from the date made, or if made available to the public in that time, 70 years from publication.[30] Where the country of origin is outside the EEA and the author is not an EEA national, the duration will be that which applies in the country of origin, provided that it does not exceed the UK term.[31]
Sound recording	Fifty years from the end of the calendar year in which the recording is made, or, if the work has been published or made available or communicated to the public in that period, 50 years from the end of the calendar year in which it was so published or made available.[32] Where the author is not an EEA national, the duration will be that which applies in the country of origin, provided that it does not exceed the UK term.[33]
Film	Seventy years from the end of the calendar year in which the death occurs of the last to die of the principal director, author of the screenplay, author of the dialogue, or composer of the music specifically created for and used in the film.[34] Where authorship is unknown, 70 years from the year made or, if made available to the public in that period, 70 years from the end of the calendar year in which it was first so made available.[35] Where the country of origin is outside the EEA and the author is not an EEA national, the duration will be that which applies in the country of origin, provided that it does not exceed the UK term.[36]

continued on next page

29 Section 12(1) of the Copyright, Designs and Patents Act 1988.
30 Section 12(2) of the Copyright, Designs and Patents Act 1988.
31 Section 12(6) of the Copyright, Designs and Patents Act 1988.
32 Section 13A of the Copyright, Designs and Patents Act 1988.
33 Section 13A(4) of the Copyright, Designs and Patents Act 1988.
34 Section 13B(2) of the Copyright, Designs and Patents Act 1988.
35 Section 13B(4) of the Copyright, Designs and Patents Act 1988.
36 Section 13B(7) of the Copyright, Designs and Patents Act 1988.

Category	Length of UK copyright protection
Broadcast	Fifty years from the end of the calendar year in which the broadcast was made. Where the author of the broadcast is not an EEA national, the duration of copyright in the broadcast in the country of which the author is a national will apply, provided that it does not exceed the UK term.[37] Any copyright in a repeat broadcast will expire at the same time as the copyright in the original broadcast.[38]
Typographical arrangement	Twenty-five years from the end of the year of publication.
Computer-generated LDMA works	Fifty years from the end of the calendar year in which the work was made.[39]

3. Related rights

In addition to copyright, the Copyright, Designs and Patents Act 1988 also covers 'related rights' which include authors' rights and performers' rights. Authors' rights and performers' rights are referred to together under the act as 'moral rights'.

Authors' rights under the 1988 act arise only in relation to copyright and are personal to the author of the work. They cannot be assigned and expire automatically on the death of the author of the work in relation to which the rights arise, except in relation to the right against false attribution, which continues for a period of 20 years after the death of the author.

The moral rights afforded to authors under the 1988 act are the following:

- the 'right of paternity'– ie, the right to be identified as the author or director of a copyright work);[40]
- the 'right of integrity' – ie, the right to object to derogatory treatment of a copyright work;[41]
- the right against false attribution of a copyright work;[42] and
- the right to privacy in respect of certain photographs and films.[43]

In addition to the moral rights of authors, the Copyright, Designs and Patents Act 1988 grants moral rights to performers (performers' rights), which are the right to be identified as the performer of a qualifying performance (the right of paternity) and the right to object to derogatory treatment of a qualifying performance (the right of integrity).

---

37 Section 14(3) of the Copyright, Designs and Patents Act 1988.
38 Section 14(5) of the Copyright, Designs and Patents Act 1988.
39 Section 12(7) of the Copyright, Designs and Patents Act 1988.
40 Section 77 of the Copyright, Designs and Patents Act 1988.
41 Section 80 of the Copyright, Designs and Patents Act 1988.
42 Section 84 of the Copyright, Designs and Patents Act 1988.
43 Section 85 of the Copyright, Designs and Patents Act 1988.

A purchaser investigating the ownership of copyright-protected works should ensure that any moral rights which may affect the future exploitation of the work in the manner intended by the purchaser after completion have been waived. For example, if it would be onerous for the purchaser to have to identify the author or a performer of the work in question every time the work is shown or issued to the public, the author of the work and the performers of the recording of the work would need to have waived their respective rights of paternity. A waiver may relate to a specific work, to works of a specified description or to works generally, and may relate to existing or future works, may be conditional or unconditional and may be expressed to be subject to revocation. If the waiver is made in favour of the owner or prospective owner of the copyright in the work or works to which it relates, it is presumed to extend to his licensees and successors in title unless a contrary intention is expressed.[44]

When investigating whether the carrying-on of a particular business or use of a specific media asset infringes on the rights of third parties, the purchaser should also consider whether any exploitation of a work will infringe any moral rights in the work.

4. Material contract types for film, television and internet broadcasts

Set out below are examples of certain specific agreement types that an acquirer is likely to see as part of any due diligence enquiry of companies involved in the creation of works in the film, television or internet broadcasting sectors, depending on the line of business. This is a non-exhaustive list but sets out some of the material intellectual property terms and issues to consider when reviewing such agreements for previous productions (where ongoing terms apply), existing productions or future productions (where agreements have been signed or are being negotiated but production has yet to commence).

4.1 Producer agreement and director agreement

Similar considerations apply to both producer agreements and director agreements since the producer and principal director of a film will be its joint authors (see Table 1 above) and therefore the first owners of copyright in the film unless they are employees and the film is created in the course of their employment.

The key questions to consider, therefore, in relation to such agreements are as follows:

- Are the producer and director intended to be independent consultants or employees?
- Does the agreement contain an appropriate assignment of all existing and future copyright in the film throughout the world (including the right to issue publicity concerning the producer's services including the actor's name, likeness, behind-the-scenes footage and other items required to promote and exploit the film)? It is common for such an agreement to appoint the production company as the producer's agent and to require it to take all steps

44 Section 87(3) of the Copyright, Designs and Patents Act 1988.

(including executing documents on the producer's behalf) towards ensuring that it gets the full benefit of such provisions.

- Has the producer/director waived his moral rights under the Copyright, Designs and Patents Act 1988 in the United Kingdom (or similar laws of other jurisdictions)?
- Is there a provision whereby the producer and director both agree that their sole remedy for breach of the agreement, or any related statute or common law, is damages? This will be important for the production company to ensure that both the producer and the director cannot rescind the agreement or otherwise seek to injunct the film, so the production schedule is not disrupted or delayed.

4.2 Commissioning/composer agreement

It is customary to call an agreement to commission music for film or TV a 'commissioning agreement' for short or lower-value productions and a 'composer agreement' for higher-budget productions.

Since the person writing and performing the music will be the first owner of the copyright in such work, the production company will usually include an assignment of the musical and literary works contained in the commissioned music and also the master recording of such music that is used in any soundtrack.

Relevant questions to consider on such agreements are as follows:

- Does the production company wish to restrict the use of session artists and musicians who are members of the Musicians' Union, in order to minimise the limitations of collective bargaining agreements to which such musicians may be subject? If any such musicians are used, it will be necessary to ensure that they similarly assign all rights in their contribution to the production company or, in the case of non-assignable rights, that they waive such rights in favour of the production company.
- What publishing royalties will the composer receive from the grant of any mechanical licence to embody the music on a sound carrier, from the grant of a synchronisation licence to reproduce the music in conjunction with audiovisual images or otherwise?
- Will the composer have the right to require the production company to reassign the copyright in the music to the composer if the film is released without the music or the film is otherwise not released within a certain period of time?
- Will the composer's services be subject to any collective bargaining agreements, guild agreements or union regulations?
- For what period will the composer be prevented from re-recording the composition?
- Given that the production company will usually request that the composer warrants that he is a member of the PRS for Music and therefore the performing rights in the music – including the right to perform or play the music in public, broadcast the music, include the music in a cable programme or authorise third parties to do the same in relation to the music

in any part of the world – will be subject to the rights of the PRS for Music and its affiliated societies outside the United Kingdom, has the composer agreed to procure that the PRS for Music grants to the production company the exclusive right and licence throughout the world (directly or through the PRS's affiliated societies) to exhibit and perform the composition?

4.3 Actor agreement

Relevant questions for this type of agreement are as follows:

- Is the actor a 'qualifying person' for the purposes of the Copyright, Designs and Patents Act 1988? The copyright in a work is protected if, generally speaking, the actor is at all material times a British national or domiciled in the United Kingdom or a country in which the relevant provisions of such act extend.
- Does the agreement contain appropriate assignment provisions whereby the actor grants and assigns (both present grants and the assignment of existing and future rights) the entire copyright and all other rights arising in all LDMA work written or created by the actor (including the right to issue publicity concerning the actor's services, including the actor's name, likeness, behind-the-scenes footage and other items required to promote and exploit the film)?
- Does the agreement contain 'further assurance' provisions to ensure that the actor will undertake all such acts as the production company may reasonably require to vest, and/or confirm the rights under this agreement of the production company, any licensees or any successors in title (including registrations of copyright in other territories such as the United States)? The production company should also seek to include a provision whereby the actor appoints the production company as agent to effect the preceding matters.
- Has the actor waived the benefit of moral rights?

4.4 Distribution agreement

A distributor's licence would typically impose its standard terms and conditions for every film it distributes, and therefore it would be unusual for there to be material deviation from these terms and conditions. Nonetheless, questions to consider are as follows:

- Will there be any form of 'holdback' whereby the distributor agrees not to exploit certain rights granted under the agreement for a certain period (eg, territorial releases being in a certain order)?
- Will the distribution rights be granted on an exclusive basis (whether in a particular territory, as would be normal, or worldwide)?
- What rights are to be granted? For example, film rights (theatrical and/or non-theatrical), free television rights (free satellite broadcast rights, free cable transmission rights, free digital terrestrial rights and/or free analogue terrestrial rights), pay-TV rights (pay satellite broadcast rights, pay cable transmission rights, pay digital terrestrial rights and/or pay-per-view rights),

video-on-demand rights (near video-on-demand rights, subscription video-on-demand rights, free video-on-demand rights and/or pay-per-view video-on-demand rights), home video rights, internet rights (internet simulcasting rights, internet streaming rights and/or internet downloading rights), mobile technology rights, new media rights, interactive television rights, ship and plane rights and/or hotel/motel rights.

- For the purposes of exploiting the film, will the distributor require a deadline for the delivering of the delivery materials (eg, prints of the film, advertising and promotional materials and trailers) by the producer/sales agent?
- What withholding, offsetting or deductions are specified in the agreement, and are these reasonable? Since a distributor is likely to be marketing a number of films at any time, it is important that there is no withholding, offsetting or deductions unless the sales agent/producer has agreed to them in advance, so as to avoid any cross-collaterisation of each film's expenses.

4.5 Option agreement

It will be important for the production company to have an exclusive option so the film may be developed without having to compete with other third parties. Further, as with other agreements entered into by a production company, it is extremely important that its rights under this agreement are freely assignable without restriction to enable such rights to be secured by any party providing production funding.

While the moral rights of the work's owner may not be assigned, it is necessary to consider whether the owner is willing to waive his right to be identified as the author of that work and/or to object to derogatory treatment of that work. There is no obligation for such a waiver to be granted but those in a weaker bargaining position – which typically include most writers – would be expected to waive their rights so that the work may be exploited without interference.

Over and above the foregoing, relevant questions are as follows:

- Will the rights owner assign its rights in the relevant work to the production company or will it license the rights?
- What categories of rights will the production company require? The company would ideally be seeking all copyright and all other rights, title and interest in the relevant work but, at a minimum, it should secure all audiovisual rights in order to enable its development, production and exploitation of the film in all media throughout the world. If only a partial assignment of copyright is obtained, it is common for the stage rights, non-dramatic radio rights and literary publication rights to be reserved by the owner of the rights (provided that the owner agrees not to exploit them before the expiry of a pre-agreed period).
- Will the owner of the work be willing to assign to the production company his 'remake rights' – ie, his rights in the film, any associated soundtrack based materially on the plot, story or characters in the work, any sequel to the work, or any adapted versions (including foreign versions, shortened/extended versions or trailers)?

- What compensation, if any, will the owner of the rights receive for any sequels and remakes?
- Will all or any of the terms of the WGGB Agreement apply to this agreement? The WGGB Agreement is a collective bargaining agreement between the WGGB and PACT which was entered into on February 3 1992 and which sets out various minimum terms and conditions to be observed in contracts between PACT members and WGGB members, based on the budget of the film.
- Will the agreement contain a 'turnaround' clause whereby the work's owner is able to receive his rights back if the production company does not exploit them within a certain time? If so, a production company would usually seek a minimum of five to seven years after it has exercised its option.

4.6 Screenplay writer agreement

The scope and validity of the assignment of rights and consents clause will be of paramount importance in a screenplay writer agreement so as to ensure that all copyright and related rights, including future rights, are assigned to the production company. Moreover, it is typical for the agreement to include a provision whereby the screenwriter acknowledges that the production company has no obligation to exploit any part of the screenplay and waives any claim for damage suffered by the screenwriter as a result. Local counsel outside the United Kingdom may also need to be considered if relevant because (for example) the US require ownership of all copyright to be registered at the US Copyright Office to allow protection.

The agreement will typically include a power of attorney in favour of the production company to enable the production company to undertake all matters required for it to receive the full benefit of the agreement. It should be noted that if there is a power of attorney, the agreement will need to be executed as a deed and the other requisite formalities followed in this regard.

In addition, three other questions are relevant to this type of agreement:

- Will the screenwriter be entitled to sole credit or co-credit? It is common for UK screenplay agreements to refer to the Screenwriting Credit Agreement 1974 and the Writers' Guild of Great Britain Screenwriting Credits Agreement, but complications can arise where, for example, more than one writer is involved or a director rewrites the script. This can be particularly problematic if another writer exists whose own agreement was subject to the Writer's Guild of America (WGA). Generally speaking, the territorial jurisdiction of the first writer will take precedence over the second writer; but attributing the contributions of the various writers can be difficult to prove. For example, if a WGA writer is only engaged as a screenwriter and is not the director, that person needs to show that he has contributed more than 33% of the screenplay as assessed by three arbitrators of the WGA (based on dramatic composition, original and different scenes, characterisation or character relationships and dialogue) in order to receive a shared screenwriting credit. This proportion rises to 50% of the screenplay if the individual is both a writer/director and a member of the WGA. However, dividing a script into such percentages is extremely difficult.

- Have the provisions of the WGGB Agreement (see section 4.5 above) been incorporated by reference into the screenplay writer agreement, or has the WGGB Agreement been disapplied in whole or in part? The production company might be keen to ensure that certain provisions of the WGGB Agreement are disapplied or otherwise amended, such as the right of the writer to repurchase the screenplay or to negotiate new terms in the event that merchandise is produced from the screenplay.
- Does the agreement contain a waiver of the screenwriter's moral rights (ie, the right to be identified as the author of the screenplay, the right to object to derogatory treatment of the work and the right to not suffer a false attribution of the work)? Under the Copyright, Designs and Patents Act 1988, such rights are conferred on the creator of the copyright and may not be assigned. It is prudent for any such waiver to also cover the producer, financiers and distributors in order to avoid any claim by the screenwriter that it does not cover changes to the work by any such party.

5. Regulation in the United Kingdom

5.1 Film

The British Board of Film Classification (BBFC) is tasked with classifying and censoring films, DVDs and certain video games on behalf of local authorities before they may be shown in the United Kingdom. Previously known as the British Board of Film Censors, the BBFC is a non-governmental organisation that has operated for more than a century in bringing a degree of harmonisation to the classification of films that are licensed to be shown in cinemas in the United Kingdom. While local authorities still have the ability to ban films or otherwise seek to change elements of the film, they generally accede to the decision of the BBFC.

5.2 Broadcasting

The Communications Act 2003 consolidated the telecommunication and broadcasting regulators in the United Kingdom and sought to promote competition and attract new investment and ideas. The act also introduced the Office of Communications (Ofcom) as the industry regulator, inheriting the duties of the Office of Telecommunications (Oftel). Among other measures, the act lifted many restrictions on cross-media ownership and for the first time allowed a non-European entity to wholly own a British television company.

5.3 Video on demand

Video on demand (VOD) providers are now commonplace throughout the United Kingdom, with the major terrestrial stations all providing 'catch-up' services on demand through platforms such as the BBC's iPlayer, ITV's itvPlayer and Channel 4's 4OD.

United Kingdom legislation provides that VOD service providers must inform regulators of their activities and act in accordance with regulations pertaining to programming content and advertising standards.

Ofcom has designated its responsibility for the regulation of VOD services in the United Kingdom to:

- the Authority for Television on Demand (ATVOD) (previously known as the Association for Television On-Demand), which monitors compliance with those rules relating to on-demand service programming, including administrative and editorial content provision; and
- the Advertising Standards Authority (ASA), which monitors advertising on VOD services for its compliance with the Committee of Advertising Practice Code.

Any decision taken by the co-regulators may be appealed to Ofcom. Service providers must notify ATVOD before providing an 'on-demand programme service' (ODPS).

In determining which services are subject to regulation and notification, it is necessary to determine whether such a service will constitute an ODPS, evidenced by meeting each of the following criteria:

- The principal purpose of the service is the provision of TV-like programmes whose form and content are comparable with the form and content of television programmes. (ATVOD has published a non-exhaustive list of examples to be taken into account when determining what is 'TV-like'). Electronic versions of newspapers and magazines are expressly not considered as ODPSs.
- It is a VOD service, thereby enabling users to select individual programmes from the various programmes available on the service, receive the programme via an 'electronic communications network' and view such programmes when the user wishes (so a DVD purchased online but delivered in the post would not constitute an ODPS). No distinction is made between instant-streaming, download-to-rent and download-to-buy services.
- The programmes provided via the service are subject to a person's editorial responsibility, even if such responsibility is exercised through a third party such as a content provider. As such, a service whereby user-generated content was uploaded for exchange without any prior modification or restriction would not be caught. In this context the Audiovisual Media Services Directive 2014[45] only covers 'mass media' whose function is to inform, entertain or educate the public, and would therefore not include content created by professional bodies or educational institutions to disseminate information about such organisation to its members.
- The services are made available by that person for use by the public in the European Union.
- That person is subject to the jurisdiction of the United Kingdom for the purposes of the Audiovisual Media Services Directive, whereby the service provider is "established in the United Kingdom" – ie:

---

45 Directive 2010/13/EU of the European Parliament and of the Council of March 10 2010 on the coordination of certain provisions laid down by law, regulation or administrative action in Member States concerning the provision of audiovisual media services.

- The editorial decisions are taken in the United Kingdom and the service provider's head office is in the United Kingdom; or
- where the editorial decisions are taken in the United Kingdom or the service provider's head office is in the United Kingdom, with the other functions being performed in a different EU member state, the place of establishment is deemed as follows:
  - the member state where a significant part of the workforce involved with the service activity operate;
  - the territory of the service provider's head office if a significant proportion of the workforce operates in each of those EU member states;
  - if a significant proportion of the workforce is located in a third member state, the place of establishment is deemed to be the member state in which the service provider first began its activity in accordance with the laws of that territory; or
  - the United Kingdom if the editorial decisions are taken in the United Kingdom but the service provider's head office is located in a third non-EU country, or vice-versa, provided that a significant proportion of the workforce is located in the United Kingdom.

(a) Advertising

The VOD Annex of the British Code of Advertising, Sales Promotion and Direct Marketing (the CAP Code) provides rules on the form and content of advertising found in an ODPS. Such rules re overseen by the ASA and provide that advertising must:

- be readily recognisable as such;
- not use techniques which exploit the possibility of conveying a message subliminally or surreptitiously;
- not prejudice respect for human dignity;
- not contain any material likely to incite hatred based on race, sex, religion or nationality;
- not include or promote any discrimination based on sex, racial or ethnic origin, nationality, religion or belief, disability, age or sexual orientation;
- not encourage behaviour prejudicial to health or safety;
- not encourage behaviour grossly prejudicial to the protection of the environment;
- not include cigarettes or other tobacco products or any prescription-only medicine;
- not, in the case of alcoholic drinks, be aimed at persons under the age of 18 or encourage excessive consumption of such drinks;
- not cause physical or moral detriment to persons under the age of 18;
- not – if such advertising contains material which might seriously impair the physical, mental or moral development of persons under the age of 18 – be made available in a manner which allows such persons to normally see or hear it;
- not directly exhort persons under the age of 18 to purchase or rent goods or services in a manner which exploits their inexperience or credulity;

- not directly encourage persons under the age of 18 to persuade their parents or others to purchase or rent goods or services;
- not exploit the trust of persons under 18 in parents, teachers or others; or
- not unreasonably show persons under 18 in dangerous situations.

In addition, the CAP Code Advice Team provides free and confidential advice on the likely compliance of advertisements under the CAP Code.

The ASA's sister body, the Committees of Advertising Practice (CAP), published in 2015 new guidance for vloggers to help them better understand how and when the advertising rules apply to their vlogs.

Service providers must notify ATVOD before providing an ODPS and must thereafter notify ATVOD of any material changes to the notified service. A fee is payable by the service provider to ATVOD in respect of each ODPS it provides, such fees being subject to public consultation each year and approval by Ofcom.

(b) Sponsorship

ATVOD also regulates product placement and sponsorship references in the United Kingdom, although there are no specific rules governing other commercial references in an ODPS. A programme included in an on-demand programme service is 'sponsored' if a person (the sponsor), other than the provider of that service or the producer of that programme, has met some or all of the costs of the programme for the purpose of promoting the name, trademark, image, activities, services or products of the sponsor or of another person. However, a person is not to be taken to have met some or all of the costs of providing a service only because a programme included in the service is sponsored by that person.

An ODPS and any programme in an OPDS is not permitted to:

- be sponsored by tobacco companies or otherwise promote tobacco (including non-tobacco products or services which share a brand name with a tobacco product that is prohibited by law from advertising in other UK media);
- be sponsored for the purpose of promoting a prescription-only medicine (although it is possible for a manufacturer of prescription-only medicines to sponsor a service or programme, or make a sponsorship announcement, if it does not contain any references to prescription-only medicines); or
- include sponsored news or current affairs programmes (although comedic treatments of news and current-affairs-related matter are permitted, and short specialist reports (including sport, travel and weather reports) may be sponsored provided they are distinct from news or current affairs programmes (eg, by using different presenters and sets).

When an ODPS is sponsored or includes a sponsored programme:

- sponsors may have an involvement in the commissioning and creation of programmes but the sponsorship must not unduly influence the editorial content of the programme that would affect the editorial independence of the service provider;
- the sponsored editorial content and announcements relating to it must not

directly encourage the purchase or rental of the goods or services, whether by making promotional reference to them, by portraying them in a particularly favourable manner or otherwise (although this does not prohibit sponsorship announcements, provided these are distinct from editorial content and not unduly prominent);

- it must not include alcohol sponsorship aimed at persons under the age of 18 or encourage immoderate consumption of alcohol (which will be judged on the content and context of the drinks displayed);
- users should be clearly informed of the sponsorship agreement (including when the service is first accessed, when browsing the catalogue or whilst viewing a programme, for example); and
- the name/logo of the sponsor must be displayed at the beginning or end of a sponsored programme to ensure users are aware of the identity of the sponsor and of the sponsor's relationship with the sponsored programme.

A 'sponsorship announcement' means anything included in a programme for the purpose of complying with the requirements to clearly inform users of the existence of a sponsorship agreement and to display at the beginning or end of a sponsored programme the name of the sponsor and the logo or other symbol (if any) of the sponsor, together with anything included at the same time as or otherwise in conjunction with such user information.

Sponsorship announcements in an ODPS must not:

- employ subliminal/surreptitious techniques (with surreptitious techniques being regarded as those by which a viewer may be aware a message has been included, but is unaware that it has been done so for the purposes of advertising); or
- prejudice respect for human dignity;
- include or promote discrimination based on sex, racial or ethnic origin, nationality, religion or belief, disability, age or sexual orientation;
- encourage behaviour that is prejudicial to health or safety or that is grossly prejudicial to the protection of the environment;
- cause physical or moral detriment to under-18s or encourage them to persuade others to purchase or rent goods or services, exploit their trust in parents/teachers et al or unreasonably show them in dangerous situations.

Sponsored programmes and services, and associated credits, that would be acceptable on broadcast television are likely to be acceptable in on-demand services.

(c) Product placement and prop placement

'Product placement' is the inclusion in a programme of, or a reference to, a product, service or trademark where the inclusion is for a commercial purpose and is in return for the making of any payment, or the giving of other valuable consideration, to any relevant provider or any person connected with a relevant provider, and is not prop placement.

'Prop placement' is the inclusion of a product, service or trademark where that product etc has no significant value and no relevant provider (or connected person) has received any payment or other valuable consideration in relation to its inclusion. The product placement rules do not apply to prop placement.

The product/prop placement rules apply to programmes produced after December 19 2009. Product placement is permitted in films made for cinema, films or series made for broadcast or on-demand television service,; sports programmes and light entertainment programmes, provided that certain conditions are met.

In this regard, product placement is not allowed:

- in children's programmes (including programmes acquired from overseas, but excluding films which were originally made for the cinema);
- of tobacco products (including cigarettes or other non-tobacco services or products which share a brand name with a tobacco product that is prohibited by law from advertising in the UK media) or of prescription-only medicines;
- on behalf of an undertaking whose principal activity is the manufacture or sale of cigarettes or other tobacco products; or
- of alcohol if it is aimed at under-18s or encourages immoderate consumption (which will be judged on the content and context of the drinks displayed).

Furthermore, product placement in an ODPS must not:

- place undue influence on the editorial content of the programme;
- encourage the purchase or renting of the goods or services;
- give undue prominence to the products, services or trademarks concerned;
- use subliminal or surreptitious techniques; or
- prejudice respect for human dignity;
- include or promote discrimination based on sex, racial or ethnic origin, nationality, religion or belief, disability, age or sexual orientation;
- encourage behaviour that is prejudicial to health or safety or that is grossly prejudicial to the protection of the environment;
- cause physical or moral detriment to under-18s or encourage them to persuade others to purchase or rent goods or services, exploit their trust in parents/teachers et al or unreasonably show them in dangerous situations.

The use of product placement must be appropriately signalled at the start and end of the programme in which it appears, and at the recommencement of the programme after any advertising breaks. Service providers may wish to use Ofcom's guidelines given in *Technical Criteria for the Universal Product Placement Logo5* in this regard, although there is no requirement to do so in respect of an ODPS.

Content containing product placement which is acceptable in broadcast TV services is likely to be acceptable in an ODPS.

Subject to the above restrictions, product placement is permitted in programmes included in on-demand programme services provided that the following conditions are met:

- The programme in which the product, service or trademark, or the reference to it, is included is a film made for cinema, a sports or light-entertainment programme or a film or series made for a television programme service or for an on-demand programme service.

- The product placement has not influenced the content of the programme in a way that affects the editorial independence of the provider of the service.
- The product placement does not directly encourage the purchase or rental of goods or services, whether by making promotional reference to those goods or services or otherwise.
- The programme does not give undue prominence to the products, services or trademarks concerned.
- The product placement does not use techniques that exploit the possibility of conveying a message subliminally or surreptitiously.
- The way in which the product, service or trademark, or the reference to it, is included in the programme by way of product placement does not:
  - prejudice respect for human dignity;
  - promote discrimination based on sex, racial or ethnic origin, nationality, religion or belief, disability, age or sexual orientation;
  - encourage behaviour prejudicial to health or safety;
  - encourage behaviour grossly prejudicial to the protection of the environment;
  - cause harm to persons under the age of 18;
  - directly encourage persons under the age of 18 to persuade their parents or others to purchase or rent goods or services;
  - exploit the trust of persons under the age of 18 in parents, teachers or others; or
  - unreasonably show persons under the age of 18 in dangerous situations.

One further condition applies only where the programme featuring the product placement has been produced or commissioned by the provider of the service or any connected person. This condition requires that the on-demand programme service in question must signal appropriately the fact that product placement is contained in a programme no less frequently than at the start and end of such a programme and, in the case of an ODPS that includes advertising breaks within it, at the recommencement of the programme after each such advertising break.

Post-completion steps for intellectual property rights

Tom Farrand
Novagraaf UK

Intangible assets typically make up more than 50% of the value of a modern business.[1] In some sectors (eg, pharma) the percentage is much higher than that. Intellectual property is usually the greater part of these assets. It is hardly surprising that purchasers of businesses and their assets should pay careful attention to the process of perfecting ownership of intellectual property.

As with the transfer of ownership of real property, there is a significant difference between agreeing to transfer and completion of formal change of ownership. The latter requires compliance with formal procedures across multiple jurisdictions and often with multiple authorities.

Advance preparation is crucial for any transfers of IP ownership. Yet, no matter how extensive IP due diligence has been, the recordal process rarely passes without hitch. Updating records is, in general, a time-consuming and often costly process, bound as it is by the cleanliness of the existing records and the vagaries of each jurisdiction's recordal system. However, there are steps that companies can and should follow to smooth the process and minimise the demands on their internal resources.

1. From agreement to completion – managing the transition

The main agreements in a transaction normally include an umbrella clause or clauses by which the ownership of IP rights will transfer from the vendor to the purchaser. Within the scope of that agreement it is important for the purchaser to know that the scope of this clause covers the IP assets that it intends to acquire and that it has all the assurances it needs from the vendor that the vendor will assist, where necessary, with the recordal process. These assurances are generally found in a "Further Assurances" clause. For a smooth post-completion process, this is a clause that a purchaser should always insist on.

2. Due diligence

As we have seen in Paul Davies' chapter on diligence, part of the early preparation work needs to include effective due diligence. As well as identifying the rights the purchaser is acquiring, the due diligence process is also vital to establish facts relating

1 According to a study by the firm Brand Finance, more than 50% of the value of businesses is made up of intangible assets. This is based on a study of 55,000 companies listed on 100 stock exchanges around the world.

to the IP rights and so to facilitate the later transfer of ownership. To ease the post-completion process, the due diligence process needs to include the following in relation to the IP assets:

- Exactly which entity is recorded as the owner of each right?
- What is the status?
- Are the rights in force?
- Are there licences in force and recorded against any rights?
- Are there charges or other interests recorded against any rights?
- Do the registered rights match those used in the business?
- Are there any unregistered rights?

Obtaining the answers to these questions in advance enables effective planning for the recording of change of ownership.

3. Good housekeeping

The extent to which companies are diligent in the registration and maintenance of IP and IP records varies. If the vendor has followed best practice, either as a matter of ongoing routine or in preparation for an asset sale, then this inevitably makes the recordal process easier to execute. When IP rights are in force, with a sensible ownership structure and up to date ownership details recorded, then this is very helpful.

If rights are not kept up to date then they are at risk in terms of validity and/or enforceability. This will come out during the due diligence process and may result in more complicated requirements for the post-completion recordals (as well as potentially impacting the sale process itself).

4. Obligations on the vendor

As indicated above, it is usual for the agreement between the parties to place an obligation on the vendor to assist the purchaser in undertaking all necessary steps to record the change of ownership of IP rights. This would include the requirement to complete whatever documents are needed in order to meet the formal requirements of recording the change. While individuals are not specifically named in the transaction documents, identifying who within the vendor's organisation will have ongoing responsibility to assist after completion provides an easier and open line of communication and thus facilitates the process.

There should also be an obligation on the vendor to provide information relating to intellectual property. This is particularly important when it comes to unregistered rights where creation and use are important factors in the ability to register or enforce rights post-completion.

The scope of the obligation on the vendor should be clear and broad enough to enable effective future protection of rights as well as enabling recordal of the change of ownership to happen without a problem.

It is in the interests of the purchaser to have as long a duration of these obligations as possible. However, there will normally be a time limit and the purchaser needs to be mindful of this limit when planning the recordal process.

5. Recording the change of ownership

5.1 Getting organised

When dealing with the recordal of change of ownership of IP rights across multiple jurisdictions it is essential to have things well organised. A well-organised administrator is much more important at this stage than a skilled lawyer.

A clear inventory of documentary requirements needs to be created. This should be done with the help of local lawyers/agents in each jurisdiction in which recordal filings will need to be made and who are up to date not just with local law, but also with the formalities, procedures and documents required by the local authorities. Local registries, local law and the required formalities differ. Being aware of what is needed and when it is needed in each jurisdiction is an important part of the planning stage.

5.2 Documentary requirements

Just as with real property, the transfer of ownership of IP rights needs to be by written instrument and executed by or on behalf of the existing owner (assignor) and, usually, the new owner (assignee). In most jurisdictions in order for the change of ownership to be formally completed and recorded on the local register it is necessary to submit an original or certified copy of the written instrument.

Often the main Asset/Share Purchase Agreement could be sufficient for this purpose, but that approach has many disadvantages, including:

Confidentiality: in many jurisdictions the documents submitted to record ownership will be open to public inspection, and these days often via the website of the local intellectual property office. The main agreement usually includes commercially sensitive information which the parties may not wish to be open to public scrutiny.

Tax implications: the payment of the consideration involved may be subject to tax in some jurisdictions. Submission of the main agreement might open up the transaction to investigation by local tax authorities. Whilst this may not be critical if the proportion of the consideration applicable to the jurisdiction in question is not significant, it may still involve unwanted complications.

Size: these types of main agreements are usually long and the practicality of providing multiple originals or certified copies should be avoided.

Parties: the existing recorded owner and the target new owner may not themselves directly be parties to the main agreement. For example, in many cases, there will be a procurement obligation on the transacting company within a group to procure compliance by subsidiaries with respect to IP rights to be held by the subsidiaries. It may thus be necessary to provide further documentary evidence of, for example, parent/subsidiary relationship.

For all of these reasons, usual practice is to create separate short-form assignment documents, sometimes referred to as "confirmatory assignments" since they are confirming the change of ownership agreed in the main agreement. These can be tailored to fit with specific requirements of local jurisdictions, and keep the information required to a minimum, thereby avoiding the presence of communally sensitive information on public registers.

Creating confirmatory assignment documents for each jurisdiction involved has the advantage of being able to be specific as to local requirements in each document.

In many jurisdictions it is still a requirement for documents to have a Notarial Certificate and to be legalised by the local authorities. A Notarial Certificate is a certificate provided by a notary[2] to the effect that, for example, the person signing for the assignor is an officer of the assignor company and is entitled to sign the document on behalf of the company. Once notarised, there are various routes to getting a document legalised,[3] including via apostille[4] or by an official of the local consulate or embassy of the jurisdiction in question. This can take time. If, therefore, the recordal in a particular jurisdiction is time sensitive and notarisation and legalisation will be required, it is important to be prepared for this and to submit the notarised documents for legalisation as soon as possible after completion.

5.3 Chain of title

It frequently happens that the vendor has not kept its portfolio of IP rights completely up to date with past ownership changes resulting from, for example, company name and address changes, mergers, acquisitions, and corporate reorganisations and restructurings.

The result is that it will be necessary to record the earlier changes before recording the latest change of ownership. Local documentary requirements will need to be met for each link in the chain of title.

This requirement should be anticipated from the pre-transaction due diligence, and planned for in the transition phase. The scope of the warranty provisions in the transaction documents may mean that the vendor updates the registers prior to completion. If not, any additional costs involved to the purchaser should be taken into account, for example by a proportional reduction in the consideration or by the vendor agreeing to cover some or all of the associated cost.

In some extreme cases it will not be possible to complete the chain of title for some IP assets. This may occur when there has been a restructuring of a group with a subsidiary ceasing to trade. The warranties given by the vendor in the main agreement should enable the purchaser to seek redress and obtain compensation for any resulting loss of rights.

---

2 A notary is a lawyer or person with legal training who is licensed by the government to perform acts in legal affairs, in particular witnessing signatures on documents. The form that the notarial profession takes varies with local legal systems.

3 Legalisation is the process of authenticating or certifying a legal document so a foreign country's legal system will recognise it as with full legal effect.

4 Apostille is a simplified form of legalisation established under The Hague Convention Abolishing the Requirement for Legalisation for Foreign Public Documents; the Apostille Convention, or the Apostille Treaty is an international treaty drafted by the Hague Conference on Private International Law.

5.4 Regulatory considerations

Some sectors are highly regulated and this may impact the ownership of IP rights and thus the transfer of rights.

One prominent example is the pharmaceutical industry in which product licences and marketing rights are just as important and valuable as IP rights such as patents and trademarks.

For transactions in these sorts of sectors, aside from ensuring that the necessary documents are completed, care needs to be taken over the transition of one ownership to another to ensure that the right to sell or distribute products is not lost and that the new owner does not fall foul of regulatory limitations. This is bearing in mind that the regulatory authorities in some jurisdictions do not process changes quickly.

These types of allied rights are in the main administered by bodies that do not deal with IP rights like patents, designs and trademarks on a daily basis. Plant breeders' rights, domain names and pharmaceutical product licenses are all examples of rights, allied to core IP rights, that may be acquired as part of a transaction but which require separate recordal.

6. Unregistered legacy rights

6.1 Unregistered trademarks and goodwill

Businesses have different policies on the registration and protection of IP rights. In some jurisdictions, including the UK, it is possible to rely on unregistered rights in trademarks utilising the common law principle of passing off or similar unfair competition rights.

Most transaction documents will include catch-all phrases and clauses by which the goodwill in the business associated with the trademarks – registered or unregistered – will pass to the purchaser.

It should be noted that one of the challenges in enforcing these unregistered rights is providing evidence to satisfy a court that the plaintiff is the rightful owner of the rights. Thus as discussed in Zarah Rasool's chapter on fast-moving consumer goods, it is advisable to ensure that the vendor provides information and evidence to show the existence and ownership of its unregistered rights.

It may be that the purchaser has a different policy on the registration of trademarks and will wish to take steps to register those trademarks that were previously unregistered by the vendor. Again, it is important that the transaction documents include the right to register and commit the vendor to provide assistance to the purchaser as required. It may be that one of the reasons why such trademarks were unregistered was because they lacked inherent distinctiveness and thus required evidence of use in order to secure registration. If so, then the vendor should be afforded the opportunity to correct matters by providing evidence of use, the bulk of which would have been use in the vendor's business.

Some trademarks, most notably those consisting of or incorporating a logo, will have copyright associated with them. IP rights are not mutually exclusive. In some cases registered ownership, and thus the ability to enforce rights, will be jeopardised if ownership of copyright does not pass to the purchaser. Copyright is of its nature an unregistered right in most jurisdictions, and can get overlooked in these situations. Logos are often designed by external consultancies, and as we have seen from Paul Davies' discussion of due diligence, the purchaser should take care to identify ownership issues around copyright and ensure that they are documented and ownership perfected, so that not only is the purchaser the owner of the trade markbut also the other rights that may be present in it.[5]

6.2 Licensed rights

As well as the changes in ownership of registered rights, post-completion the formal change of ownership of licensed rights needs to happen.

For in-bound licences, the licence agreements should be amended or re-executed as appropriate and where the licences are recorded at the local intellectual property office, that change should be recorded.

Similar comments apply in the case of out-bound licences except that it is ownership details that change on the official record and not necessarily the recorded licence although the local requirements on this point should be checked. Again, local formalities for recordal may apply. As with registered rights, it is important to be aware of these as soon as possible.

These details are important. In some jurisdictions, recordal of a licence is required in order to maintain full enforcement rights and/or to be able to collect royalties.

6.3 Creation of hybrid trademarks

In some situations, the purchaser will be acquiring the whole of a business including the entire registered company/legal entity. The purchaser may opt to retain the ownership of IP rights with the legacy legal entity rather than undertake a large scale project to record change of ownership. Occasionally this can cause problems when part of what is effectively a merger and the newly merged business creates a new corporate brand. If the new brand is a hybrid of the two businesses' brands then the ability to register the new corporate brand may be adversely affected by the pre-existence of legacy trademark registrations standing in the name of the (old owner) vendor company.[6] Such issues are not often insurmountable, but increase cost, are inconvenient and in extreme situations can affect ability to enforce rights. As we have seen in the chapter on corporate agreements, the more appropriate way to solve this is for there to be a target entity for ownership of IP rights in the newly formed business and for legacy rights to be assigned to the target entity.

---

5 A good example of this scenario was the expensive fight over the Innocent Smoothie logo – see OHIM Appeal Board decisions on CTMs 1815612 and 4769832.

6 For example
a. Company A trades under corporate brand A
b. Company B trades under corporate brand B
c. Company A acquires/merges with company B
d. Newly merged company trades under new corporate brand AB
e. Company AB leaves ownership of legacy brands A and B where they are
f. Applications to register AB as a trademark held up by prior legacy registrations of A and B in the old names
g. A real life example was merged company GlaxoSmithKline

The correct way to solve this is for there to be a target entity for ownership of IP rights in the newly formed business and for legacy rights to be assigned to the target entity.

6.4 Creation of conflicting trademarks

There are situations where only part of a branded business is sold off. This can create a situation where there is a new owner of a trademark relating to part of the business for which it is registered, and where the existing owner retains the rights to the remaining business.

For example, the owner of a brand used for cleaning products might sell off the industrial cleaning products division. The vendor may choose to retain the domestic cleaning products division of the business. In commercial terms this may be logical and may not create a commercial conflict. However, it will create a challenging legal situation where a solution will need to be found. If there is a single trademark registration covering "cleaning products", who will own it? It will be a challenge to find a solution that allows ownership by different entities of identical trademarks registered by different entities for potentially identical goods. With cross consent the registration might be divided into "industrial cleaning products" and "domestic cleaning products". In many jurisdictions this situation is not permitted, and the only practical solution may be single ownership and a licensing arrangement.

Similar considerations may arise in relation to patented products, ingredients, methods or components.

The compelling commercial benefit of a transaction may override these IP specific obstacles, but it is helpful to have some forward thinking about potential solutions and agreement to cooperate to execute them post-completion.

6.5 Prosecution of existing registrations

At the time of completion of a transaction there will normally be some applications for registration of trademarks, patents, or designs in train. In some jurisdictions completion of the recordal of the change of ownership may not be possible until after the completion of the registration process. In these situations, it is necessary to empower the purchaser and its representatives to take over the prosecution of pending applications for registration so that the process can be completed.

In some cases the application to record a change of ownership will be in its pendency at the same time as the application for registration of the right itself is pending. This can add to the complexity of the prosecution of both, but should not prevent either happening correctly.

More complicated is the situation where there are ongoing opposition proceedings before an intellectual property office, or litigation before the courts. In this situation it will normally be necessary to seek leave of the tribunal or court to change the parties involved in the proceedings.[7] It may be necessary for the vendor to remain involved and for the purchaser to be added as a party to proceedings.

---

7 The tribunal section of the UK IPO has practice guidance on this based around the judgment in *Pharmedica* [2000] RPC 536.

Again, the purchase agreement should place sufficient obligations on the vendor to ensure cooperation, and the pre-transaction due diligence and disclosures should reveal any such ongoing proceedings.

In the case of ongoing litigation where remedies such as damages are sought, it should be made clear which party is entitled to them post-transaction. If the damage was done pre-transaction then, logically perhaps, damages should be to the benefit of the vendor, but this should be made clear by agreement.

7. Pitfalls and practical tips to avoid them

7.1 Record changes now or delay/defer?

The process of recording change of ownership of a large IP portfolio is a costly exercise. Best practice is to record as soon as possible after completion of the transaction. Delay in recordal can have an adverse affect on validity and enforceability of rights in some jurisdictions and in some circumstances. For example, in the UK, if change of ownership is not recorded within six months a claimant can lose the right to damages in any litigation in relation to the right in question incurring after the six month cut-off point until the date of recordal. Further, any litigation needs to be brought in the name of the owner of the right, so the litigation process (including if necessary an application for interim relief) could be delayed pending final recordal of ownership.

On the other hand, some businesses choose to defer some of the cost by delaying recordal until there is a compelling need. For example, this could be when a right requires a renewal payment or when litigation/license is contemplated.

Although this approach will spread the overall cost of recordal over potentially several years, the absolute total cost of the exercise will usually end up being significantly higher than a single mass recordal project. There are economies of scale and the ability to negotiate reduced fees with local agents/law firms for attending to the recordal process. In most jurisdictions, local official fees are lower for multiple recordals than for piecemeal recordals. The cost of recordal of ownership varies significantly from country to country. The overall costs for a large portfolio of rights – large in number of rights and number of countries – can be very significant. As a guide, you could budget for costs of between £300 and £2k per country, depending on the number of rights involved in each.

By not updating ownership changes in a systematic way, IP owners face increased portfolio management costs, as well as exposure to business and legal risk, including the inability to enforce their valuable IP Rights and/or benefit from IP-related royalties. Instead, IP record management should play an integral part of sound IP portfolio management practice, and that means updating all changes to ownership records (whether assignments, name changes, mergers or address updates) in a timely manner.

As mentioned earlier, the transaction documents are likely to be confidential documents and include commercially sensitive information such as purchase price. That is why it is common to create a confirmatory assignment to put on public record. Legally, ownership of IP assets is transferred at the point of completion even where there is no recordal. So if the purchaser comes across a problem before recordal it is possible, though not often efficient, to take action by accelerating the recordal process in a specific jurisdiction or in relation to a specific IP right, for example in the case of impending infringement action.

It is easy to understand why a company might fall behind in updating IP asset ownership details. It is possible that in this situation there may be be a backlog of changes from previous transactions not yet recorded. This may mean recording several changes of ownership prior to taking action, and this may present a challenge in obtaining all the supporting documents in order to perfect the change of title. This work is time-consuming and heavy in administration. Even in cases where companies have filed the requisite paperwork in the relevant jurisdictions within the timescales allocated, it is not uncommon for that paperwork to be flawed or incomplete, leaving the IP owner exposed to portfolio management risk. Similarly, many companies report that although they may start title update work in good time, they often struggle to finish due to a lack of available resources, expertise and time. However, it is important to be alive to the potential risks and pitfalls of a failure to record in a timely manner. Ultimately, it will be a commercial decision based on a cost–benefit analysis but there are adverse implications that can stem from a failure to record.

8. Pitfalls

8.1 Potential issues and problems to solve:

Is the schedule of rights listed on the final assignment reflected by the records held by the relevant patent and trademark offices? Are the records held in the correct starting entity name? Look out for even minor discrepancies, eg, between plc/ltd status. Errors here create delay, or worse, may invalidate the registered rights.

Contact an agent in every country – the purchaser should use its own agents (rather than agents of record) asking what their relevant intellectual property office requires or would accept to make the changes.

Using your own agents ensures that there is no potential conflict of interest. Using local agents is usually essential so as to have knowledge of local law and rules and because local rules may require a representative to be locally resident and/or registered, and there may be local language requirements.

Getting documents signed: This has to work for both signatories (selling and buying). They have to be available. Do they have the right to sign on behalf of their company. What happens if they leave after sale? It is often helpful to have the parties sign a general power/authorisation empowering an attorney to complete all documents needed to confirm and record the assignment. This means that documentary requirements that arise after completion may be met without the need to track down authorised signatories from either party.

In most jurisdictions there is not a thorough examination of the documents filed in support of an application to change ownership. In some cases there is no examination at all. This means that the first and only time that the supporting documents are scrutinised is during litigation. At this stage lawyers on both sides will examine the documents and their validity. A primary defence may be that the trademark registration is not, in fact, owned by the claimant. If the ownership documents are faulty it will come out just when the new owner needs it least. For that reason it is important to ensure that every step of the process in every jurisdiction is taken correctly.

For patents, it may be the inventor as well as the owner who needs to complete documents. Inventors who are not or no longer employed by the owner may be difficult to find, particularly post-completion. This is another reason why identification of issues as early as possible in a transaction is important to facilitate the smooth running of post-completion steps.

Deadlines – these are usually critical in the prosecution and maintenance of IP rights, particularly in relation to patents, which require payment of annual or regular maintaining fees. If not met, the right can be lost. As responsibility changes from one owner to another owner and from one representative to a new representative, the risk of error or omission increases markedly. It is thus critical to ensure an effective transition through good cooperation and communication between the parties involved. It is also important to ensure that any foreign representatives are notified promptly. The sharing of a forthcoming diary list is extremely helpful.

Outlined below are common portfolio management issues that surface when chain of title and IP recordal work are not properly updated:

- Difficulty tracking and identifying which IP assets have been updated and which have not;
- Erroneous record of title may jeopardise the validity of the IP in some jurisdictions;
- Recently filed applications can be held up by IP registered in the old name;
- Original evidentiary documents could be irretrievably lost;
- Prior owners may go out of business, cease to exist, move or change names;
- Prior owners may be unwilling to cooperate after the passage of too much time, especially if personnel have changed since original transaction;
- Default in applications and registered IP may occur if official documents are delivered to old owners and answer deadlines are missed, potentially causing the rights to be lost;
- Inability to file suit against infringer if IP is in wrong name;
- Inability to get temporary restraining order in infringement matters;
- For trademarks, third parties may be more likely to adopt conflicting marks if they think the owner is defunct; and
- May make divestiture of assets more difficult or may get lower offer if ownership appears split or the chain of title is not up to date.

9. Local quirks

9.1 Examples

- Under UK law, companies are barred from recovering damages or costs in infringement proceedings in the UK courts where the chain of title has not been properly updated within the six-month limit, even where the company is the rightful owner of the intellectual property.

- The penalties are equally harsh elsewhere; in the United Arab Emirates, for example, significant fines are incurred if an assignment isn't recorded within six months of the effective date of transfer.
- In many countries, it is the formality requirements that can prove challenging. In South Korea, a Corporate Nationality Certificate (CNC) must be submitted by the same signatory as appears on the Deed of Assignment in order to effect a legal transfer, unless the CNC has previously been incorporated into the Deed. That means that if the signatories are no longer available by the time the assignment application is filed, the owner will struggle to complete the recordal.
- Confidentiality – many local IP offices publish all documents as a matter of course. That means that the change of ownership and the documents supporting its recordal will all be on the public record and open to inspection. In some cases the information will be available via the IPO website – examples are USA, UK and EU (OHIM – the Office for Harmonisation in the Internal Market). Thus the parties should take care that the documents filed do not contain any confidential and/or commercially sensitive information.
- Paper – in most cases all the documents supporting a change of ownership recordal will have to be completed and filed on paper. In many cases this will need to be the original documents.
- Certificates – in a few countries it will be necessary to produce an original certificate of registration for endorsement with the change of ownership. These certificates will need to be part of the information and files passed from the Vendor to the Purchaser.
- Copyright – in most cases copyright is an unregistered right. This poses a challenge in record keeping since enforcement of rights will require proof of ownership. Proof of ownership in turn requires a chain of written transfers of ownership going back to the originator of the copyright work. Good record keeping relating to copyright assignments is critical.
- Copyright – in some jurisdictions there is a requirement for registration of copyright works in order to obtain full rights – notable examples are USA, China and Argentina.
- Onerous documentary requirements need to be met in some jurisdictions, eg, in China separate sets of forms need to be completed and filed for each and every individual right that is being assigned. In Saudi Arabia, documents need to be legalised with fees amounting to hundreds of dollars.
- In some jurisdictions moving responsibility from one local agent/representative to another may not be simple. In lots of cases a (new) power of attorney will be required. For example in China, there is an official fee of c$85 per record to appoint a new representative and pass the relevant file to them.
- Timescale – many jurisdictions take a long time to record a change of ownership on their records.

10. Some words on the recommended underlying process

We have already emphasised the importance of planning. Below we outline the recommended underlying process that can be adopted in a project to record the change of ownership of a registered IP portfolio.

Step 1 – Transfer of information and responsibility

The purchaser should have a schedule of registered IP rights and pending applications. This may sometimes be included as a schedule to the transaction documents. This will be the starting point and an up to date version should be passed to the purchaser and its IP team (internal or external) and it is vital that this includes information relating to upcoming deadlines.

The vendor should notify its own IP team plus all external agents and advisors that responsibility as of a certain date passes to the purchaser and the purchaser's agents and advisors.

There needs to be a thorough round of communication to all relevant parties to ensure that the change of responsibility is understood.

The vendor and its agents/representatives should take steps to transfer all relevant files to the purchaser and its own agents/representatives – particularly in the case of pending applications and other pending matters.

Step 2 – Checking information; entering information

The purchaser and its agents/representatives should take steps to verify that the information with which they have been provided is correct and reflects the present state of the official record in every jurisdiction.

The purchaser should start by evaluating the IP assets in question: identify the countries where they are registered; assess the chain of title and identify integrity issues; and select foreign agents in each country to carry out the work on their behalf.

The purchaser's IP team (internal or external) will usually enter/transfer details of the portfolio onto their own IP management system – including, importantly, upcoming deadlines to ensure nothing is missed.

In order to adhere to these strict formalities it's important that IP transactions, such as transfers of ownership or changes against the official record, must not only be notified to the appropriate patent and trademark offices in a timely manner, but also managed and stored appropriately within the organisation itself.

In order to build an IP recordal management programme to deliver this, companies need to first understand and identify the complexity, the dangers and the requisite level of expertise needed to manage this work successfully. This can depend on a number of factors, but is most often driven by: the number of countries across a portfolio; the number of changes of ownership that need to be updated; the presence of multiple owners within a given portfolio; any uncertainty about the current status of official ownership records; the need to update the chain of title before recordals can be made; and the number of foreign agents in the same country that are engaged in (and therefore need to be managed through) the IP recordal process.

Step 3 – Confirming documentary requirements for recordal

Take local advice in each and every jurisdiction where rights are to be transferred. Requirements vary from country to country and local practice and rules can be rather fluid.

Requirements within a single jurisdiction can be different for different types of intellectual property. Don't assume that a single document will suffice for all intellectual property.

Prepare a complete schedule of requirements.

Prepare a complete set of documents ready for completion with instructions on how to complete each one.

Bear in mind that documents will often require the signature of both the old and new owners.

Documents typically required are:

- Confirmatory Assignment;
- Certificate of Incorporation;
- Power of Attorney.

In many jurisdictions notarial certificates and legalisation stamps will also need to be obtained and applied.

Step 4 – Completing the documents

Documents will usually need to be signed by executives of both the vendor and purchaser companies and their signatures may need to be witnessed by a notary.

Logistically it is simpler to have a single signing session for each party with a complete set of documents signed in one session.

Next, prepare your documents for the updates, including confirmatory deeds and/or evidentiary documentation and Power of Attorney documents; arrange for documents to be signed in the presence of a notary and factor in time for additional preparation depending on the laws of each country involved. Those that require legalisation should be sent promptly to the relevant authorities (embassies and consulates).

Step 5 – Applications to record

The completed documents will normally accompany an application form and fee by which the application to record the change of ownership is formally recorded.

This will mostly be carried out by local agents/representatives acting under the authority of a power of attorney.

Instruct your agents in order of priority; factor in time to chase agents for timely responses and to update internal records as and when responses are received.

Step 6 – Tracking progress and updating internal records

The speed with which the local authorities process applications to record changes vary enormously from a few days to, in the most extreme cases, several years.

The purchaser's IP team needs to keep track of this, and maintain internal records to reflect the status and up to date details.

Step 7 – Recordal complete

Confirmation of the recordal of the change of ownership will come from the authorities in each jurisdiction by way of certificate or some other formal communication.

Finally, make sure you receive all confirmations of the updates by monitoring the files. Updated recordals should be registered as receipts, and you'll need to check and address errors and omissions with agents as they arrive. You also need to factor in the time needed to manage foreign agent invoices, the updating of internal records and the budgeting and costs for staff time, among other things.

11. Conclusion

The work involved in post-transaction recordal of changes of ownership of IP rights requires a blend of skill and knowledge; for example, you need expertise in international IP administration as it relates to updating IP ownership on a global basis; you need access to, or knowledge of, the current international rules and documentary requirements for filing ownership changes; and you need to manage competing deadlines and multiple lines of communication. Importantly, you also need access to a knowledgeable network of local representatives in all the jurisdictions where IP rights are held.

Accordingly, it is a sound practice to select resources that can safely and cost-effectively manage such a project through to completion. If you choose to utilise internal resources, consider their qualifications, track record and existing workloads; if you choose to recruit outside resources or commission the work to an outside party, try to balance experience, expertise and cost. However you choose to manage the process, it's imperative to invest time and effort in the project. Although the process may appear to be complicated, it is easy to manage it if the correct support is in place.

IP valuation

Michelle Korman
Stephen Robertson
Metis Partners

1. Introduction

1.1 Intellectual property

Intellectual property, an intangible asset, created and developed through innovation, plays an enormous part in today's economy. Formal IP rights enable the creator to commercially exploit their innovation for a limited period of time. Formal, registered intellectual property includes copyright (eg, books, films, software); patents (technological inventions); and trademarks (words, symbols). These IP rights can also be sold or licensed if, for example, the intellectual property is a non-core element of the business. There are a number of categories of informal intellectual property including customer databases; brand and reputation; trade secrets and know-how. For many companies, it is often the intellectual property that drives revenues and underpins their competitive advantage, rather than traditional, tangible assets that historically dominated the manufacturing age of business.

It is evident from statistics that European industries are moving towards a knowledge-based economy and this hastens the need for the recognition of intangible assets as a central business asset and creator of competitive advantage, which will underpin business goals. It is estimated that 50% of EU industries rely on IP assets and that these industries generate almost 40% of total GDP in Europe.[1] Governments worldwide have recognised the growing interest in intellectual property as a key strategic tool for businesses and are encouraging investment in innovation in order to secure sustainable economic growth; emerging economies are looking to expand their economic base using intellectual property and more mature economies are focusing on intellectual property in order to maintain their competitive position in global markets.

Increases in innovation in technology, internet and mobile applications and a growing number of collaborations in innovation have had an impact on how companies are using, licensing and protecting their intellectual property. Despite an increased focus on intellectual property, many companies have no strategy in place for investing, protecting or monetising their IP assets, with management often failing to recognise that their companies have valuable intellectual property that is

1 *Intellectual property rights intensive industries: contribution to economic performance and employment in the European Union; Industry-level Analysis Report*, September 2013. A joint project between the European Patent Office and the Office for Harmonisation in the Internal Market.

underpinning competitive advantage. As a result, this vital asset class is overlooked, and consequently undervalued. There is no statutory requirement to value intellectual property, in contrast to other assets that are recognised in the financial statements, and this is likely to be the reason that there is an absence of formal guidance on the process of IP valuation.

1.2 Current obstacles in IP valuation

In 2014 there was a flurry of reports commenting on the state of IP valuation, including the *Final Report from the Expert Group on Intellectual Property Valuation*[2] commissioned by the European Commission and *Banking on IP?*[3] commissioned by the UK Intellectual Property Office. The overarching theme appears to be the general lack of knowledge and confidence in IP valuation as a sustainable value proposition. As a result, many IP-rich companies, and in particular small and medium-sized businesses, find it difficult to raise external finance despite the significant investment they have made or created in the form of IP assets. These companies are often innovation rich, cash poor, with few tangible assets to offer as security for debt finance.

It is widely accepted that this will inevitably change and that the global economy's increasing reliance on intellectual property will drive innovation and consequently the need for:

- companies to develop specific IP strategies;
- regular IP audits for companies in order to identify key IP assets and ensure their adequate protection and exploitation;
- finance providers to develop non-equity finance products for IP-rich companies; and
- a robust and transparent process of IP valuation that is accepted and relied upon by equity and non-equity finance providers.

1.3 Proposals for the development of IP valuation

The main obstacle for IP valuation and for companies attempting to secure IP-related finance is the lack of transparency around IP transactions. The market for trading intellectual property is relatively immature and there is limited information about IP-related transactions that support the validity of IP valuation. The Expert Group[4] noted in its report that the increasing reliance on intellectual property in Europe had created "a clear need to increase market actors' confidence and certainty in IP valuation methods as a way to stimulate IP transactions, to support IP based financing and to give companies the tools to provide information about their IP". The Expert Group[5] made a number of recommendations intended to increase the use of IP valuation and to improve the transparency and reliability of IP valuations. These included:

---

2 Commissioned by European Commission and published November 2013.

3 Intellectual Property Office, *Banking on IP? The role of intellectual property and intangible assets in facilitating business finance. Final Report.* Published November 2013.

4 *Ibid.*

5 *Ibid.*

- establishing a data source containing information on IP transactions, which could enhance credibility of IP valuations and create a market-based benchmark for valuations; and
- introducing an additional reporting section for intangible assets and intellectual property to increase transparency of IP value within company accounts, providing essential information to lenders, investors and stakeholders.

In 2014 the intellectual property office in Singapore announced an IP-based financing scheme enabling companies to use their granted patents as collateral for bank loans. The scheme is partially underwritten by the Singaporean government, which has recognised the need to mitigate the risk of securitising this relatively new asset class. The scheme was set up in response to increasing levels of intangible value within the Singaporean market, reported in Brand Finance Singapore 100[6] at an estimated value of US$144 billion in 2011, representing 35% of enterprise value and US$195 billion in 2012, representing 42% of total enterprise value.

In 2014 the Malaysian Intellectual Property Office (IPO) launched an IPR Marketplace portal,[7] which aims to connect investors, individuals and companies in the commercialisation and trade of IP rights. The portal enables companies to list IP rights, including patents, trademarks and copyright, available for sale or licensing. In addition to the objective of facilitating an IP marketplace and assisting the IP community to monetise its IP assets, the portal also provides education tools and resources for companies to learn about commercialising their intellectual property. This followed the launch in Malaysia in 2013 of an IP financing scheme, which was set up to pursue the increasing interest in using intellectual property as an alternative form of security for finance. The Malaysian IPO also set up a framework for the training and qualification of IP valuers in order to support its IP financing framework.

1.4 International standard on valuation

In 2010 the International Organization for Standardization (ISO) published the first standard on IP valuation,[8] setting out the principles that should be applied when valuing a brand. The ISO requires that the valuer declares the purpose of the valuation (eg, tax planning, financial reporting, litigation support, strategic planning) as this affects the basis of the valuation and the assumptions used in forming the valuation opinion. The ISO recommends that all of this be transparent to the user in the valuation report. The ISO requires three types of analysis to be conducted prior to forming the valuation opinion:

- legal analysis – the bundle of intangible assets and IP rights that are being valued must be clearly identified. These could include names, term, signs, symbols and logos that contribute to the potential economic benefits that

---

6 *The Brand Finance Top 100 Singapore Brands Report 2013* (on Singapore's intangible assets and brands).

7 See Malaysian IPO website: www.myipo.gov.my/.

8 ISO 10668: *2010 Brand Valuation – Requirements for monetary brand valuation*, issued by the International Organization for Standardization in October 2010.

could be earned by the branded company. The valuer must also identify and assess the legal protection of the valued intellectual property. The ISO[9] insists that extensive due diligence and risk analysis is required to capture the legal protection by type of intellectual property, territory and company category, since the valuation opinion could be affected by the scope of use or registration, notoriety of the brand and the ability of the owner to enforce the rights associated with the brand being valued.

- behavioural analysis – the ISO[10] requires valuers to investigate and form opinions on the potential stakeholder behaviour in each of the geographical, product and customer segments in which the brand operates. To do this effectively the valuer must assess the sustainability of the future returns generated by the brand. This assessment must take account of:
  - market size and trends;
  - how the brand contributes to the customer's decision to purchase;
  - the likely long-term demand for the brand and any risks that would affect this; and
  - the total economic benefits that the brand helps to generate.
- financial analysis – the ISO[11] requires a detailed financial analysis to be performed as part of the valuation process and specifies the three valuation methods that can be adopted for the brand valuation: market; cost; and income (all of which are discussed in detail below). Brands are unique and the lack of market comparables limits the use of the market approach for valuing brands. The cost method is rarely used for brands as the inherent value in a brand rarely equates to the costs incurred in creating them. The income method is predominately based on the future returns that can be generated by commercialising the IP rights associated with the brand and, as a result, is the most relevant and commonly used method of valuation.

It is not surprising that IP valuation is considered to be a professional specialism. The Expert Group[12] noted in its report that:

Valuation involves assumptions and judgement by the valuer derived from and justified based on a bespoke, rigorous analysis of the IP within its business context, together with its importance versus other business drivers, broader industry and competitor constraints, dynamics and economic outlook.

All of these factors must be considered in forming the valuation opinion as they could have an impact on either the opinion itself or the underlying assumptions on which it is based. Furthermore the Expert Group[13] recognised that IP valuation is "an interdisciplinary study drawing upon law, economics, finance, accounting and investment".

---

9 *Ibid.*
10 *Ibid.*
11 *Ibid.*
12 *Ibid.*
13 *Ibid.*

1.5 Integrated reporting

Under generally accepted accounting rules, internally generated intellectual property does not typically meet the definition of an asset, as required by accounting standards, and therefore does not appear on a company's financial statements. As a result, intellectual property has been overlooked as an asset class, despite commonly being the most important factor that underpins a company's competitive advantage. Many company directors have selected to provide additional narrative disclosures detailing the company's intellectual property, its potential for market traction, its place in the corporate strategy and the probability that it will provide future economic returns for the company, in order to enhance the information available to stakeholders.

The increased interest in what is commonly referred to as integrated reporting enables companies to communicate to investors and other stakeholders what the directors see as the key drivers of future performance that are not necessarily reflected in the financial statements. Integrated reporting offers directors the opportunity to provide narrative about:

- the vital role of intellectual property in driving company revenues;
- the company's strategy to develop and protect its intellectual property; and
- the potential of the intellectual property to limit or block potential competitors.

The International Accounting Standards Board recommends that the management commentary,[14] a narrative report that accompanies the statutory financial statements, includes information that is useful and relevant to stakeholders in order for them to make their assessment of the company's future performance and help them in their subsequent investment decisions. For IP-rich companies this will be an essential part of their reporting to stakeholders as it is the company's intellectual property that will underpin future returns.

2. IP valuation and corporate transactions

2.1 Purpose and nature of IP valuation opinions

Despite being at a relatively early stage of development, IP valuation has an integral part to play in many corporate transactions. This is due to the fact that intellectual property is increasingly the key driver of future revenues for many companies. This means that intellectual property is inevitably at the centre of many of the decisions companies will make including:

- resource allocation and investment decisions;
- target markets and product development;
- strategic partnerships or ventures;
- potential mergers or acquisitions; and
- management of risk, both internal and external to the company.

---

14 *IFRS Practice Statement: Management Commentary; A framework for presentation.* Issued in 2010 by the International Accounting Standards Board.

Valuation opinions are often likened to legal opinions. They are, by their nature, subjective and judgemental, but when performed by experienced professionals that follow accepted methodologies and a transparent and rigorous process of investigation, there is no reason why they cannot be relied upon. In fact, IP valuations are already used to support many corporate transactions. The process relies on the valuer formulating key valuation assumptions that are developed by performing a detailed analysis of:

- the IP assets being valued;
- the financial position of the business at the date of valuation;
- the current position and future prospects of the market in which the business operates.

This chapter will consider how IP valuation is used to support corporate transactions and the main methods used in the process.

2.2 IP valuation and merger and acquisition activity

IP-rich companies are often attractive acquisition targets by virtue of the future revenue streams and market share to which the intellectual property can give access. The acquiring company's management, having identified the target IP assets, will then typically consider the best course of action to pursue in order to gain access to the intellectual property and the underlying rights associated with it. The IP-rich target company could be acquired, thus giving access to the intellectual property inherent in the business. The acquirer may not have the funds for this or may have identified that other elements of the target company do not fit with its overall corporate strategy. In this case, it may be more beneficial to attempt to take a licence in similar intellectual property. This may prove to be a more cost-effective route to securing the competitive advantage and future related revenues. A valuation of the relevant intellectual property is a vital part of the investment decision-making process as it enables the acquiring company to assess the potential investment and potential related returns. It will also support and facilitate acquisition price negotiations, irrespective of the solution that is pursued.

2.3 IP valuation and purchase price allocations

The International Accounting Standards Board responded to an increasing level of merger and acquisition activity by amending its guidance for accounting and reporting for business combinations.[15] Purchased goodwill is determined by comparing the consideration transferred with the fair value of the net assets acquired. Typically, the value of internally generated intangible assets such as a valuable company or product brand, customer loyalty or trade secrets is not reflected in financial statements because these assets fail to meet the recognition criteria in the accounting standards. However in arriving at the value for purchased goodwill, the acquirer is required to assess the fair value of all the company assets that exist at the

15 International Financial Reporting Standard (IFRS), 3 *Business Combinations*, issued in January 2013 by the International Accounting Standards Board.

date of acquisition. This includes categories of intangibles that may not previously have been permitted to be recognised by the developing company. The existence of a third party that is willing to pay more than the balance-sheet value for a company implies that there is value in the intangible assets and if a financial value can be reliably attached to these assets they can be recognised on the acquirer's financial statements.

Acquiring entities that do not allocate the premium on purchase to separately identifiable assets run the risk of having a large value being recorded as "purchased goodwill" within its consolidated assets. This goodwill is subject to an annual impairment review, and companies could find that they are subject to significant annual impairment losses being charged to profit when operating in times of economic decline or where there are changes to the underlying economy in which the company is operating.

The accounting standard, IFRS 3 *Business Combinations*,[16] requires that all assets that are capable of being identified and reliably measured, in accordance with IAS 38 *Intangible Assets*,[17] be separately disclosed on acquisition. IP asset valuation provides companies involved in mergers and acquisitions with an independent assessment of the identifiable IP assets they are purchasing. Separate types of intangible assets, including brands, databases and customer lists can then be recognised within group assets, rather than recording a lump sum in an unspecified category, "purchased goodwill".

2.4 IP valuation and raising finance

The Athena Alliance Report, entitled *Maximising Intellectual Property and Intangible Assets*,[18] stated: "Uncertainty surrounding intangible asset valuation is the most significant obstacle to greater interest and activity in IA finance." Having an agreed set of professional standards governing IP valuation is often cited as the way to overcome this uncertainty. However, the methodologies that are used in IP valuations have existed for decades. The three methods discussed below, market, cost and income, are recognised worldwide as valid approaches to valuation. The development of professional standards and guidance on IP valuation is likely to come from market need, as we have seen with, for example, accounting standards. When the business environment changes this creates or uncovers new risks or transactions that require guidance – the standard setters then react to develop guidance for how best to deal with these risks or transactions. Many of the world's economies now acknowledge that intellectual property is a significant element of innovation, which is necessary to drive economic growth. As intellectual property increases in importance as an identifiable asset class, so will the need to regulate its valuation and measurement.

The need for IP valuation regulation will no doubt come from pressure from

---

16 *Ibid.*

17 International Accounting Standard (IAS), 38 *Intangible Assets*, issued in January 2012 by the International Accounting Standards Board.

18 *Maximising Intellectual Property and Intangible Assets: Case Studies in Intangible Asset Finance*, published in November 2009 by Athena Alliance.

groups that are relying on IP valuations in their decision making and have most exposure to risk – corporate debt and equity providers. Debt providers are yet to have non-equity finance solutions as a regular offering to IP-rich companies. However, grant-awarding bodies exist (nationally and internationally) to cover the risk element of securitised lending using a company's intellectual property, in an effort to stimulate growth and innovation. Insurance products have also been developed to mitigate the lender's risk of securitised IP lending.

2.5 IP valuation and pension schemes

Pension-led funding and pension deficit funding have both been increasingly evident in recent years. Asset-backed pension deficit funding was developed to enable companies that did not have cash resources available to make increased contributions to their company pension scheme. Pension funding partnerships were created that enable companies to transfer their intellectual property into special purpose vehicles, which can then be leased back to the company. Intellectual property has been included in these asset transfers. In 2010 GKN transferred assets,[19] which included trademarks and property with a value in excess of £300 million, in order to fund its pension deficit. TUI Travel[20] used its Thomson and First Choice brands as security to fund a pension deficit of more than £400 million.

Pension-led funding operates on a much smaller scale, targeting SMEs, and offers alternative financing options involving business owners' accrued pension benefits that are used to fund their own organisation. Pension-led funding injects new capital into the company, with the benefit of having the intellectual property now held within a creditor-protected pension environment. The intellectual property can be sold and licensed back to the company or the pension fund can extend a loan to the company, secured on IP assets. Regardless of how the deal is structured, the related intellectual property must be professionally valued in order to protect the pension scheme assets.

2.6 IP valuation and business structures

Prior to entering a joint venture or partnership, companies should assess the value of any IP assets that they plan to use in the new corporate structure or activity. Only then can appropriate contractual agreements be drafted that protect the IP rights that each party is bringing to the business arrangement. It is often vital for maintaining competitive advantage that a company is able to ring-fence its intellectual property in order to protect it. A valuation of this intellectual property will ensure entities that are investing in ventures or alliances can quantify their investment to enable them to assess the potential return on investment in addition to protecting the value of the intellectual property they have invested in.

---

19 As reported in *The Daily Telegraph* on April 28 2010: www.telegraph.co.uk/finance/newsbysector/industry/7640353/GKN-reveals-plan-to-cut-pension-deficit.html.

20 As reported in *Investment and Pensions Europe* in May 2011: www.ipe.com/uk-travel-firm-tui-plugs-pension-fund-deficit-with-brand-names/40582.fullarticle.

2.7 IP valuation and enforcement of IP rights

Every company should aim to protect its IP rights in order to secure its future revenue potential. Management will take responsibility for managing the risks that could have an impact on revenues and profitability. This will include identifying any infringement of the company's IP rights. Where infringement is evident, the management has two obvious options: to pursue the infringement through court action or consider licensing the intellectual property.

This is a strategic decision that must be supported by IP valuation. The management will want to pursue the most commercially beneficial action; either suing in order to receive a lump sum in damages or licensing to receive a regular income. This decision cannot be made until the management can identify the value of the intellectual property in question.

2.8 IP valuation in litigation

Where an infringement of IP rights has been identified, the directors of a company must decide on appropriate action. The most obvious options, as noted in section 2.7, are to either pursue litigation or to negotiate a licence. An assessment of the damage or loss to the company resulting from the infringement of its IP rights is likely to be the basis of the valuation where litigation is pursued. This valuation approach would take account of the economic conditions existing in the market that affect the level of competitive advantage to which the IP rights provide access.

EU Directive 2004/48/CE[21] states that when infringement damages are set authorities should "take account of all appropriate aspects, such as negative economic consequences, including lost profits, which the injured party has suffered, any unfair profits made by the infringer...". There are various ways to value the option of pursuing litigation, including assessment of a rights holder's actual loss, the profits made by the infringing company and the potential compensation based on a hypothetical licence. These valuations are typically performed by valuers that specialise in IP litigation.

2.9 IP valuation and business strategies

IP valuation assists management in budgeting and forecasting, essential elements of resource allocation within the company and critical to decision making around corporate transactions. The starting point is often to perform an IP audit to identify core and non-core intellectual property within the company. This will ensure that investment is effective and made only in areas most likely to offer reliable future returns. Decisions can then be made on how much to invest in developing and protecting core IP assets and whether non-core intellectual property should be sold or licensed, or be allowed to lapse if the intellectual property is obsolete. Management typically use investment appraisal techniques when deciding on resource allocation, calculating the value of an investment versus the expected returns on that investment. Intellectual property valuation will assist in this process

21 European Union (EU) Directive 2004/48/EC of the European Parliament and of the Council of 29 April 2004 on the enforcement of intellectual property rights.

and allow management to benchmark and assess this value against the expected future returns the intellectual property is expected to generate both in business operations and transactions.

2.10 IP valuation and financial distress

It is becoming more common for IP assets to be identified, marketed and sold from distressed corporate scenarios. This provides evidence that there is value inherent in IP assets. Prospective buyers and bidders will require an IP valuation before making a decision about whether or not to bid for the intellectual property and if so, at what price.

3. Valuation methods

3.1 The process of IP valuation

Many IP assets are unique and this makes IP valuation more complex. There is often no obvious comparable IP asset to provide a reliable market valuation, but an increase in reported IP transactions would enable an adjusted valuation based on similar assets. This model is already successfully used in estimating the value of some tangible assets such as property. There is an element of judgement involved in IP valuation, just like in any other asset or business valuation. This does not mean, however, that the IP valuation is less reliable, providing the judgement is exercised by an experienced valuation professional and is the result of a rigorous and transparent valuation process. A valuation opinion is often likened to a legal opinion: it is not an exact science; another professional could offer a different but equally valid opinion; but it can be relied upon, provided it is given by an experienced professional with a track record of providing opinions in a similar area.

Given the complex nature of the process, a key element in the process of obtaining a reliable valuation for IP assets is to engage a valuation specialist. Nonetheless, most IP valuation specialists would agree that there are three standard models of IP valuation: market, cost and income.

3.2 Market method

The market approach can, in theory, offer a good indication of IP value as it involves benchmarking against actual comparable transactions within the relevant sector or marketplace in order to ascertain the likely value of similar IP rights. However, the market approach requires an active marketplace with access to public records of transactions and prices. Until recently, IP assets were not being bought, sold or licensed frequently enough to establish value based exclusively on direct market-based comparables; there was simply no market for IP assets. Even with the recent increase in IP commercialisation activities, it is still difficult to access the IP purchase or licence prices associated with these transactions. Furthermore, where the intellectual property in question is particularly unique, as is the case with a new invention, no comparable information will be available. This will render this valuation method unsuitable for many IP assets.

Even when a market exists for the intellectual property being valued, and public data is available regarding the purchase price or royalty rates agreed, the market methodology still requires context-based analysis. When identifying a potentially comparable transaction, it is necessary to consider the context in which the transaction took place, which will of course affect the valuation. Naturally, if the transaction was forced through litigation or financial distress then, again, a comparable may not be available.

Nonetheless, if a suitable market with reliable data can be located, the market-based valuation methodology can be "considered the most direct and systematic method for accurately valuing intangible assets such as IP".[22]

3.3 Cost method

The cost method of valuation, rather than ascertaining value based on comparability, focuses on substitution. The value of the relevant IP asset is considered to be equivalent to the costs to obtain or reproduce it. This is based on the assumption that potential buyers would not pay more for an IP asset than the cost of recreating it themselves. There are two methodologies within the cost-based approach: (1) reproduction cost and (2) replacement cost. The former considers the cost necessary to reproduce the exact same IP asset, whereas the latter measures the cost to develop an asset of similar quality.

Not all costs accrued during development of an IP asset can be included; only those required to duplicate the asset, or an asset of similar utility, can be considered. Direct expenditures comprise "materials needed in the development process, labor costs and some overhead items".[23]

The cost-based IP valuation is not the equivalent of costs incurred at the time the IP asset was created. Cost-based valuation must take account of the costs as at the date of valuation rather than the date at which the historical expenditures actually took place. This is a significant distinction with significant impacts. Firstly, if the cost of any of the relevant components, or means of making those components, has changed since the IP asset's initial inception, the current cost level needs to be incorporated into the valuation calculation. The cost, whether it has gone up or down, can be affected by such forces as the time value of money or technological obsolescence; certain IP assets could conceivably be developed faster and at a lower cost, based on advancements and economy of effort over time.

Cost-based IP valuation can be useful in particular scenarios – for example, in relation to pre-revenue, high-tech companies where the income and market methods are inappropriate as no income has been generated or the intellectual property is unique, and therefore there are no comparables in the market. Nonetheless, cost-based valuation is often considered to be the least reliable of the various valuation methodologies because it is difficult to assume a correlation between expenditure on an IP asset and its value. If the relevant intellectual property offers significant economic advantage and can be used to generate substantial revenues, the use of the

---

22 Weston Anson, Want to Value Your Intellectual Property? Here Are Three Approaches, *IP in Brief*: www.ipinbrief.com/three-approaches-to-value-ip/.

23 David Drews, The Cost Approach to IP Valuation: Its Uses and Limitations: www.ipmetrics.net/Cost%20Approach.PDF.

cost method may understate its actual value. Conversely, if development has been inefficient or lengthy, the use of the cost method might overstate its value.

3.4 Income method

Income-based approaches to valuation aim to identify the value that is generated by a company as a result of its ownership of the intellectual property. In practice, the income approach is the most commonly used and relevant method of valuing intellectual property. This approach has a number of methods that can be adopted but all with one common feature: they rely on making assumptions about the future use of the intellectual property and typically require the company to provide forecast information about the likely revenues and post-tax returns from using the intellectual property. The main challenge is allocating the income that is attributable to each identifiable IP asset. The most commonly used approaches are as follows.

(a) Relief from royalty method

This approach views the value of the intellectual property as equal to the capitalised amount of the royalties that would be due if the intellectual property was licensed rather than owned by the company. This method requires the use of a comparable royalty rate and the valuer will investigate the market and sector in order to reach a conclusion on a suitable royalty rate for each identifiable IP asset. In addition, assumptions are made about how long the IP asset is likely to contribute to revenues (ie, the economic useful life of the intellectual property). The valuation uses forecast revenues, discounted to their present value. The discount rate used is normally an estimated cost of the capital of the company. Adjustments are also made for tax and risk. The forecasts are adjusted for tax at the rate applicable at the valuation date, on the assumption that if the company were paying a royalty for the use of the intellectual property it would receive tax relief on this as a deductible business expense. The valuer must exercise considerable professional judgement in arriving at an appropriate adjustment for risk as this covers company, product, sector and market risks. Adjustments for risk must take account of:

- the uncertainty within the sector and whether there is a long-term need or desire for the products/services;
- the likelihood that competitors' intellectual property would affect future returns and how well the company has protected the intellectual property that underpins future revenue streams;
- the ability of the company to achieve its forecasts and whether the company has the technical capability and financial resources to achieve its forecasts; and
- management's experience level in preparing reliable forecast information, assessing the reliability of the forecasts that underpin the valuation calculations.

(b) Premium profits method

With this method the valuation can be based on the price premium and/or the estimated volume premium that the intellectual property is expected to generate compared with a competitor that has no or limited access to similar intellectual property. This method relies on forecast financial data, so again it would be necessary to apply a suitable discount factor in order to restate the earnings to their present value. This method values the intellectual property based on the additional value that it adds to the future revenue of the company as a whole. This can be particularly relevant for assessing the value of a brand; for example, a brand could be valued by comparing the price premium a branded product can generate compared with an unbranded or weakly branded comparative product or service. In practice, however, it is often difficult to identify unbranded comparators.

(c) ***Incremental cash flow method***

This method follows a similar principle to the premium profits method, by identifying the incremental cash flows that the intellectual property can generate through both increased revenues and reduced costs. This is a more detailed and complex approach to valuation and so is not as common as, say, the relief from royalty method. However, it is particularly relevant for negotiations when, for example, forming strategic partnerships or ventures.

(d) ***Residual methods***

There are two approaches within this method, which establishes the valuation of the intellectual property using a more indirect process. The income-split method starts with net operating profit and makes an adjustment for the contribution expected to be made by the total tangible capital employed. This then assumes that any remaining profits are attributable to the total intangible assets in the company. Detailed analysis would then investigate how much of this remaining profit could be allocated to each identifiable IP asset. The value of an IP asset would be assumed to be the present value of the profits that are assessed to be attributable to it. The multi-period excess earnings method is similar but values all the identifiable individual tangible and intangible assets employed other than the key asset it is attempting to value. The attributable profits are allocated to each asset and any excess is deemed to be the present value of the residual earnings over the remaining useful life of the IP asset in question.

4. IP trolls – tbc

Patent, trademark or copyright holders who amass a portfolio of patents, trademarks or copyright respectively with no intention of commercialising the underlying inventions are known as non-practising entities or, pejoratively, patent, trademark or copyright trolls (collectively IP trolls).[24] The negative connotation stems from the perception that IP trolls are mere opportunists, emerging solely to accuse unsuspecting companies that have a particular technology of, for example, patent

24 There is some debate regarding which moniker to use; the term 'non-practising entities' is sometimes criticised for its inclusion of entities whose primary purpose is to develop and transfer their technology, such as universities, which is not seen as abusive conduct. The US Federal Trade Commission has adopted the term 'patent assertion entities' to refer to firms whose business model primarily focuses on purchasing and asserting patents, which narrows the definitional scope.

infringement in order to extract licensing royalties or damages from them.[25] Look to companies like Lemelson Medical, Education and Research Foundation, which has earned an estimated $1.2 billion in licensing revenues since 1988, or to Eolas Technologies, which was awarded over $500 million in a suit against Microsoft, and it is not difficult to understand the popular maligning of these entities.[26]

But apart from claims that IP trolls stifle innovation, what consequences do these IP 'aggregators' have for valuation? The effects are twofold, and somewhat contrary.

IP rights were, historically, meant to protect revenues associated with a patent-, trademark- or copyright-protected product sold by the IP owner by granting them a legal monopoly. More recently, however, IP rights have begun to be seen as a monetisable asset class of their own. Companies who have a vast patent portfolio, most of which is lying dormant, may seek to license or sell its patents as a way to bring an influx of capital into the company. Licensing in particular helps demonstrate the value in intellectual property since, according to Generally Accepted Accounting Principles, internally generated IP assets cannot be represented on company balance sheets as assets.[27]

This "monetisation movement has spawned a burgeoning secondary market" for IP rights, and although the market is still in its infancy, *The Economist* magazine estimates that this market is expected to grow by 20 to 30% in the near future.[28] While there are potential concerns regarding IP trolls, including an increase in patent litigation, excessive damage awards, difficulties in identifying and clearing patent rights and concerns over patent quality, a 2011 Federal Trade Commission report also identified that a new marketplace of patent transactions is developing.[29] This marketplace accounts for certain practices which, though heretofore considered detrimental, may actually have net benefits in this new context. Patent assertion entities can actually provide remuneration to individual inventors who otherwise lack the capability, financial or otherwise, to exploit the technology.[30] Supporters of the patent assertion entity business model argue that when patent assertion entities purchase patents from independent inventors and small and medium-sized enterprises, they provide them with compensation and funding these inventors could not otherwise receive.[31] Interestingly, patent assertion entities have also been

---

25 Patent Trolls: Unfair Name-Calling or Threat to Patent System? Drinker Biddle, June 2005: www.drinkerbiddle.com/Templates/media/files/publications/2005/intellectual-property-update-2005-6-30.pdf.

26 JP Mello, Technology Licensing and Patent Trolls, *Boston University Journal of Science and Technology Law* (2006) 12: 388.

27 Financial Accounting Standards Board, Accounting Standards Codification § 350-30-25-3 ("Costs of internally developing, maintaining, or restoring intangible assets that are not specifically identifiable, that have indeterminate lives, or are inherent in a continuing business and related to an entity as a whole, shall be recognized as an expense when incurred.")

28 Malcolm T Meeks and Charles A Eldering, Patent Valuation: Aren't We Forgetting Something – Making the Case for Claims Analysis in Patent Valuation by Proposing a Patent Valuation Method and a Patent-Specific Discount Rate Using the CAPM, *Northwestern Journal of Technology and Intellectual Property* (2010) 9: 194.

29 Federal Trade Commission, *The Evolving IP Marketplace: Aligning Patent Notice and Remedies with Competition*. Washington, DC: Government Printing Office 2011.

30 *Ibid.*

31 *Ibid.*

32 *Ibid.*

heralded for their ability to negotiate royalty payments from large operating companies that individual inventors cannot credibly threaten themselves.[32]

Most illustrative of this position, however, is the fact that patent assertion entities have been the catalyst for propagating a new type of asset class, with patents most frequently at its centre. In downstream or secondary patent markets, these entities can provide liquidity for patent transactions as well as valuation comparisons for fair market benchmarking.[33] They also provide the means by which both large and small companies can find buyers for patent portfolios they do not need or do not wish to maintain.[34] Selling these portfolios may allow a company to recoup a return on the associated R&D investment, create capital for investing in new innovation or even provide funds with which to compensate a company's creditors.[35] Conversely, they may also benefit manufacturing companies looking to purchase patents that will provide them with the freedom to operate in a new product area or market.[36]

At the same time, so-called IP trolls may skew public perception of IP valuation, particularly in relation to high-profile cases resulting in astronomical damage claims. They operate on the premise that certain IP rights have infringement value, that is, are valuable due to the potential damages the IP troll can receive as a result of IP infringement suits. As typical valuation methods rely, in some part, on the exploitation value of IP rights, changing the model to focus on economic rent seeking[37] distorts their true economic value.

---

33 *Ibid.*
34 *Ibid.*
35 *Ibid.*
36 *Ibid.*
37 Often used in relation to property, the definition is equally relevant to intellectual property: "when property rights are weakened and the ownership of someone's wealth or goods is debatable, people can gain more by trying to appropriate that wealth than by producing themselves." David J Marotta, What is Rent Seeking Behaviour?: www.forbes.com/sites/davidmarotta/2013/02/24/what-is-rent-seeking-behavior/.

The relationship between IP law and competition law

Jonathan Cornthwaite
Wedlake Bell LLP

1. Tensions

1.1 Introduction

Viewed from a distance, the law can give the impression of being harmonised and consistent. But if one takes a closer look, internal tensions within it swiftly become apparent; and few of these are more deeply rooted than the tension between IP law on the one hand and competition law on the other. It is not hard to see why, for the two come from very different directions. Intellectual property law, in essence, is all about restricting unauthorised trade: for example, a patented invention will entitle the patentee and its licensees to stop others from exploiting the invention without consent within the jurisdiction in which the patent has been granted. By contrast, competition law is in principle uncomfortable with trading restrictions and exclusive arrangements: it favours permitting people to trade, not restricting them from so doing. Boiling it down even further, one could say that IP law involves the erection of trading barriers, whereas competition law favours their dismantlement.

1.2 Reconciling the tensions

How are these tensions reconciled? The approach adopted by the Court of Justice of the European Union has been to draw a distinction between the existence of an intellectual property right on the one hand, and its exercise on the other.[1] The jurisprudential reasoning is that the courts will not interfere with the existence of the IP right, but that, in the interests of (for example) the internal market, they will intervene to police how that right is exercised. An analogy might be drawn here with a bi-lateral co-existence agreement, in which the two sides – despite their opposing interests – reach a modus vivendi by making reciprocal concessions. Competition law gives ground by conceding that, in certain specified circumstances, softcore IP restrictions will be deemed not to violate the prohibitions on anti-competitive agreements. And, in its turn, intellectual property law 'backs down' by accepting that certain commercial practices that (for example) promote the internal market will not constitute IP infringement – major derogations, in other words, from the exercise of IP rights. By virtue of these compromises the tensions between these two bodies of law are reduced, though they are certainly not removed altogether.

1 *Consten and Grundig v Commission* [1966] ECR 299 *et seq.*

1.3 Examples of reconciliation

Examples are worth a thousand words of theory, and we therefore set out below an example of each of these types of concession, one by competition law and one by IP law.

A prime example of competition law giving ground is the EU's Technology Transfer Block Exemption (TTBE).[2] This important piece of legislation is a regulation, and thus (unlike directives, which are addressed to member states and which therefore have to be transposed into domestic law) is directly binding on EU citizens and businesses. It grants to certain categories of IP assignments and licences a major exemption from the prohibition in EU law on anti-competitive agreements, provided always that specified conditions are met; and it is called a "block" exemption in order to differentiate it from individual exemptions that are granted only on a case-by-case basis. (Although the TTBE is sometimes described as a "safe harbour", IP rights holders need to be alive to the fact that the harbour walls are far from all-encompassing. Thus, the exemption will not apply if specified market shares are exceeded, and in any event whole categories and sub-categories of IP rights – trademarks, for example, and non-software copyright – are not covered at all by the TTBE.)

Conversely, a classic example of a major derogation from the exercise of IP rights can be found in the law on the free movement of goods (closely related to EU competition law, for both laws are aimed ultimately at securing and upholding the internal market) in the form of the exhaustion of rights principle. This important precept holds that, once a product has been placed on the market within the European Economic Area (EEA) by an IP rights holder or with its consent, the latter's entitlement to use those rights to control how the product is subsequently distributed will be exhausted. This principle is enshrined not just in case law, but in national statutes: for example, the UK Trade Marks Act stipulates that (subject to certain exceptions):

> *a registered trade mark is not infringed by the use of the trade mark in relation to goods which have been put on the market in the European Economic Area under that trade mark by the proprietor or with his consent.*[3]

The objective of ensuring the internal market within the EEA thus takes such priority that it has given rise to statutory defences to infringement which have been inserted in national statutes.

From a jurisprudential standpoint, the reconciliation of divergent legal principles is a fascinating subject. But in this chapter we shall take a more pragmatic approach to the issue, and shall review how, under the law applicable in the United Kingdom, the tension between IP law and competition law is handled in practice by legislators, courts and regulators.

---

2 Commission Regulation (EU) number 316/2014 on the application of Article 101(3) of the Treaty on the Functioning of the European Union to categories of technology transfer agreements.

3 Trade Marks Act 1994, section 12(1).

2. Red flags

2.1 Introduction

A full discussion of the complex interface between IP law and competition law is beyond the scope of this section, where the approach will be limited to discussing a list of red flags that should be waved when certain IP transactions are being contemplated. It needs to be emphasised that this list is selective and non-exhaustive, and that whether or not the red flag proves to be justified in any individual case will depend on a mixture of fact (including, for example, the respective market shares of the parties involved) and law (including, for example, whether any applicable exceptions or exemptions may be available).

However, before listing these red flags we need to outline the prohibitions that the red flags are designed to highlight. The best starting point is the Competition Act 1998, which, in admirably concise language, outlaws two main categories of anti-competitive behaviour under UK law. The first of these categories is the subject of what is known as the Chapter I Prohibition,[4] which (unless they fall within one or more of the various statutory exceptions) forbids agreements between undertakings, decisions by associations of undertakings and concerted practices that may affect trade within the United Kingdom, and that have as their object or effect the appreciable[5] prevention, restriction or distortion of competition within the United Kingdom. The second category is dealt with by the Chapter II Prohibition,[6] which outlaws any conduct on the part of one or more undertakings that amounts to the abuse of a dominant position in a market if it may affect trade within the United Kingdom. Essentially, therefore, the first prohibition is aimed at contracts and arrangements, whereas the second is aimed at conduct. Of the two, the second prohibition is arguably the more dangerous: for, unlike the first prohibition, it can be infringed by purely unilateral behaviour, and there are hardly any exceptions to it.

The Chapter I and II Prohibitions faithfully reflect those that are enshrined in Articles 101 and 102 respectively of the Treaty on the Functioning of the European Union (TFEU), the language of which is indeed used almost verbatim in the British statute. It is therefore very helpful that, unlike the position with mergers and acquisitions (where there is clear blue water between UK law and EU law), the prohibitions in the Competition Act harmonise with those in the TFEU.

2.2 Anti-competitive agreements

Below we outline categories of contractual provisions that may cause the IP transactions in which they feature to suffer adverse attention from competition law regulators.

---

4 Competition Act 1998, section 2.

5 Although the word "appreciable" does not appear in the relevant wording of the statute, the Chapter I Prohibition is interpreted by the courts and the regulators as meaning that, unless so-called "hardcore" restrictions are involved, the effect of agreements between parties with small market shares that fall below specified levels is considered to be insufficient to constitute an infringement of the Chapter I Prohibition.

6 Competition Act 1998, section 18.

(a) *The cartel offence*

There is little doubt that the reddest of the red flags needs to be waved whenever there is a bilateral or multi-lateral arrangement that, if operated in the United Kingdom as the parties intend, would:

- directly or indirectly fix a price for the supply of a product or service to a third party;
- limit or prevent the supply of a product or service;
- limit or prevent production of a product;
- divide up between the parties the supply of a product or service to a customer or customers; and/or
- divide up between the parties customers for the supply of a product or service.

The reason why these types of arrangement are potentially so heinous is that, in addition to the risk of civil liability under the Chapter I Prohibition and/or Article 101, they may also incur criminal liability on the part of an individual who made the agreement by virtue of constituting the so-called 'cartel offence',[7] which, in addition to the fines that may be imposed, is punishable on summary conviction by up to six months' imprisonment, and on indictment by up to five years' imprisonment. It is sometimes forgotten that people have already been not only convicted but sent to prison in this country for having committed this offence: thus, in the infamous *Marine Hose* case,[8] the defendants were convicted of having dishonestly engaged in price fixing, bid rigging, the allocation of markets and the restriction of supplies, and were given sentences of imprisonment of up to three years, although these were subsequently reduced by the Court of Appeal. And the risk of such liability has increased since April 2014, when the previous requirement of "dishonesty" was removed from the offence,[9] thus making it easier for the prosecution to prove.

(b) *Resale price maintenance*

But even if it does not constitute a criminal offence, an IP transaction can still be regarded as going against the principles of competition law. A classic example is resale price maintenance which, though it falls outside the parameters of the cartel offence, will nevertheless be very likely to violate the prohibitions on anti-competitive behaviour. So if, for example, the royalty rates that I have set in my patent licence have the object or effect of fixing the price at which the patented products are resold by the licensee, there would be a clear risk of the licence infringing the prohibitions under Chapter I and/or Article 101. Indeed, "the restriction of a party's ability to determine its prices when selling products to third parties" is at the very top of the list of "hardcore restrictions" contained in the TTBE, which will automatically disallow the applicability of the exemption where the parties are competing undertakings.[10] And, even where I have merely recommended

---

7 Enterprise Act 2002, section 188.
8 *R v Whittle et al* [2008] EWCA Crim 2560.
9 Pursuant to the Enterprise and Regulatory Reform Act 2013.
10 TTBE, Article 4.1(a).

resale prices to my licensee, that can still be regarded by the competition law regulators as offensive if I have pressured the licensee to accede to my recommendation, or offered it incentives to do so.

(c) ***Restrictions on the licensee's use of its own technology***

What if I have included in my licence an obligation on the licensee to assign to me – or to license to me exclusively – the improvements that it has made to my patent? Again, that will definitely warrant a red flag, for the obligation is specifically listed by the TTBE as having the effect of disallowing its exemption.[11] Indeed, any restriction of the licensee from exploiting its own technology rights or (unless it is indispensable to prevent the disclosure of licensed know-how) from carrying out research and development would be risky.[12]

(d) ***Post-expiry restrictions***

Another danger area is where restrictions imposed on a licensee purport to endure after the expiry of the licensed IP rights. For example, if I oblige my licensee to continue to pay me royalties on its use of my patent not only during its term but after its expiry date, I could be skating on very thin ice indeed.

(e) ***Output restrictions***

There are certain commercial situations where the contractual imposition of output restrictions in an IP licence may be justifiable, if not pro-competitive. For example, output restrictions could be necessary for the licensor to disseminate its technology as widely as possible; and, unless it is permitted to limit the licence to a particular production site with a specific capacity, the licensor might be reluctant to license its technology to its competitors at all, which would thus have a negative effect on competition.[13] Nevertheless, it needs to be remembered that the limitation of output features prominently on the TTBE's list of hardcore restrictions[14] and should therefore be treated with great caution.

(f) ***Territorial exclusivity***

The question of territorial exclusivity for IP licences is an especially tricky area, which is unfortunate to say the least, as it repeatedly arises in practice. It is, after all, very normal for IP licensors to wish to grant exclusive rights in a particular territory to one (and only one) licensee; yet such an arrangement can all too easily run the risk of contravening competition law, which often views territorial exclusivity with suspicion, namely as a means of dividing up markets and erecting unjustified barriers to trade. This is therefore a classic example of the tension between IP law and competition law referred to in section 1.

---

11 TTBE, Article 5.1(a).

12 TTBE, Articles 4.1(d) and 5.2.

13 See further the Guidelines on the application of Article 101 on the Treaty on the Functioning of the European Union to Technology Transfer Agreements: Commission Communication 2014/C89/03 (the Commission Guidelines) at section 4.2.3.

14 TTBE, Article 4.1(b).

Whether in any particular case a clause in an IP licence granting territorial exclusivity will contravene competition law will depend on a range of factors, including (*inter alia*) the parties' respective market shares, whether they are actual or potential competitors, whether the contract includes reciprocal licences, and whether a selective distribution system is in place. For the purposes of this short section, therefore, the most that can be done is to refer to a general rule of thumb: regulators traditionally distinguish between prohibitions imposed in an exclusive licence on active sales (ie, sales made pursuant to an active marketing policy outside the exclusive territory) on the one hand and passive sales (ie, the sales made in response to unsolicited orders emanating from outside the exclusive territory) on the other. A ban by the licensor on the former will tend to be regarded more benevolently by the regulators than a ban on the latter. So, for example, if I purport to impose an absolute export ban on my Hungarian copyright licensee from selling its licensed products to any other member state, or to prohibit it from selling the products online,[15] the red flag will need to be waved vigorously; if, by contrast, I merely prohibit it from (for example) establishing a sales branch or distribution depot in another member state in which I have granted exclusive rights to another licensee, the risk should be considerably lower.

(g) Settlement agreements

The use of compromise agreements, co-existence contracts, non-assertion agreements and other types of settlement are obviously a frequent and familiar way of resolving IP disputes, since they avoid the expense – and risk – of a trial. But in the heat of negotiating and drafting such instruments, it can often be forgotten that competition law has decidedly mixed feelings about them.

On the one hand, competition law acknowledges that a settlement is in principle a bona fide way of finding a mutually acceptable compromise to a legal dispute, and can indeed promote the public interest by saving courts and other tribunals the burden of trying and judging them. On the other hand, IP settlements usually involve arrangements between actual or potential competitors that incorporate restrictions on trading, which is precisely the sort of situation where red flags need to be waved from the competition law standpoint.

Patent settlements: A clear indication of how seriously the regulators view this issue is the fact that the European Commission has to date published no fewer than five successive reports on its monitoring of patent settlements in the pharmaceutical sector. The most recent of them[16] provides a useful insight into the Commission's approach to the subject. Firstly, it divides pharmaceutical patent settlement agreements into two broad categories: namely, Category A, which comprises those that permit the generic company to enter the market and compete freely, or that do not oblige it to leave the market; and Category B, which comprises those settlements that impede or ban the generic company from entering the market with its own

15 Case C-439/09: *Pierre Fabre Dermo-Cosmétique SAS v Président de l'Autorité de la Concurrence et al.*
16 *Fifth Report on the Monitoring of Patent Settlements*: 5 December 2014: Competition DG.

product. The difference between the two from a competition law viewpoint is that the former agreements are generally unobjectionable, whereas the latter are potentially problematic.

Category B agreements are therefore subdivided depending on whether or not they contain a transfer of value from the originator company to the generic company. Those that do not (Category BI) will be unlikely to encounter problems with the regulators unless exceptional circumstances apply; those that do (Category BII), on the other hand, are clearly at risk of attracting adverse regulatory attention. Indeed, in the years 2013–14 alone the European Commission imposed fines of almost €0.6 billion on parties to arrangements that delayed generic entry on to the market.[17] The rule of thumb, therefore, is that a large red flag must definitely be waved whenever "pay-for-restriction" or "pay-for-delay" provisions feature in a patent settlement agreement.

Other types of IP settlement agreements: Even if your compromise agreement is careful to avoid any restriction of generic entry, it can still run into competition law problems. For example, a settlement deal whereby the parties agree to cross-license each other and to accept restrictions on the use of their respective technologies could well be risky, especially where the parties have a significant degree of market power, and/or where the deal has the effect of preventing them from gaining a competitive lead over the other or reducing their incentive to innovate.[18]

Another type of provision often encountered in IP settlements (including, in particular, trademark co-existence agreements) is the delimitation of territorial markets. Such provisions need to be drafted with great care, especially if they are combined with restrictions on the use of the intellectual property after the expiry of the applicable licence: the *Chiquita/Fyffes* case[19] is a good example of how such a combination can incur the wrath of competition law regulators.

Finally, no-challenge clauses are often encountered in IP settlement agreements. These are discussed in section 3.1 below.

(h) Joint ventures

Joint venture arrangements are often used as vehicles for the collaborative exploitation of IP rights. But the range of different commercial operations that describe themselves as joint ventures means that they can be treated in a bewildering variety of ways by competition law: for example, the establishment of a cross-border jointly owned company might fall to be assessed under the Merger Control Regulation,[20] whereas a purely domestic research and development collaboration might fall to be considered by reference to the Chapter I Prohibition. Distinguishing which regime (if any) will apply will depend on (*inter alia*) whether or not the joint

17 For example, Cases T-460/467/470/471/472/13 (the *Lundbeck* cases) and Cases T-677/679/680/684/691/701/705/14 (the *Servier* cases), although all these cases are subject to appeal at the time of writing.

18 Commission Guidelines, paragraphs 240–241.

19 Commission Press Release IP/92/461, 4 June 1992.

20 Council Regulation (EC) No 139/2004 of 20 January 2004 on the control of concentrations between undertakings.

venture is full-function, whether it has a cooperative or concentrative element, and whether a community dimension is present. In a chapter of this length, there is insufficient space to explore these criteria; suffice it to say therefore that this is a complicated area of law where the potential applicability of competition law is very often present, and where it is prudent to tread carefully. With specific reference to IP joint ventures, those that involve the assignment or licensing of IP rights may often be able to avail themselves of the TTBE, and those that involve joint research and development might find that the EU research and development block exemption regulation[21] can be helpful.

2.3 Abuse of a dominant position

In the preceding section we have outlined a range of commercial situations in which IP transactions can all too easily contravene the prohibition of anti-competitive agreements under Chapter I and/or Article 101. We now turn to consider a different set of red flags that may need to be hoisted, namely where the exercise of IP rights may amount to the abuse of a dominant position contrary to Chapter II and/or Article 102.

It is important for IP rights holders to understand that, in certain circumstances, their rights may directly or indirectly cause them to occupy a dominant position under one or more of the relevant markets. For the purposes of EU jurisprudence a 'dominant position' is taken to mean:

> *a position of economic strength enjoyed by an undertaking which enables it to hinder the maintenance of effective competition on the relevant market by allowing it to behave to an appreciable extent independently of its competitors and customers and ultimately of consumers.*[22]

While the occupation of a dominant position on the relevant market or markets does not itself contravene Chapter II or Article 102, the abuse of that position certainly can do; and we set out below a number of such situations with particular reference to intellectual property.

(a) Refusal to license

Few, if any, commercial situations highlight the tension between IP and competition laws more starkly than where the refusal by a rights holder to license its IP rights causes it to be accused of abusing a dominant position. From the IP viewpoint, a rights holder should obviously be free to choose whether (and, if so, how and to whom) to license its IP rights. But from a competition law standpoint the proprietorship of IP rights may in certain circumstances amount to a dominant position on the relevant market, and an arbitrary refusal to license them can – exceptionally – be abusive and thereby unlawful.

A good example from UK case law is the Court of Appeal's decision in *Intel v Via Technologies*,[23] in which the court held that, in exceptional circumstances, a refusal to

---

21 Commission Regulation (EU) No 1217/2010 of 14 December 2010 on the application of Article 101(3) of the Treaty on the Functioning of the European Union to certain categories of research and development agreements.

22 *Nederlandsche Banden Industrie Michelin v Commission* [1983] ECR 3461.

23 *Intel Corporation v Via Technologies Inc. et al* [2002] EWCA Civ 1905.

grant a licence in respect of a product could constitute a contravention of Article 102 even where the product in question was not new.

Comparable decisions have been made, too, at the EU level. For example, in *IMS Health*,[24] the European Commission ruled that IMS Health occupied a dominant position in the market for collecting and compiling data about the sales of pharmaceuticals, and that its conduct – which included using its copyright to enjoin other suppliers from using the same compilations, and refusing to grant licences to them under that copyright – was *prima facie* evidence of abuse. And, of course, one of the largest single fines ever imposed by the European Commission (almost €0.5 billion) was in respect of a breach of Article 102 by Microsoft for its refusal to provide to its competitors the data that they needed in order to be able to develop new products capable of interfacing with Microsoft's desktop operating systems.

Extracting a consistent *ratio decidendi* from these contrasting cases is beyond the scope of this chapter. Suffice it to say that, if you are considering rejecting a request for a licence under your IP rights from someone who wants to bring a new product to market, give thought to whether there might be a Chapter II/Article 102 problem, especially if your refusal would cause a downstream market to fail to be satisfied.

(b) Tying and bundling

Even if you agree to license your IP rights, you can still get into serious trouble with Chapter II and/or Article 102 if you 'tie' or 'bundle' – or, in the more formal words of the legislation, if you make "the conclusion of contracts subject to acceptance by the other parties of supplemental obligations which, by their nature or according to commercial usage, have no connection with the subject of the contracts".[25] Again, EU law and practice show how severely the regulators view this type of practice. For example, IBM was required to amend its practices as a result of objections by the European Commission that its so-called 'memory bundling' – namely, only selling its central processing units with memory included – was tantamount to an infringement of Article 102. Microsoft's practices, too, have had to be amended as a direct result of accusations by the European Commission that the tying of Internet Explorer, its web browser, to its client PC operating systems was an abusive 'bundling' contrary to Article 102.

(c) Patent ambush

Finally, even if your IP exploitation practices avoid refusals to license, and steer clear of tying and bundling, red flags may still need to be waved if the royalty rates that you set in your patent licences are considered to be unreasonable. This is precisely what happened to Rambus Inc, a US company whose patent portfolio covered technology required for compliance with industry-wide standards set for categories of electronic memory. Rambus was accused by the European Commission of having arranged a so-called 'patent ambush' – namely, deliberately refraining from disclosing the existence of patents and patent applications that were relevant to the

24 European Commission press release IP/03/1159.
25 Competition Act 1998, section 18(2)(d).

said standards – which led it to set the royalty rates in its patent licences at an unreasonably high level. As a result of these accusations Rambus was obliged to submit to binding commitments to alter its practices.[26]

2.4 Anti-competitive agreements combined with abuse of a dominant position

There can sometimes be nightmare scenarios in which the exploitation of intellectual property may simultaneously contravene both the prohibition of anti-competitive agreements and the prohibition of abuse of a dominant position. The European Commission's decision in the *Servier* case[27] (though under appeal at the time of writing) provides a salutary example of such a scenario.

The case involved patent settlement agreements between Servier and five producers of generic variations of Servier's best-selling blood-pressure medicine, perindopril. The European Commission found that these arrangements simultaneously contravened Articles 101 and 102. The former, it held, was breached because the settlement agreements had the object or effect of preventing or delaying the entry onto the market of cheap generic versions of perindopril; and the latter was breached because, by having induced the settlement agreements, Servier had abused its dominant position in the market for perindopril. The aggregate fines imposed on Servier and the generic producers exceeded €0.4 billion, which does not include the sums being separately claimed from Servier by the alleged victims of its anti-competitive practices, including health authorities in England, Wales and Scotland. In this latter respect, IP rights owners need to bear in mind that the inevitable result of the implementation next year of the EU anti-trust damages directive[28] will be to increase the incidence of civil litigation by those who claim that they have been damaged by anti-competitive agreements or abuses of dominant position.

3. White flags: IP transactions with a low risk of contravening competition law

While (as demonstrated above) there are various types of IP transactions that will warrant the waving of a competition law red flag, there are other categories where the risk of competition law violation will be low or indeed non-existent. We review some of them below:

3.1 No-challenge and termination clauses

As a general rule, a clause that prohibits (whether directly or indirectly) a licensee from challenging the validity of the IP rights licensed to it will not enjoy the benefit of the TTBE's exemption.[29] However, the European Commission is inclined to take a more favourable view of such a clause if it relates to licensed know-how that is likely to be impossible or very difficult to recover once it has been disclosed. In that sort of

---

26 European Commission press release IP/09/1897.
27 European Commission press release IP/14/799.
28 Directive 2014/104/EU of the European Parliament and of the Council of 26 November 2014 on certain rules governing actions for damages under national law for infringements of the competition law provisions of the Member States and of the European Union.
29 TTBE, Article 5.1(a).

situation, the Commission's thinking is that a prohibition on the licensee from challenging the licensed know-how will in fact promote dissemination of new technology, in particular by allowing weaker licensors to license stronger licensees without fear of a challenge once the know-how has been absorbed by the licensee, and that it can therefore be pro-competitive.[30]

Furthermore, a clause in an exclusive licence that merely entitles the licensor to terminate the contract in the event of such a challenge is now viewed much less sternly by the regulators, and would not necessarily forfeit the TTBE's exemption.[31]

3.2 Prescribed minima

Provisions in IP licences that include obligations to pay minimum royalties, or to produce a minimum quantity of products incorporating the licensed technology, are sometimes thought to be a danger area from the standpoint of competition law. But the Commission Guidelines state that such obligations are not generally restrictive of competition within the meaning of Article 101.

3.3 Other obligations

Obliging the licensee to help the licensor to enforce the licensed IP rights, or prohibiting it from sub-licensing, are, like the pro-competitive output restrictions discussed above, other examples of typical provisions in IP agreements that are unlikely to occasion adverse consequences under competition law.[32] Nor is the imposition of a prohibition on the licensee from using the licensed IP rights after the date of termination of the contract likely to be objectionable from a competition law standpoint, provided that those IP rights remain valid and in force.[33]

4. National and supranational regulation

4.1 Structure

(a) The EU level

The European Commission is the body that oversees the competition law framework at EU level. The principal elements of this framework are Articles 101 and 102 of the TFEU and the EU Merger Control Regulation,[34] but there are also links to the rules on the free movement of goods,[35] public procurement, and state aid (though the two latter elements are rarely applicable to IP issues).

(b) The UK level

The UK's principal competition regulator was for a long time the Office of Fair Trading, but the latter was abolished by the Enterprise and Regulatory Reform Act

---

30 Commission Guidelines, paragraph 140.
31 TTBE, Article 5.1(b).
32 Commission Guidelines, paragraph 183(b) and (d).
33 Commission Guidelines, paragraph 183(c).
34 See note 20.
35 See section 1.3 above.

2013 and has been replaced by the Competition and Markets Authority (CMA), an independent non-ministerial department which has assumed all the competition law functions not only of the Office of Fair Trading but also of the Competition Commission. In addition to these responsibilities, the CMA plays a collaborative role with other regulators both within the competition law arena (as part of the UK Competition Network) and in other fields (as part of the UK Regulatory Network, in which it collaborates with the Financial Conduct Authority, the Civil Aviation Authority and other such bodies).

4.2 Enforcement

(a) Penalties and powers

It used to be the case that the UK's national competition regulator was not empowered to enforce the prohibitions in what are now Articles 101 and 102 of the TFEU, but since the EU's so-called Modernisation Regulation[36] all national competition authorities throughout the EU member states have had the decentralised power to enforce those prohibitions (in respect of their national markets) concurrently with the European Commission. Of the various weapons in the regulators' arsenal, the power to impose very substantial monetary penalties – often, though inaccurately, called "fines" – on infringers is the best known. These penalties can reach 10% of worldwide turnover, though they will often be reduced where advantage is taken of the various leniency policies that are designed to encourage whistleblowers to confess all to the regulators. Other enforcement measures include the power to order the cessation of anti-competitive behaviour or conduct, to impose interim measures while an investigation is in progress, to execute unannounced inspections – often, though again inaccurately, called "dawn raids" – and, where mergers or acquisitions are involved, to order divestment or indeed to prohibit the merger altogether.

(b) Other adverse legal consequences

In addition to the above, a contractual provision that contravenes the Chapter I Prohibition and/or Article 101 will be unenforceable; and, unless it can be severed from the remaining clauses, it may cause the entire contract to be unenforceable.

Anti-competitive agreements or conduct can also trigger civil ligation in national courts for damages and other remedies from those who claim to be the victims of the infringement. This is a phenomenon that is occurring more often, and, as discussed above, will inevitably be accelerated as a result of the EU's antitrust damages directive.[37]

(c) Other adverse non-legal consequences

The legal and management costs of having to deal with a regulatory inspection will

---

36 Council Regulation (EC) No. 1/2003 of 16 December 2002 on the implementation of the rules on competition laid down in Articles 81 and 82 of the Treaty.

37 See section 2.4 above.

be irrecoverable from the regulators, even if they subsequently decide to discontinue the investigation. And a finding of infringement will be highly likely to increase the risk of regulatory surveillance in future. Finally, and sometimes worst of all, the adverse publicity following a public finding of infringement can be very damaging indeed, if not catastrophic.

5. Conclusion

If even senior courts and experienced regulators sometimes struggle to reconcile IP law and competition law, it is hardly surprising that IP rights holders (and those who advise them) can find it a difficult task. But it is a task that needs to be undertaken, for the risks of inadvertently overlooking the potential applicability of competition law to IP transactions can be very serious indeed. As discussed in this chapter, there have been all too many examples in recent years alone of IP rights holders who have encountered major anti-trust problems. The interface between IP law and competition law is a tricky channel to sail, and a good navigational chart always needs to be close at hand.

About the authors

Richard Binns
Partner, Simmons & Simmons LLP
richard.binns@simmons-simmons.com

Richard Binns is widely recognised as a leading commercial IP lawyer. Having advised both public and private sector clients on IP aspects of corporate transactions and on complex, high-value, international IP deals across a range of sectors, he is familiar with the IP issues that can arise in such deals. He has extensive experience of technology transfer and licensing, as well as advising on related competition law and regulatory issues. He has advised on numerous collaboration agreements, R&D agreements and consortium agreements, and he regularly assists corporate lawyers in the sale of shares and assets of companies and in financings where intellectual property is involved.

Mr Binns has written a substantial number of articles for legal and industry journals and he lectures extensively in the United Kingdom and elsewhere on IP-related matters. He sits on the healthcare committee of the Licensing Executives Society, is a member of the IP committee of the Confederation of British Industry and is a past member of the IP subcommittee of the City of London Solicitors' Company.

Jonathan Cornthwaite
Partner, Wedlake Bell LLP
jcornthwaite@wedlakebell.com

Jonathan Cornthwaite specialises in IP law and competition law at London-based law firm Wedlake Bell LLP, where he has been a partner since 1988. He also lectures and publishes extensively on these subjects in the United Kingdom and abroad. He was educated at St Paul's School, London, and the Universities of Oxford and Cambridge.

Mr Cornthwaite is a member of the Society for Computers and Law, the Federation against Software Theft Legal Advisory Group, the Intellectual Property Lawyers' Organisation, the Licensing Executives' Society, the Competition Law Society and the British-Spanish Law Association. He is a fellow of the Royal Society of Arts and an honorary fellow of the Association of Fellows and Legal Scholars of the Centre for International Legal Studies. He sits on the electronics, IT and e-commerce committee of the Licensing Executive Society International; and he serves as honorary secretary of the City of Westminster and Holborn Law Society, of which he is a director.

Neil Coulson
Partner, Baker Botts LLP
neil.coulson@bakerbotts.com

Neil Coulson is an IP lawyer with a broad-based practice focused on dispute resolution and the exploitation of IP rights – including advising on protection strategies and the full range of commercial agreements. Mr Coulson has worked in all key industry sectors, including oil and gas, engineering, chemicals, electronics, and pharmaceuticals and biotechnology. He has represented clients asserting and defending their

IP rights before the UK courts, as well as in patent matters before the UK and European Patent Offices and in trademark and design matters before the UK Intellectual Property Office and the Office for Harmonisation in the Internal Market. In transactional matters, Mr Coulson advises on cross-border technology licensing issues, on stand-alone IP agreements and on intellectual property in the context of corporate and commercial transactions. Mr Coulson also advises on matters related to data privacy and has a particular interest in advertising and sponsorship matters.

Paul Davies
Head of intellectual property, EverEdgeIP
p.davies@everedgeip.com

Paul Davies is a global leader on the commercialisation of intellectual property, with significant experience in a number of facets of technology commercialisation. Mr Davies has been heavily involved in negotiating commercial deals (particularly licensing deals between technology firms and large multinationals) as well as providing advice on multi-million-dollar transactions in IP and associated business units.

Before joining EverEdgeIP, Mr Davies held a number of senior positions with patent attorney and law firms internationally, before moving into IP strategy and portfolio management. Mr Davies has worked with a host of companies, from technology start-ups to multi-billion-dollar US multinationals, developing and implementing strategies for intellectual property held in registered forms, such as patents, or unregistered forms, such as trade secrets and know-how.

Mr Davies is a New Zealand-registered patent attorney and has been recognised by *IAM* magazine as one of the top 300 IP strategists in the world.

Tim Davison
Senior associate, Baker Botts (UK) LLP
tim.davison@bakerbotts.com

Tim Davison has significant experience in the areas of technology and telecommunications, media and entertainment, life sciences and healthcare. He advises on a wide range of transactions, including corporate finance, mergers and acquisitions, reorganisations, joint ventures and other general corporate and commercial matters. In addition, he advises on general company procedure, corporate law and governance.

Within the technology sector, Mr Davison's practice includes advising on strategic alliances, licensing, and complex technology and sourcing transactions covering the whole range of hardware, software, security and data usage, online assets, IT services, engineering assets, 'cleantech' and alternative energy. In the media and telecoms industries, he advises clients on digital media, online and offline brands, mobile and other telecoms, film, broadcasting, games, television channels, distribution and content.

Tom Farrand
Managing director, Novagraaf UK
t.farrand@novagraaf.com

Tom Farrand is a registered trademark attorney, with more than 30 years' experience in the IP field. His expertise includes: providing strategic IP advice; filing and prosecuting UK, EU and international trademark applications and oppositions; coordinating litigation and dispute resolution; dealing with UK and Registered Community Design (RCD) registrations; and advising on copyright and unregistered design rights. Mr Farrand is a mathematics graduate, an alumnus of the London Business School and has spent many years in senior management in the IP sector.

Mr Farrand provides expert advice for established and growing companies on the protection and exploitation of intellectual property, including trademark clearance, registration and licensing. He has hands-on experience of IP auditing, including establishing copyright ownership, changes of ownership, and inbound and outbound licensing advice and support. Mr Farrand utilises an extensive network of skilled colleagues and contacts, aimed at helping businesses succeed through innovation and the exploitation of intellectual property.

Mark Heaney
Partner, Baker Botts LLP
mark.heaney@bakerbotts.com

Mark Heaney is a partner in the IP practice of Baker Botts. He has experience in contentious matters and his practice covers a broad range of IP work, with a focus on patents, confidential information, and copyright and related rights. He has a particular interest in matters that relate to computers, electronics and telecommunications and has been involved in a large number of such cases. The majority of Mr Heaney's work involves international disputes, with litigation taking place in multiple jurisdictions and usually involving either the United Kingdom and the United States or the United Kingdom and other European jurisdictions.

Mr Heaney has a BSc degree in computer science and was employed as a software and electronic engineer before qualifying as a solicitor in 1998.

Michelle Korman
Senior analyst and IP valuation manager,
Metis Partners
michelle@metispartners.com

Michelle Korman works across the breadth of Metis Partners' business, carrying out assignments ranging from managing IP valuation assignments in advance of fundraising, investment, restructuring or exit, to IP audits, licensing negotiations and IP strategy. Ms Korman has significant experience in identifying, valuing and marketing critical IP assets in both solvent and distressed scenarios, and has worked on a number of high-profile IP sales and IP valuations during her time at Metis Partners. She is also the voice behind many of the Metis Partners blogs.

Ms Korman has gained four degrees, the most recent of which is an LLM in internet law and policy.

Colin McCall
Senior associate, Taylor Wessing
c.mccall@taylorwessing.com

Colin McCall is a senior associate in Taylor Wessing's IP department. His practice focuses on the life sciences, healthcare and technology sectors (with a particular focus on med-tech and clean technology), and he advises on both non-contentious and contentious matters. Key areas of his practice include: commercial agreements (eg, patent and know-how licensing, R&D agreements, collaborations and distribution agreements); contract disputes in the life sciences and technology sectors; and IP aspects of mergers and acquisitions, joint ventures and investments.

Chambers and Partners recently named Mr McCall as a key individual for having impressed clients with his "very practical" approach and his ability to give business-like solutions. Mr McCall has a first-class degree in cell biology from Durham University, and he holds both a diploma in IP law and practice from Bristol University and an MSc in energy, environmental technology and economics from the London City University.

Christoff Pienaar
Partner, Cliffe Dekker Hofmeyr Inc
Christoff.Pienaar@dlacdh.com

Christoff Pienaar is a director (partner) in the technology, media and telecommunications practice of Cliffe Dekker Hofmeyr Inc. He advises on commercial, IT and IP law, specialising in IT and commercial matters with particular expertise in technology outsourcing, business process outsourcing, systems integration, IT consultancy services, managed services, disaster recovery services, software development, and software licensing and support transactions. He also advises on general commercial and IP issues across a diverse range of industry sectors, especially financial services.

Mr Pienaar is a solicitor of the senior courts of England and Wales and an attorney of the High Court of South Africa.

Zarah Rasool
Associate, Baker Botts LLP
zarah.rasool@bakerbotts.com

Zarah Rasool is an associate in the IP team at Baker Botts. She has a broad-based IP practice covering contentious and non-contentious matters; in particular, she advises on the exploitation, protection and enforcement of IP rights across all areas of the IP field (including patents, trademarks, copyright, designs and confidential information). Ms Rasool has extensive experience advising on IP aspects of corporate transactions – including licensing, research and development, confidentiality, and vendor and purchaser due diligence relating to acquisitions in the retail, design, engineering, chemical, and food and beverages sectors.

Stephen Robertson
Director, Metis Partners
stephen@metispartners.com

Acknowledged as one of the world's 300 leading IP strategists by *IAM* magazine, Stephen Robertson founded Metis Partners in 2003 with the aim of assisting businesses with the maximisation of value from their IP assets. He has advised a range of enterprises, including FTSE-quoted companies, small and medium-sized enterprises, global banks, insolvency practitioners and public sector organisations across Europe and the United States. Mr Robertson's experience includes valuing and monetising IP assets, providing IP due diligence, delivering IP strategies and IP asset brokerage. He also provides expertise with IP commercialisation, using IP assets as security in order to restructure debt, and IP infringement and invalidity. Mr Robertson has 20 years' experience in corporate finance and has worked in banking, 'business angel' investment and the public limited company sectors.

Mr Robertson graduated with a degree in law before qualifying as a chartered accountant with Deloitte and Touche. He is currently chairman of the Licensing Executives Society (LES) for Scotland and is a member of the LES Council for Britain and Ireland.

Clive Thorne
Partner, Wedlake Bell LLP
cthorne@wedlakebell.com

Clive Thorne is a partner at Wedlake Bell LLP. He specialises in IP and IT disputes, in which he has more than 40 years' experience in the United Kingdom and Far East. He has acted in numerous leading IP cases, including coordinating multi-jurisdictional litigation and arbitration. He has a particular interest in the arbitration of IP disputes, especially patent disputes.

Mr Thorne is a fellow of the Chartered Institute of Arbitrators and sits as a World Intellectual Property Organization (WIPO) domain name panellist. He is also on the WIPO arbitration panel. Mr Thorne is admitted to practise law in England, Australia and Hong Kong.

Lydia Torne
Supervising associate, Simmons & Simmons LLP
lydia.torne@simmons-simmons.com

Lydia Torne is a member of the IP team at Simmons & Simmons. She advises on a range of contentious and non-contentious IP matters, with a particular focus on commercial IP transactions (including commercial licensing, collaboration agreements, R&D agreements, consortium agreements, monetisation agreements and related commercial arrangements for public and private corporate transactions and financings). Ms Torne advises clients in a wide range of sectors, including fast-moving consumer goods, telecommunications media and technology, life sciences, financial institutions, and energy and infrastructure.

Amy Williams
Associate, Baker Botts LLP
amy.williams@bakerbotts.com

Amy Williams advises on a wide range of intellectual property law and has experience of advising on all areas of IP rights, in both contentious and non-contentious matters. She advises on IP licence and contract interpretation, as well as IP issues in corporate transactions; she has also advised on contentious matters relating to software copyright ownership and branding disputes. Her professional experience includes acting for international corporations in the United Kingdom's High Court, Court of Appeal and Intellectual Property and Enterprise Court, and coordinating multi-jurisdictional litigation across Europe.

Ms Williams has a degree in physiological sciences from Oxford University and is particularly experienced in advising on patent actions across a number of different sectors, including the telecommunications, biotechnology and chemical industries.